THE WEST GERMAN MODEL

III. WEST GERMAN MODEL

THE
WEST GERMAN
MODEL

Perspectives on a Stable State

Edited by

William E. Paterson

and

Gordon Smith

FRANK CASS

First published 1981 in Great Britian by
FRANK CASS AND COMPANY LIMITED
Gainsborough House, 11 Gainsborough Road,
London, E11 1RS, England

and in the United States of America by
FRANK CASS AND COMPANY LIMITED
c/o Biblio Distribution Centre
81 Adams Drive, P.O. Box 327, Totowa, N.J. 07511

British Library Cataloguing in Publication Data

The West German model.
  1. Germany, West-History-Addresses, essays, lectures
  I. Paterson, William F.   II. Smith, Gordon
  943.087   DD259

ISBN 0-7146-3180-9 (Case)
ISBN 0-7146-4034-4 (Paper)

This group of studies first appeared in a Special Issue on
'The West German Model: Perspectives on a Stable
State' of *West European Politics*, Vol.4, No.2,
published by Frank Cass & Co.Ltd.

Typeset by Barron Print & Setting, Thornton Heath, Surrey
Printed and Bound in Great Britain by
Robert Hartnoll Ltd., Bodmin, Cornwall

Contents

Notes on the Contributors

William E. Paterson is Volkswagen Senior Lecturer in German Politics, Warwick University. He is author of *The SPD and European Integration* (Saxon House, 1974), co-author with I. Campbell of *Social Democracy in Post War Europe* (Macmillan, 1974) and has co-edited *Social and Political Movements in Western Europe* (Croom Helm, 1976) with M. Kolinsky, *Special Democratic Parties in Western Europe* (Croom Helm, 1977) with A. Thomas, *Foreign Policy Making in Western Europe* (Saxon House, 1978) with W. Wallace and *Sozialdemokratische Parteien in West Europa* (Bonn, 1979) with K. Schmitz.

David P. Conradt is Professor of Political Science at the University of Florida. During the 1978/79 academic year he was a Fullbright Research Professor at the Universität Konstanz. *The German Polity* (1978), *The West German Party System* (1972) and contributions to *The Civic Culture Revisited* (1980) and *Germany at the Polls* (1978) are among his publications.

Kenneth Dyson is lecturer in the Department of Political Theory and Institutions of the University of Liverpool. He has published *The State Tradition in Western Europe* and *Party, State and Bureaucracy in West Germany*, as well as numerous articles on West European and West German politics and public administration.

Jonathan Story is Associate Professor in the European Business Environment Department INSEAD at Fontainebleau, France, and a member of the Institut Français des Relations Internationales, Paris. His publications include *Euro-Communism: Myth or Reality?* (Penguin, 1979), *North Sea Oil: Its effects on Britain's Economic Future* (INSEAD, 1975), *South Africa: The Limits of Growth* (INSEAD, 1975), and chapters in *Foreign Policy Attitudes of Socialist Parties in Western Europe* (ed. Werner Feld, Committee on Atlantic Studies, 1977) and *Social Democratic Parties in Western Europe* (ed. William Paterson, Croom Helm, 1977).

Roger Morgan is Head of the European Centre for Political Studies, Policy Studies Institute, London; he is also an Associate Member of Nuffield College, Oxford, and a Visiting Professor at the University of Surrey. His publications include *The German Social Democrats and the First International* (1965), *Britain and West Germany: Changing Societies and the Future of Foreign Policy* (with Karl Kaiser) (1971), *The United States and West Germany, 1945-1973* (1974), and *West Germany's Foreign Policy Agenda* (1978).

Helga Michalsky is Assistant Professor of Political Science at the University of Heidelberg. She is the author of *Bildungspolitik und Bildungsreform in Preussen* (Weinheim, Basel, Beltz Verlag 1978), and has published several articles on the economic and social policies of the two German states.

Geoffrey Pridham is Lecturer in European Politics at Bristol University. His books include *Christian Democracy in Western Germany: The CDU/CSU in Government and Opposition, 1945-76* (1977), *Transnational Party Cooperation and European Integration: The process towards direct elections*, with Pippa Pridham (1981) and *The Nature of the Italian Party System: A regional case study* (1981).

Peter Pulzer has been Official Student (i.e. Tutorial Fellow) in Politics at Christ Church, Oxford since 1962. He is the author of *The Rise of Political Anti-Semitism in Germany and Austria, Political Representation and Elections in Britain* and numerous articles on British and German politics.

Richard J. Evans has been Lecturer in European History at the University of East Anglia, Norwich, since 1976. He is the author of *The Feminist Movement in Germany 1894-1933* (1976) and other books and articles on German history. In 1980 he was Visiting Associate Professor at Columbia University in the City of New York, and he is currently a Research Fellow of the Alexander von Humboldt Foundation at the Free University of Berlin, where he is preparing a study of twentieth-century German historiography.

R. B. Tilford is Professor of Modern Languages and Chairman of the Postgraduate School of Studies in Language and European Studies, University of Bradford. He has broad interests in contemporary West German politics with, in recent years, particular interest in the governance of West German universities and the relationship between the university and the state in that country. His publications include (with R. Preece) *Federal Germany. Social and Political Order* (Oswald Wolff, London, 1968), (ed.) *The Ostpolitik and Political Change in Germany* (Saxon House, London 1975), and a number of articles on different aspects of West German politics in political science journals.

Gordon Smith is Reader in Government, London School of Economics and Political Science. He is the author of *Politics in Western Europe* (Heinemann, 3rd edition, 1980), *Democracy in Western Germany* (Heinemann, 1979) and *Party Government and Political Culture in Western Germany* (Macmillan, forthcoming).

Preface

In recent years the Federal Republic has become almost synonymous with the idea of political stability. Casual observers tend to regard Western Germany in a quite uncritical light as an unqualified 'success story', her achievements a reward for unstinting effort, her stability as the ultimate prize awarded only to the most well-behaved of liberal democracies.

There is no doubt that the Federal Republic has exerted a powerful fascination on political scientists precisely because of her stable politics, even if the motivating interest at an earlier stage was whether the absence of a basic crisis was not just a temporary phase. For whatever reason, the fortunes of the republic have been subjected to a scrutiny equally close as that given to the misfortunes of the Weimar Republic.

As a general concept, or as an expression of approbation, the concept of stability does not present too many difficulties; in a broad way it is easy enough to propound answers as to why the second republic has been so successful and why the first was not. Yet the more one studies contemporary West German politics, the more difficult it becomes to make easy generalisations: it has to be admitted that the conditions of stability are complex and elusive, and they are just as difficult to pin down as are the obverse conditions of crisis. It was with such a view of Western Germany in mind that the present collection of essays was conceived, to offer in fact a series of *Perspectives on a Stable State*, rather than embark on a search for a 'total' explanation.

At one level the picture that emerges from these articles is the familiar one of variations on the seamless web of stability, the *Modell Deutschland*. Underpinning all else is a massively prosperous economy, insulated from direct politicisation by its rational framework for economic policy-making, and by its continued success. This sustained performance led in turn to the development of a supportive political culture, now no longer exclusively dependent on a high level of economic growth, but closely related to the political institutions as well. This effect is strengthened by factors which together encourage the successful functioning of these institutions: the absence of deeply divisive social cleavages, the orientation of the major political parties towards the winning and exercise of governmental power, and the resources provided in the office of Federal Chancellor for the exercise of political leadership. The internal stability is buttressed by a network of international relationships which guarantee security, assure the freedom of West Berlin, and provide outlets for an export-oriented economy.

Yet stability is not some permanently immobile condition, but the resultant of dynamic factors. These factors, both internal and external, may have more than one aspect, and in West Germany, at least, they seem often to have an inherently dual, sometimes contradictory character. The Federal Republic's commitment to a market economy is in tension with stubbornly anti-market features of German society. If economic prosperity were to be sharply halted, those anti-market forces could assert themselves with disturbing effect. The unique way in which the universities and the state have combined in Germany to produce both a conforming, state-supporting majority as well as a deeply-alienated minority in the student body, points to an important weakness in a key area of West German society. Richard Evans' view that West German society, like other industrial societies, is becoming increasingly ahistorical emphasises another duality. In one sense this absence of tradition is a condition of contemporary stability, but in a period of uncertainty the very lack of tradition could be a destabilising influence.

The governmental orientation of West German political parties contributed to an election in 1980 characterised by the appearance of stability, normality and predictability. It also meant, however, that the election failed to articulate some important long-term problems, a failure that may be potentially unsettling in the long term. This same contrast between present security and possible future crisis is also apparent in relation to the position of the Chancellor. Helmut Schmidt, the most popular and powerful chancellor since Adenauer, has created for himself an enviable governmental and popular basis. This has, however, been achieved to some extent at the cost of sacrificing support within the SPD and indicates possible future difficulties for Schmidt and his Government.

The factors that contribute to stability and instability are perhaps most finely balanced in the relationship West Germany has with its external environment. The massive benefits the Republic has drawn from its present pattern of relationships, incline it to be conservative; yet the conditions of its industrial pre-eminence point also to revisionism. The international environment plays a unique and critical role in relation to the two Germanies in shaping and constraining their relationship. The advent of détente threatened the stability of East Germany by forcing the regime to accept much more contact with West Germany. A move away from détente and a sharpening of the GDR's policy of *Abgrenzung* might well contribute to a sense of insecurity in the Federal Republic, since by making the division of Germany even more painful, it could reawaken the quasi-dormant national question.

Our views of the Federal Republic can be described in terms of a 'delicate balance' or as containing 'tensions within harmony'. What we would assert is that politics in Western Germany have by no means 'come to an end' in a stifling consensus, nor have certain unresolved strains been expelled. What these essays do indicate, perhaps, is that in all its dealings the Federal Republic operates within various bands of constraint. To overstep them could well invite entirely new perspectives.

W.P.
G.S.

The Chancellor and His Party:
Political Leadership in the Federal Republic

William E. Paterson*

The dazzling success of Konrad Adenauer's first years as chancellor helps to explain why early attempts at analysing political stability in the Federal Republic focused on the role of the chancellor as political leader. Helmut Schmidt's success in fulfilling public expectations of that leadership role has served to reawaken interest in analysing the potentialities and limitations of chancellorial power. Discussion has centred on the question of the relationship between the leader of the executive and the political party which supports him; in particular, has the SPD become just a *Kanzlerwahlverein* for the re-election of Helmut Schmidt? A related area of discussion is provided by analysis of the election results where we have the apparent paradox of the electorate rewarding not the political party of the overwhelmingly popular candidate, but that of its junior coalition partner.

THE CHANCELLOR AND HIS PARTY

'The powers of his office leave nothing to be desired. At the moment of election his stallion is bridled and saddled; he only needs to be able to ride it.' (Wilhelm Hennis)[1]

Renate Mayntz's recent excellent analysis of the formal institutional complex within which the chancellorship is embedded has indicated a number of factors which serve in practice to qualify this view of a chancellor with unlimited power to affect his political environment.[2] More important than the constitutional structural determinants, however, are the constraints which flow from the nature of the relationship between the head of government and the governing party elites.

Lewis Edinger has suggested that at both the federal and sub-national level of politics, there are basically two different modalities in the relationship between the head of government and the governing party elites:

> One is characterised by the autonomous and authoritative leader of an executive centred elite coalition who dominates his party and considers it his instrument. In the other, the formal chief of government is, in fact, the chairman of a team of more or less equal party leaders, and party elites inside and outside the legislature may play a much greater role in fashioning government policy.[3]

In the following section Edinger's concept will be used as the framework for discussion of the relationship between former chancellors and their

*The author would like to thank the Nuffield Foundation for financial support in connection with research for this essay.

parties. The relationship between Helmut Schmidt and the SPD will then be considered in a more detailed manner.

Christian Democratic Chancellors

(i)   Konrad Adenauer. When Konrad Adenauer became Chancellor in 1949, the CDU was a very recent creation and, indeed, was not to hold its first National Congress until 1950 in Goslar. The CDU therefore grew up around Adenauer in office and adherents were attracted to the CDU through identification with Adenauer in his role as federal chancellor. During this period of office as both party chairman and federal chancellor, Adenauer normally completely dominated the CDU and the relationship is adequately described in terms of Edinger's first model, though as Arnold Heidenheimer has pointed out this applied much more to foreign and security policy than the domestic policy.[4]

(ii)   Ludwig Erhard. Adenauer's successor as federal chancellor, Ludwig Erhard, was unable to sustain chancellorial dominance over the CDU. Adenauer had been permitted to remain as party chairman of the CDU on his retirement and he used the full resources of his office to resist chancellorial domination of the CDU. Adenauer was much aided in his efforts to sabotage the Chancellor by the attitudes and behaviour of Franz-Josef Strauss, the chairman of the CSU who had been ousted from ministerial office over the *Spiegel* affair. Together they formed a formidable intra-party opposition to the Chancellor. This opposition ostensibly grouped around foreign policy orientations, 'Gaullists' versus 'Atlanticists', but it is much more accurately described as a struggle of the 'outs' against the 'ins', and the division played a major role in the internal life of the CDU/CSU in 1963-66. The existence of this internal opposition necessarily led to decision-making power in the still dominant governing party being shifted to its leaders in the *Länder* and in the Bundestag. It was during this period that the Chairman of the Parliamentary Party, Rainer Barzel, experienced a marked rise in influence.

Erhard, finding himself unable to use the CDU as an instrument to support his policies in the Adenauer manner, attempted to rely on public opinion, to play the part of a plebiscitary *'Volkskanzler'*. This enabled him to win the election of 1965 but his authority, mortgaged to electoral success, was completely eroded by the disastrous result from the CDU perspective in the North-Rhine Westphalian *Landtagswahl* in Summer 1966. Erhard's incumbency is clearly better described by the second of Edinger's two models.

(iii)   Kurt-Georg Kiesinger. As leader of the CDU in a government of equals with the SPD, Kiesinger was in an unprecedented and very difficult position. The exigencies of coalition maintenance meant that very often it was not possible to press forward on issues that were very popular in the CDU. Lewis Edinger argues that the CDU in the Grand Coalition was still an executive-centred coalition, that in contrast to the Erhard government, the Grand Coalition made party authority identical with governmental authority.[5] This seems to be a mistaken view. Liberated from the disciplin-

ary constraints provided by the existence of government and opposition roles, the *Fraktionen* of both the CDU/CSU and the SPD asserted themselves against their governmental representatives. Indeed, it can be argued that the crucial figures in the functioning of the Grand Coalition were Helmut Schmidt as the chairman of the SPD *Fraktion*, Rainer Barzel as the chairman of the CDU/CSU *Fraktion* and Baron Von Guttenberg, who acted as a link between the chancellery and the CDU/CSU *Fraktion*. It can therefore be argued that the relationship during the Kiesinger period was very close to Edinger's second model of the chancellor as chairman of a team of more or less coequal party leaders, with party elites inside and outside the legislature playing a much greater role in fashioning government policy.

Social Democratic Chancellors

(i)   *Willy Brandt.*

> 'One of Brandt's principal weaknesses was to listen rather too much to the Social Democratic Party and to take his cue too often from arguments proceeding within it.' (*Nevil Johnson*)[6]

> 'In contrast to Brandt, who maintained close ties to his party and could be seen as executor of its will in a domestic reform programme, Schmidt aspires to relative autonomy as chancellor and national leader.'   (*Renate Mayntz*)[7]

Both these quotations indicate that the authors believe the advent of a social democratic chancellor meant a changed relationship between the head of government and the mass membership of the governing party. If they are correct, then neither of Edinger's models would apply since policy-making would not simply be the outcome of interaction between governmental and party elites, but would reflect more closely the views of the mass membership.

At one level, there is some supporting evidence for these views. The SPD though it had called itself a *Volkspartei* since Bad Godesberg, a decade before, could never hope to completely expunge its hundred-year-old tradition of being a major source of alternative ideas on the governance of society. The internal life of the party which had shown marked signs of stagnation was refreshed by a large influx of new, more youthful members after 1969 who were intent on asserting ideas of party democracy against the prevailing orthodoxy of representative democracy. Brandt did raise expectations of domestic reform, of 'daring more democracy' in his inaugural governmental declaration in 1969.

And yet the arguments against this view are overwhelming. The SPD has been in coalition with the FDP since 1969. Coalition consensus, rather than articulation of party policy has been the dominating structural imperative. Paradoxically, when the SPD emerged as the largest party from the 1972 election and was arguably less dependent on the FDP, Brandt announced that henceforth his governmental policy was to be based on the new centre

(*Neue Mitte*).[8] The *Neue Mitte* did not correspond to the SPD position but to that of the SPD-FDP coalition.

Again, although the youthful radicals may have wanted to press party goals on to government, they were in no position to do so. Power in the party remained located in the Presidium and to a much lesser extent the Party Executive. The Presidium was almost completely composed of members of the federal government, *Land* governments and *Bundestagsfraktion*. Brandt was chairman of the party, and the parliamentary party chairman, Herbert Wehner, saw his role in terms of ensuring the the *Fraktion* supported governmental policy.

Most importantly, however, these critics have misunderstood Brandt's conception of his role. As Renate Mayntz has pointed out, Brandt in practice used his authority not as spokesman for domestic reform but in order to pursue foreign policy goals.[9] The foreign policy goals which he pursued, although popular in the SPD had grown not out of 'listening hard' to members of the SPD but had been developed independently in conjunction with Egon Bahr.[10] It was also always central to Brandt's view of the *Volkspartei* that the chancellor be seen as relatively autonomous from the party, that he make it clear that he was not bound by party directives. As early as 1960, Brandt told the SPD party conference when accepting the nomination as chancellor candidate: 'I am perhaps not making a statement that will win easy popularity when I declare that I cannot simply be an instrument for expressing the will of the party, but that after earnest thought and on my own responsibility, I shall have (if elected) to make decisions which are vital to the interests of our nation'.[11] In 1969 Brandt reminded delegates at the party conference that governmental policy would have to be asserted even against party friends,[12] and in 1972 Brandt asserted, with even less respect for party shibboleths, that party conference resolutions may have an effect but are in no sense a substitute for governmental policies.[13]

Brandt's conception of his role differs from that of the first model, where the party exists solely to support the chief executive. Whilst Brandt successfully asserted his autonomy as chancellor from party demands and was loyally supported by the *Bundestagsfraktion*, his conception of the role of party chairman was one which was very tolerant to a great deal of programmatic activity within this party, as long as it was not seen as binding on the incumbent government. Thus while he saw a major function of the party, and arguably the sole function of the parliamentary party, as supporting the government, he regarded other activities such as the drafting of long-term programmes and the articulation of social democratic values as legitimate.

There is a sense in which Brandt moved from the first to the second model in the transition from the first to the second term. In the first term Brandt set the objectives in the field that he considered important, foreign policy, and was supported by a united party on that issue. In the second period with the achievement of his major foreign policy goals, he lost momentum and had begun to be replaced as the most important policy maker, at least in relation to the domestic policy by Helmut Schmidt before the formal transition.

(ii)   Helmut Schmidt

"I am ill adapted to toeing the line."
Helmut Schmidt at SPD Party Conference, Berlin, 1979.

On Brandt's resignation as chancellor in the early summer of 1974 he was succeeded, at his own suggestion, by Helmut Schmidt. Brandt remained as chairman of the SPD and Wehner continued as chairman of the *Bundestagsfraktion*. This triumvirate has functioned very well, resting as it does on a division of labour and talents:

> The Chancellor meets the public's need to be governed efficiently and, indeed, perfectly; the party chairman absorbs and channels everything that goes beyond matters of state, he preserves the identity of the party and keeps the chancellor free for his task, and finally, the parliamentary party leader reconciles the necessities of government and conflicting trends within the party. Despite internal conflicts and tension, this trio, which can be taken as representative of the party as a whole, has proved itself splendidly.[14]

HELMUT SCHMIDT AND THE BUNDESTAGSFRAKTION

The resignation of Erhard Eppler in July 1974 removed any possibility of opposition to Helmut Schmidt from other Social Democratic members of the Cabinet. Schmidt continued, however, to be dependent on the support of the *Bundestagsfraktion*. Herbert Wehner remained a key figure and saw his role as ensuring that support: 'The party must . . . not allow itself to become the opposition, as it were, to government in which it is the bigger partner. It must support the Social Democrats in the executive. The line of conflict has to run principally between the Social Democrats and their political opponents and not between the party on the one hand, and its government members on the other, or between different groups within the party'.[15]

The poor electoral performance of the SPD in 1976 reduced the coalition majority to ten and made parliamentary party unity a vital consideration deputy *Auschussobmänner* and cutting down the holding of many offices the necessary unity by involving as many members as possible in routine work. This was effected both by creating many new posts, such as those of deputy *Auschussombmänner* and cutting down the holding of many offices simultaneously (*Ämterhäufungen*). These reforms meant that almost half the members of the SPD Fraktion had a *Fraktion*-responsibility for some area or other.

Despite these changes *Fraktionsdisziplin* remained a problem throughout the whole legislative period. This first became apparent during the parliamentary debate on the Traube affair. Traube was an atomic physicist whose home had been bugged by the Office for the Protection of the Constitution with the agreement of the Interior Minister, Werner Maihofer. The debate which led to the resignation of Maihofer and his replacement by Baum made it clear that there was a small number of SPD members who were unresponsive to appeals to coalition loyalty and the necessity of supporting the government.[16] This incident prompted Schmidt in a speech to the *Fraktion* to talk of 'so-called governing' since he had to spend 85 per cent of his strength and time in justifying decisions he had made. This, he claimed, only left five per cent over for thought and decision since ten per cent was needed for administration and implementation.[17]

The first major test for the second Schmidt government arose from the refusal of some members of the left-wing of the *Fraktion* to accept the tax-reform package of midsummer 1977. This package was seen by the left as clearly hostile to their constituents, since a planned decrease in *Vermögenssteuer* was to be accompanied by a rise in the rate of value-added tax. The leadership of the SPD was very unhappy at the prospect of relying on opposition votes to carry this measure and massive pressure was put on 'the tax dissidents'. A meeting took place on 6 June 1977 between the leadership of the *Fraktion*, the Finance Minister and the most instransigent dissidents — the deputies Coppik, Gansel, Meinike and Conradi. Wehner also wrote to the deputies Hansen and Schöfberger. In effect, support of the tax-reform legislation was made a question of confidence on the future of the social-liberal coalition. In the final vote taken on 16 June 1977 only Coppik and Hansen voted against the package, while Meinike, Schöfberger and Waltemathe abstained. The proposals were adopted by the narrow margin of 259 to 256 votes.[18]

An even greater challenge to governmental leadership was posed by the controversy surrounding the passing of the *Kontaktsperrgesetz* which placed grave restrictions on the freedom of defendants to communicate with their lawyers in terrorist cases. The measure, introduced against a backdrop of public near-hysteria in the wake of the abduction of Hanns-Martin Schleyer, was an all-party resolution. In the final vote on 29 September 1977 four members of the SPD voted against the measure (Coppik, Hansen, Lattman and Thüsing) and 11 further members of the SPD abstained. In the debate Wehner had launched a strong attack on the dissidents and all 15 of them signed an open letter to Wehner asserting that as chairman of the parliamentary party Wehner also had a duty to defend minorities within it. 157 members of the *Fraktion* replied with a public letter of solidarity for Wehner.[19]

Dissent in relation to anti-terrorist measures rumbled on throughout 1977 and 1978. Coppik, Hansen, Lattman and Meinike continued to oppose changes in the criminal law in relation to terrorism and the 'anti-terrorist law' was passed against their votes by a margin of only 245 to 244 on the 16 February 1978. Indeed the measure was only passed at all by means of massive pressure on individual SPD deputies. Peter Conradi made a personal statement in the Bundestag declaring his opposition to the measures involved but stating that he would nevertheless vote for them in order to keep the coalition in power.[20]

The dissidents in the eighth legislature although small in number had posed a consistent problem for Helmut Schmidt. Unlike their *Fraktion* colleagues and members of former SPD *Bundestagsfraktionen*, they were not prepared to give absolute primacy to upholding an SPD-led government. They were opposed to what they saw as the conservative policies of Schmidt and did not feel as deputies that they fell within the *'Richtlinienkompetenz'* of the chancellor. That their number remained so small and did not encompass all the members of the left in the *Fraktion* (about 35-40) indicates the pressures that are available to the governmental and *Fraktion* leadership. These include appeals to solidarity, co-option into responsibility, helping or hindering of political careers of deputies, questioning the legitimacy of dissent — since it is argued that electors cast a party vote rather than for an individual deputy, placing the responsibility for the government's survival on the dissidents. The eighth legislative period was one in which, despite dissidents, Wehner was able to deliver majorities for the SPD-led government. This was not accomplished without difficulty however, and it did mean that the coalition abstained in its last one-and-a-half years of office from introducing measures for which it would be very difficult to secure a majority.

It is as yet unclear how the relationship between chancellor and *Fraktion* will operate in the present Bundestag. The coalition majority has increased but the weight of the FDP with the majority (1976/80: 214 SPD, 39 FDP; 1980/84; 218 SPD, 53 FDP) has increased. Herbert Wehner who has hitherto acted as the coupling-rod between government and parliamentary party is to remain as chairman of the *Fraktion*. He has however said in a number of speeches that there is a problem about preserving the identity of the *Fraktion* and has indicated that both he and the government could live with variable majorities on different issues — a view which he has most strenuously opposed in the past.[21] This change was a recognition of a growing potential dissidence, as shown in a motion tabled by 24 *Fraktion* members attacking SPD defence policy and demanding a 1000 million DM spending cut, the saving to be used for overseas aid.[22]

THE PARTY AND HELMUT SCHMIDT

In the preceding section we have established that the SPD *Bundestagsfraktion* far from becoming a *Kanzlerwahlverein,* on the model of the CDU/CSU in the 1950s, became during the eighth legislative period a slightly less pliable instrument of the chancellor than it had been hitherto. In the following section we shall look at the developing relationship between Helmut Schmidt as chancellor and the SPD as a whole.

After taking over as chancellor in 1974 Schmidt was content to remain as a Deputy Chairman of the SPD, relying on Willy Brandt to manage the party as a whole. Brandt, freed from governmental responsibilities, was very successful in this task. He managed to integrate the party around the policy of détente, support for a North-South policy, and in favour of mild revisionism on a number of policies he had supported in office, such as the *Radikalenerlass.* He was, however, always loyal towards the SPD Government and encouraged the party to follow his example.

There were, however, a number of critics of Schmidt's governmental policy who were unresponsive to Brandt's appeals for solidarity with the

SPD government. While the dissidents in the *Bundestagsfraktion* were
small in number and distant from the centres of power, the critics in the party
at large, while still clearly a minority, were much more numerous and
represented about a quarter of the membership of the Party Executive,
although they only had one member on the more important Presidium.[23]
The two most vocal critics were Erhard Eppler and Jochen Steffen.[24] Their
priorities — full employment, protection of the environment, reduction of
the North-South gap and social security measures — could only be realised
in the long term, whereas Schmidt's emphasis on financial stability and
combatting inflation was associated by opponents and adherents alike with a
philosophy of 'crisis management'.[25]

Schmidt's initial response to these critics was to ignore them! Faced with
this policy of benign neglect Jochen Steffen resigned from the Executive in
1976. He eventually left the SPD in 1979 and launched himself on a new
career as political cabarettist. His place as chairman of the *Grundwerte-
Kommission* was taken by Eppler and the *Kommission* reported in 1977.
Schmidt let it be known that he regarded the report as being of little
relevance to his governmental activity.[26] He had earlier made it clear that he
regarded 'the *Orientierungs Rahmen* 1980-5' as sharing in this lack of
relevance.[27]

Schmidt's critics, in a permanent minority of the Party Executive and
scarcely represented in the Presidium, placed their faith in changing the
Chancellor's policy in the SPD party conference. There was little reason for
this since even if they had been successful in mobilising a majority of the
conference against the chancellor's policy, Brandt had, as we have seen
earlier, already successfully established the convention that a social democratic chancellor could not be forced to represent a position which he felt to
be wrong. This was a convention which Schmidt took great pains to
reinforce:

> Please understand this: we social democrats in the Bundestag and in
> the Federal Government carry out the wishes of many millions of
> voters, the wishes of a million members of our own party, the wishes of
> our own party conference and of our own parliamentary party.
> However the Basic Law spreads the responsibility on far too few
> shoulders. That means: the members of the federal government must
> be able to take responsibility for what they do or do not do.
> I hope I have become more tolerant as the years have gone by.
> Nevertheless, I cannot as *Bundeskanzler* represent any position
> which I do not believe, after examining my own conscience and for
> which I cannot therefore take responsibility.[28]

An analysis of the selection process for delegates to the party conference
and a look at the membership of the SPD as a whole will help make clear why
the dissident minority on the party executive had such a difficult task in
mobilising a conference majority against the *Bundeskanzler*. The ordinary
party member is separated from the federal party conference by two
delegative steps. He votes for a delegate from his local association to
represent his views at the district conference (*Bezirksparteitag*). In turn,

the district conference decides on those delegates who are to represent the district at the national congress. This double process of delegation clearly filters the wishes of the rank-and-file members. Secondly, the selection of national delegates at the district conference means that only in exceptional cases are ordinary members without party office chosen to attend the national conferences. Wildenmann noted in his study of the SPD of the fifties: 'For all practical purposes, therefore, selection for the party conference goes along with some sort of party function. In structure, then, the party conference is essentially the association of the functionary cadre of the party, out of which the leadership staff arises like an erratic block.'[29]

Thirdly, the party conference plays only a minor role in the policy-making process within the party. Although the regional and local organisations are able to submit proposals, the party executive, with its own series of proposals, is able to exert considerable influence on the outcome of the various debates. It controls the agenda and often appeals for solidarity from the delegates when the votes are taken. 'Solidarity' is interpreted by the majority of delegates as support for the Executive's line. In addition, many of the resolutions passed are simply referred to the Executive or the *Fraktion*, where they can be forgotten or shelved on the basis of their unfeasability. The delegates, then, who generally lack the detailed and specialist knowledge required to participate in policy formulation, are left to ratify or turn down the proposals from the Executive and the *Fraktion*. Chalmers has rightly concluded: 'The congresses thus often turn into rituals in which party symbols are prominently displayed and emotional ties to the party are reaffirmed'.[30]

A number of authors have suggested that the influx of younger academically-educated members into the SPD has increased the potential for radicalisation and opposition to the moderate line represented by Helmut Schmidt. In a typical example of this argument Nevil Johnson has recently written that:

The influx of highly educated and articulate party members tends to produce in the lower reaches of the party organisations at least a rather different view of the purposes served by a party than any that has so far been dominant. For such members parties quickly take on the character of organisations dedicated to the production of programmes: the *Willensbildung* is seen as being directed to the formulation of policy opinions and commitments . . . Not surprisingly such a view is likely to be associated with a rather critical approach to many traditional party activities. Electoral campaigning begins to appear to many as a slightly regrettable diversion from the main task of forming opinion on policies inside the party on the basis of rational argument and analysis.[31]

This view is arguably mistaken. We have already pointed out the advantages that have always accrued to the party leadership due to the nature of the selection process of conference delegates and the organisation of the conference itself. Johnson further assumes a static long-term correlation between education and commitment to party democracy. What

evidence we have suggests that this correlation is much less close than may
be supposed and can change if the surrounding environment changes.[32] The
greatest weakness in this explanation, however, is that it ignores the extent
to which the SPD has become a *Partei des Öffentlichen Dienstes*. The
over-representation of public officials in the party membership is even more
apparent among party office-holders, delegates to the party conference, and
party members who hold public office. This over-representation of public
officials among party members is normally associated with a hostility to
party democracy and an identification with administrative rather than
political values. Moreover, they are likely to accord a very high priority to
electoral campaigning since their career prospects as public officials are
bound up with electoral success.[33]

The Party Conference of 1977

The party conference of 15-19 October 1977 in Hamburg was expected to be
a very difficult one for Schmidt. A major area of confrontation, nuclear
power, was the only area in which his critics were not clearly in a minority.
On the eve of the party conference, the party executive had passed by one
vote (against the votes of all governmental members of the SPD present) a
resolution which recommended an end to the building of all nuclear power
stations for the time being.[34] Nuclear power deeply divided the SPD since it
exposed a cleavage between the 'post-materialist' orientations of many
younger Social Democrats who gave priority to protection of the environment and other party members including Schmidt and the vast majority of
the trade unionists in the party, who gave priority to the energy needs of the
economy. In the event, the expected confrontation between chancellorial
prerogative and party opinion failed to materialise. The party conference
was held in a spirit of euphoria in the wake of the successful freeing of the
hostages and the captured Lufthansa in Mogadishu. This action was seen
both by the delegates to the party conference and German public opinion at
large as legitimising Schmidt's 'crisis leadership'. In this atmosphere it
proved possible to cobble together a resolution on nuclear energy which left
all options open to the federal government.

The 1979 Party Conference — Parteitag des Kanzlers?

> Notwithstanding Helmut Schmidt's cautious attempts at conciliation
> and accommodation with his party, Hamburg remained more a party
> conference of the party than of the chancellor. This time in Berlin he
> made no concessions on issues important to him to the party. It was the
> unvarnished Helmut Schmidt and just because he was honest, hard,
> precise, without any visions to offer, he was convincing — a man of
> governmental policy without any qualifications. (Rolf Zundel)[35]

As this view indicates, the chancellor was in an even stronger position by the
time of the Berlin party conference in December 1979. His economic policy
appeared to have been crowned with success both domestically and internationally. The domestic economy was performing well in 1978 and interna-

tionally he was seen as playing a major and constructive role in the management of the global economy. Those successes were reflected in a very high personal standing in terms of public popularity. At the end of 1978, Schmidt reached his hitherto highest point in public opinion surveys (64 per cent rated him highly), and at the same time the coalition parties overtook the opposition in popularity for the first time since the federal election of 1976.[36]

Party conferences immediately preceding federal elections are normally characterised by a high degree of identification with the party's representatives in the coming election. This factor making for solidarity has been immeasurably strengthened by the adoption of Franz-Josef Strauss as chancellor candidate for the CDU/CSU on the 2 July 1979. Those members of the SPD who were most critical of Helmut Schmidt were also those who were most appalled by the prospect of a Strauss victory. Strauss's candidature strengthened their solidatity with Schmidt as no other political event could have done.

The major issues at the Berlin Party Conference were those of energy policy and security. On the question of energy policy Eppler had managed to get the regional party conference of the Baden-Württemberg SPD on 15 July 1979 to adopt a resolution calling for a moratorium on the building of atomic power stations. Schmidt insisted that the government must retain the future expansion of nuclear power production as one of its options. In the final vote Schmidt was able to secure clear majorities for his policies on energy and defence. The delegates also made clear their overwhelming endorsement of Schmidt as the candidate for chancellor in the unprecedented high number of votes he received as deputy chairman of the party.[37] From a longer-term perspective, however, Schmidt could not but be concerned at the size of the minority (35-40 per cent) who continued to oppose his policies on what he considered to be key issues. The Berlin party conference thus had a dual significance for Schmidt. He had been able both to secure a triumphal endorsement as the candidate of the party for the chancellorship and to defend successfully his policies against their critics, but the size of the opposition to individual governmental policies was bound to make him wary of achieving too large an electoral success, since it was clear that freed from the constraints of defeating Strauss, his party comrades would put renewed pressure on him on these issues.

THE STRANGE CASE OF THE DISAPPEARING CHANCELLOR BONUS

A standard cliché in West German political science assumes that the bonus in popularity which normally accrues to an incumbent chancellor will be spent by the electors in favour of the party he represents. The gap between Helmut Schmidt and Franz-Josef Strauss in public opinion ratings was very wide;[38] yet the SPD was only able to show an increase from 42.6 per cent in 1976 to 42.9 per cent in 1980, while the FDP showed an increase from 7.9 to 10.6 per cent.

A major problem for the SPD during the campaign had, in fact, been the discrepancy in popularity between Schmidt and his party.[39] This difference continued throughout the campaign since Schmidt presented himself as a

Koalitions-Kanzler rather than an SPD chancellor. This strategy was very effective in terms of coalition maintenance, and he remained a very popular choice with FDP voters even though his popularity with them dropped in the last month, when bowing to party pressure, he identified himself somewhat more with the SPD.[40] Schmidt's conduct of the campaign, not surprisingly, failed to please many in the SPD and was subject to some robust criticism from Wehner after the election.[41] The SPD had of course, given the logic of the situation arising from Schmidt's immense popularity, been prevented from criticism of Schmidt's conduct during the election.

The Schmidt campaigns of 1976 and 1980, when compared with Brandt's campaign of 1972, reveal some interesting differences in how they resolved the tension between being a chancellor of a continuing coalition and the most prominent representative in government of the SPD. Brandt, as we have seen earlier, whilst insisting as much as Schmidt on his autonomy as chancellor once in office, fought the election as chancellor and chairman of the SPD clearly as the SPD candidate. His image as representing a *Neue Mitte* in the coalition was only unveiled after the election was over. In this case any chancellor 'bonus' would go to the SPD. Schmidt, by contrast, although endorsed by the SPD was not its party chairman. He presented himself, as we have seen, in the electoral campaign as spokesman for the coalition. It is hard to imagine Brandt saying, as Schmidt did after the unexpectedly good result for the SPD in the NRW election in May 1980, that an absolute majority for the SPD would be *lebensgefährlich*. In this case, it is not at all surprising that the SPD is not the sole or even perhaps the main beneficiary of any chancellor bonus. In view of the degree of opposition to Schmidt's policies, though not his person — to whom the SPD appears irredeemably mortgaged — it can be safely assumed that this swing towards the FPD was not totally unwelcome to the chancellor.

CONCLUSION

This article has focused on the role of the chancellor in providing political leadership in the Federal Republic of Germany. The analysis of the relationship between the chancellor and his party makes clear the resources the chancellor has for providing political leadership. Yet it is equally clear that talk of a *Kanzlerwahlverein* only really applied to the CDU for part of the Adenauer period. Even a chancellor as popular and formidable as Helmut Schmidt is not able completely to dominate the SPD, in the way he can use his chancellorial prerogatives and wide expertise to dominate the Cabinet.[42] Many SPD members continue to oppose Schmidt's policies and many who do support Schmidt also vote FDP. The chancellor is the outstanding political leader in the Federal Republic, but it is very far from being a 'Chancellor Democracy'.

NOTES

1. This citation is from Renate Mayntz 'Executive Leadership in Germany: Dispersion of Power or "*Kanzlerdemokratie*" ' in Rose R. and Suleiman E. (eds.) *Presidents and*

Prime Ministers, Washington: American Enterprise Institue, 1980, pp. 138-70, op, cit. p. 144.

2. See note 1 above, *passim.*
3. Lewis Edinger, *Politics in West Germany,* Boston: Little Brown 1977, p. 189.
4. A. J. Heidenheimer, Foreign Policy and Party Discipline in the CDU, *Parliamentary Affairs,* 1959, pp. 70-84. *Ibid.,* 'Der starke Regierungschef und des Parteiensystem: Der Kanzlereffekt in der BRD', *Politische Vierteljahresschrift,* No. 2 1961, pp. 241-62.
5. Edinger, op. cit, p. 19.
6. Nevil Johnson, 'Parties and the Conditions of Political Leadership' in Döring H. and Smith G. *Party Government and Political Culture in Western Germany,* Macmillian, forthcoming.
7. Mayntz, R. op, cit. p. 169.
8. See R. E. M. Irving and W. E. paterson, 'The West German General Election of November 1972', *Parliamentary Affairs,* 1973, p. 218-39.
9. See Renate Mayntz, op, cit. p. 146. Chancellors will acitively set policy goals and formulate directions only in one or a very few selected fields, limiting themselves to managing the process of collective decision-making. Adenauer as well as Brandt had a selective interest in foreign policy, the first more directed to the West, the second to Eastern countries. In this field both had strong convictions, formulated goals, and used all their influence to bring Cabinet and parliament in line with them. Erhard and Schmidt had a similarly selective interest in economic questions. Schmidt does not wait for a cabinet consensus to form but takes a stand on economic issues (including the controversial one of nuclear energy) on the basis of his personal knowledge and convictions, trying to sway dissenters by use of his personal authority. In matters beyond their selected areas, chancellors are content to play a more reactive role within the framework of collective cabinet divisions.
10. See W. Paterson, 'Parties and the Making of Foreign Policy in West Germany', Warwick Working Paper 23.
11. Cited in G. Braunthal, 'The Policy Function of the German Social Democratic Party', *Comparative Politics,* July 1977, pp. 127-45, p. 142.
12. Ibid.
13. Ibid.
14. *Die Zeit,* 22 Dec. 1978.
15. *Die Neue Gesellschaft,* Vol. 26, No. 11, Nov. 1979, p. 3.
16. For this section on the Chancellor and the *Fraktion,* I have benefited from the excellent chapter by Ulrich Sarcinelli entitled 'Regierungsfähigkeit und Parteibasis der SPD: Politik im Konflikt Zwischen Pragmatischem Regierungshandeln und Struktureller Innovation', in H. Kaack and R. Roth (ed.) *Handbuch des deuschen Parteiensystems,* Vol. 2, Opladen: Leske 1980, pp. 32-56.
17. *Frankfurter Allegemeine Zeitung,* 26 March 1977.
18. This account relies heavily on Sarcinelli, op. cit.
19. Text of both letters, *Frankfurter Rundschau,* 6 Oct. 1977.
20. Ibid.
21. *Die Zeit,* 17 Oct. 1980.
22. *The Times,* 27 Jan. 1981.
23. The membership of the Presidium in 1979 was: Brandt (party chairman and MdB), Schmidt (party vice-chairman, MdB and federal Chancellor), Hans Koschnick (party vice-chairman and mayor of Bremen), Wehner (Chairman of Parliamentary party), Egon Bahr (federal party general secretary and MdB), Friedrich Halstenberg (federal party treasurer and former minister in the North Rhine-Westphalia), Walter Arendt (former federal minister), Holger Börner (premier of Hessen), Erhard Eppler (Baden-Württenberg party chairman and *Landtag* member), Antje Huber (federal minister), Johannes Rau (premier of North Rhine-Westphalia), and Hans-Jochen Vogel (federal minister. See *Jahrbuch der SPD 1977-1979,* p.334.
24. Erhard Eppler, *Ende Ohne Wende,* Stuttgart, 1975.
25. Jochen Steffen, *Krisenmanagement oder Politik?,* Hamburg: Rowolt, 1977.
26. Interviews with members of the SPD *Bundestagsfraktion.*

27. Ibid.
28. Speech to SPD party conference, Berlin, 1979.
29. R. Wildenmann, *Partei und Fraktion, Meisenheim am Glan*, Anton Hain, 1955, p. 18.
30. D. A. Chalmers, 'The Social Democratic Party of Germany', *From Working-Class Movement to Modern Political Party*, Newhaven: Yale U.P., 1960, p. 134.
31. Nevil Johnson, in Döring and Smith, op. cit.
32. Wolf-Dieter Narr, Herman Scheer and Dieter Spöri, *SPD-Staats Partei oder Reform partei*, Munich: R. Piper, 1976.
33. See W. E. Paterson, 'Problems of Party Government in West Germany: A British Perspective', in Döring and Smith, op. cit.
34. Sarcinelli, op. cit. p. 42.
35. *Die Zeit*, 7 Dec. 1979.
36. Traumnoten für den Kanzler, *Frankfurter Allgemeine Zeitung*, 28 Feb. 1979.
37. Helmut Schmidt received 365 out of a possible 420 votes, a total exceeded only by the party's favourite Herbert Wehner with 407 out of 425 for his position in the executive.
38. An indication of the gap between SPD and CDU/CSU candidates is shown by result of public opinion polls in the period 1972-1980, most strikingly in 1980. The data contained in the two tables below have kindly been made available by Professor Max Kaase and originate from the Forschungsgruppe Wahlen e.V. Mannheim.

Chancellor Preference 1972–1980

Preferred Candidate	1972 Sept %	Oct %	1976 June %	Aug %	1980 June %	July %	Sept %
SPD-Candidate	55	58	48	50	65	65	61
CDU/CSU Candidate	26	26	40	41	24	22	29
Neither of the Two	12	10	11	8	10	11	9
Don't know	8	6	1	1	1	1	1
	100	100	100	100	100	100	100

Chancellor Preference 1980

Preferred Candidate	June Total %	SPD %	CDU/CSU %	FDP %	July Total %	SPD %	CDU/CSU %	FDP %	September Total %	SPD %	CDU/CSU %	FDP %
Schmidt	65	97	21	88	65	97	21	90	61	95	15	80
Strauss	24	1	64	2	22	1	61	2	29	1	72	3
Neither	10	2	14	10	11	2	17	8	9	3	12	17
Don't know	1	0	1	0	1	0	1	0	1	1	1	0
	100	100	100	100	100	100	100	100	100	100	100	100

39. This had also been true in 1976.
40. See table, 'Chancellor Preference 1980'.
41. *Süddeutsche Zeitung*, 7 Oct. 1980.
42. See Note 9 for Schmidt's dominance of Cabinet. On his general conception of political leadership, see Peter Glotz, *Die Innenausstattung der Macht — Politisches Tagebuch* 1976-78, Munich: Steinhausen, 1980, pp. 49-50.

Political Culture, Legitimacy
and Participation

David P. Conradt*

West Germany's poiitical culture — the values, attitudes and opinions of its citizens toward political objects — has been intensively studied during the three decades of the Republic's existence. The state of his culture has been by no means a purely academic concern, but an important political question throughout most of this period. The victorious Western allies together with segments of the post-war German political elite were sceptical and uneasy about the capacity of Germans to measure up to the demands of citizenship in a liberal, representative democracy. Supporting this view was a large academic literature which emphasised the relative absence of democratic values and norms in the culture and the dominance of various forms of authoritarianism.[1] Although a socio-economically 'modern' society with a 'model' democratic constitution, the attitudes and values supportive of democracy were not sufficiently present among the great mass of the populace. The bulk of the citizenry, it was argued, enthusiastically supported the Third Reich at least until the outbreak of war in 1939 and could hardly be expected, in spite of Nazism's crushing defeat, to become convinced democrats overnight.

Thus the post-war constitution emphasised the representative rather than the plebiscitary or participatory aspect of democratic government. No significant political official was to be directly elected, nor could elected officials be recalled by the electorate. Referenda were only sanctioned at the *Land* or state level. Popular participation was in effect limited to periodic voting; the actual process of policy-making was restricted to party, interest group, and bureaucratic elites well-insulated from direct popular influence.

At the same time the public was carefully watched and studied through the medium of public opinion polls, commissioned in many cases by various governmental and party agencies. The majority of these surveys focused on one central question: were German political and social attitudes changing in the direction of more supportive orientations towards the institutions, values and processes of liberal democracy or would the post-war system suffer the same fate as its predecessor and become a 'Republic without Republicans'?

These surveys provide us with a unique opportunity to examine the process of cultural change which has occurred. As Sidney Verba pointed out several years ago:

*The generous support of the German-American Fulbright program facilitated the collection and analysis of the data presented in this article. The assistance of Professor Elisabeth Noelle-Neumann and the staff of the Institut für Demoskopie is gratefully acknowledged.

. . . in terms of the amount of data about basic political attitudes the researcher is probably better equipped to deal with Germany than with any other nation. There is a large volume of survey material available for Britain and the United States as well, but little of it displays the constant, self-conscious concern with questions of basic political orientation and the acceptance of democracy.[2]

In recent years the analysis of these data has produced a sizeable literature.[3] Significantly, in spite of different analytical techniques, theoretical approaches and data bases the numerous scholars working in this area are in general agreement on the basic pattern and trends during the past thirty years.

(1)   The early post-war years were characterised by a widespread indifference to politics of any kind. Most Germans, reacting to the intense politicisation of the Nazi years, had withdrawn to their primary (personal life, family, friends) sphere of concern. This indifferent majority had little understanding of basic democratic values and institutions. For example, only about half of the adult population in 1950 wanted more than one party to participate in political life and less than 50 per cent felt that a parliament was needed. There was also significant (about 20-30 per cent) residual support for past regimes: the Hohenzollern Monarchy and National Socialism.[4] Opposition to the post-war Republic was, however, largely passive and latent. Supporters of the Monarchy or the Nazis were no more likely to participate actively in political life during these years than those indifferent to politics and were significantly less active than supporters of the Republic.

(2)   The emergence in the mid-1950s of an 'instrumental' or specific attachment to the post-war system. Policy successes, above all the 'economic miracle' produced a widespread sense that 'the system works' and was therefore worthy of support. Much of Konrad Adenauer's electoral appeal was based on this theme. The five-nation political culture study of Almond and Verba, *The Civic Culture*, included Germany and was based on a survey conducted in 1959. In comparison with such 'established' democracies as Great Britain and the United States, Germans in 1959 had an 'output oriented, detached, over-pragmatic, almost cynical attitude toward politics'. There was a 'lack of commitment to the political system independent of system output'. Political participation, communication and interest were also low in comparison to Britain and the United States. But above all there was little 'system affect' or emotional attachment to the Bonn Republic; no 'reservoir of good-will' which could see it through a major crisis. This interpretation, which essentially implied that post-war German democracy, while stable and functioning well, could not survive a major social or economic crisis, dominated much of the scholarly writing about the Federal Republic throughout the 1960s and even well into the 1970s.

(3)   The analysis of time-series data, however, from the early 1950s until the present has found significant changes in the Almond and Verba portrait. By the mid-1960s the substantial support found earlier for the Monarchy and National Socialism in the early 1950s had largely disappeared. Between 70

and 90 per cent of the adult population were supportive of basic democratic institutions, values, and norms: parliament, representation, political competition, freedom of expression. Moreover, these high support levels were over time becoming widespread across all major socio-economic strata. Even those citizens who did not benefit, for example, from the 'economic miracle' were by the mid-1960s nonetheless supportive of the system's basic structures and processes. In fact much of the aggregate change in support over the first fifteen to twenty years came from less-advantaged groups (lower income, education, occupation) and those opposed to the CDU governments of Adenauer and Erhard.

ATTITUDES TOWARD THE BASIC LAW

An example of this process can be found in the development of post-war attitudes toward the Federal Republic's constitution.[5] One component of a country's political culture certainly involves attitudes towards its basic institutional structures as delineated in its constitution. In the United States and Great Britain the 'Constitution' is also a political symbol which can be employed to generate and maintain effective support.[6] American surveys have found strong support for the document; in one study over two thirds of the adult population agreed with the statement that, 'the Constitution is as near perfect as it can be and no important changes should be made in it'.[7] In the case of post-war Germany the political system established in 1949 was structured according to a 'Basic Law'. The term constitution (*Verfassung*) was avoided because it connoted permanence, something most West Germans, still hoping for reunification, wanted to avoid.

In addition, the widespread privatisation and resultant disinterest in politics during the immediate post-war period meant that only a relatively

TABLE 1
ATTITUDES TOWARDS THE CONSTITUTION, 1955-1978
(IN PER CENT)

	1955	1972	1978
Positive	30	52	71
Negative (1978: a new constitution is needed)	5	9	14
Undecided	14	17	15
'Don't Know Anything About the Constitution'	52	22	—
	100	100	100

Source: Institut für Demoskopie, Survey Nos. 0083, 2085, 3061 Question Texts (1955 and 1972): What do you think about our present constitution, I mean our country's Basic Law? Do you find it good or not so good, or haven't you been very interested in it? In 1978: The Basic Law was written almost 30 years ago under the supervision and control of the Western powers. Some people are of the opinion that we should make a new constitution, which would better meet our needs and interests. Others say that the existing constitution has proven itself to be effective and a new one is not needed. What is your opinion?

small proportion of West Germans even knew about the new 'Basic Law' and still fewer could express an opinion about it. And as the data in Table 1 indicate as late as 1955, six years after the founding of the Federal Republic, 51 per cent of the adult population stated that they did not know 'anything' about the Constitution. Those respondents who admitted to some knowledge, however, were generally supportive. Nonetheless, in 1955 the dominant attitude toward the Federal Republic's Basic Law was either ignorance or indecision. By 1972, however, positive attitudes toward the Basic Law were held by 52 per cent of the adult population while the 'don't knows' and undecided proportion declined to 39 per cent. In a 1978 survey the proportion with a positive orientation toward the Basic Law rose further to 71 per cent.

When we examined the sources of this change, we discovered a pattern common to other political cultural items.[8] The greatest increase in support for the constitution over this 23-year period occurred among those segments of the population traditionally identified as the least interested in politics and the most parochial. Particularly striking is the change in attitudes toward the constitution among women. In 1955 only 19 per cent of the female population had a positive attitude toward the constitution as compared to 43 per cent among males. Sex was indeed a major predictor of responses to this item in 1955; the correlation (gamma) between sex and support for the constitution was a substantial .53. By 1978, however, a considerable convergence between males and females in their attitudes had taken place (Table 2); the predictive power of the sex variable had dropped to .19. Another dramatic change took place among Protestants. Perhaps as a response to the success of the Christian Democratic Union in 1949 and 1953, a party whose leaders and active members were disproportionately Catholic and the strongly pro-Western orientation of the then Chancellor Adenauer

TABLE 2
SUPPORT FOR THE CONSTITUTION BY SEX, EDUCATION, AND RELIGION:
1955-1978
(percentage positive)

SEX

	1955	1972	1978
Male	43	61	78
Female	19	45	66
Gamma =	.53	.32	.19

EDUCATIONAL LEVEL

Low	26	46	69
Medium	44	63	73
High	58	73	77
Gamma =	.43	.38	.11

RELIGION

Catholic	34	53	71
Protestant	18	53	72
Gamma =	.30	.02	.01

Source: See Table 1

who was widely suspected of placing the Western Alliance above reunification with the largely (80 per cent) Protestant eastern territories including Prussia, only 18 per cent of Protestants as compared to 34 per cent of Catholics supported the constitution in 1955. Seventeen years later, however, there was no significant difference between Catholics or Protestants in their attitude toward the Constitution. But the increase in support among Protestants (35 per cent) was greater than the gain among Catholics (19 per cent). Clearly the disappearance of religion as a major predictor of attitudes towards the constitution (1955 Gamma:.31; 1972:.02) was due to acceptance by Protestants. Apparently seventeen years of experience with the constitution had convinced many Protestants that the Bonn Republic was not a 'Catholic' creation. A similar pattern was found for the education variable. (Table 2)

The disappearance between 1955 and 1978 of sex, religion and education as major demographic predictors of support for the constitution is an indication that between 1955 and 1972 a broad consensus was developing on the Basic Law. Further evidence for this proposition was found when we examined the relationship between a major norm or rule of the post-war democracy, political competition, and support for the constitution. In 1955 these two variables were related (gamma = .47). That is support for the principle of political competition was dependent upon favourable attitudes toward the constitution, and conversely those Germans opposed to the constitution were also far more likely to support the idea of one-party rule. Fully 30 per cent of those opposed to the democratic constitution favoured a one-party state as compared to only 8 per cent who thought the Basic Law was 'good'. But by 1972 there was little polarisation between supporters and opponents of the constitution on the principle of political competition, it had now become a system norm. Likewise, support for a system of several parties was only weakly related to the constitution in 1955. Support for competitive politics rested largely (44 per cent) upon the support of Germans ignorant of the constitution; by 1972, however, the principle had become more firmly rooted among supporters of the constitutional system. In 1955 only 37 per cent of those favourably oriented to competition supported the constitution, by 1972 almost 60 per cent of competitive politics supporters came from the ranks of Germans who approved of the constitution.

One could argue on the basis of these data that in 1955 Germans were only paying lip-service to the idea of a competitive party system. It was the right thing to say; by 1972, however, this support was more firmly based on a knowledge of and favourable attitudes towards the constitution which established this system rule. There was, in other words, a greater *congruence* between system rules and norms. It is at this point, as we discuss below, that very visible behavioural manifestations of this development became apparent.

The development of an attitudinal consensus on the basic norms and values of parliamentary democracy was largely completed by the late 1960s. Most analysts have found the following factors to have had the most importance in explaining this change: (1) the socialisation of post-war generations into a stable, successful and 'functioning' political system; (2) the absence, for the great majority of the population, of any credible alternative to 'middle-class' democracy after 1945;(3) post-war socio-economic modernisation particularly the integration of Catholics, farmers and workers and (4) system performance, the domestic and foreign political policy successes of the first post-war governments.[9]

The behaviour of West German citizens between 1949 and the late 1960s, however, was only weakly related to the political values they professed. While the principle of political competition was widely endorsed, the same party held power at the national level for twenty years; although a solid majority perceived the system to be one in which freedom of political expression existed, only a small minority engaged in political conversations or other more 'difficult' forms of political participation; although over 70 per cent by 1964 stated that a parliament was needed only 42 per cent in that year believed that their own deputy would pay any attention to their concerns.[10] The emergence of a closer fit between regime norms and mass behaviour only becomes noticeable by the late 1960s, the politicisation of university students and the growing interest in more 'direct' democracy, the *Machtwechsel* of 1969, the use of the parliamentary vote of no confidence (1972), the increase in mass involvement in election campaigns (1969, 1972) and the citizen initiative group movement.[11]

The data we have examined thus far have revealed far more about the stability and security of the post-war democracy, than they have about the quality and extent of democracy in West Germany. Moreover, the post-war consensus was measured by very elementary questions tapping the basic components of political culture, which are poor predictors of the future development of the West German polity and the changing relationship between political culture, system structure and mass behaviour. Fortunately, however, a number of recent surveys enable us to make a preliminary examination of these developmental questions.

CONTEMPORARY CONCEPTIONS OF DEMOCRACY

The contemporary image or conception of democracy held by the West German public was one theme of a 1978 nation-wide survey. In this study the respondents were asked with the aid of a list containing twenty-two items[12] to describe the 'ideal democracy': What was needed for a society to be fully democratic? Later in the interview the respondents were asked to judge the extent to which these same characteristics or requisites of an 'ideal democracy' were actually present in the Federal Republic. The two questions thus enable us to compare a more abstract conception of democracy with the present political order in the Federal Republic. The responses to the two questions are presented in Table 3.

The divergence between the 'ideal democracy' and the actual democracy in the Federal Republic is greatest in two related areas: citizen participation and 'socio-economic democracy'. Those Germans who conceive of democracy as a system with frequent, extensive and direct citizen involvement in decision-making perceive the Federal Republic as falling short in this area.

TABLE 3

CONCEPTIONS OF DEMOCRACY, 1978

	Needed for Democracy %	Actually Present in the Federal Republic %	Difference %
Political Competition	79	90	+11
Freedom of Movement (Travel)	80	87	+ 7
Religious Freedom	78	87	+ 9
Freedom of Expression, Press	86	76	-10
Free Elections	75	82	+ 7
Political Equality (one man, one vote)	72	79	+ 7
Political Opposition	67	66	- 1
Independent Judiciary	69	62	- 7
Equality before the Law	85	56	-29
Freedom to Choose an Occupation	79	52	-27
Federalism	43	68	+25
Effective Co-Determination in Industry	55	46	- 9
Citizenry Capable of Direct Participation in Policy Making	53	35	-18
Responsive Political Elite	63	32	-31
Freedom from Want, Distress	60	34	-26
Referenda on Important Policy Issues	56	26	-30
An Army for Internal Security	34	26	- 8
Direct Popular Participation in Policy-Making	51	26	-25
Non-Discrimination against Extremists	36	11	-25
Only Moderate Differences in Income	35	9	-26

Source: Institut für Demoskopie, Survey No.3061

TABLE 4

THE DEMOCRATIC CONSENSUS, 1978

Item	Consensus* %
Political Competition	76
Freedom of Movement (Travel)	74
Freedom of Religion	73
Freedom of Expression, Press	70
Free Elections	69
Political Equality	63
Political Opposition	53
Independent Judiciary	51
Equality before the Law	51
Freedom to Choose an Occupation	45
Federalism	38
Effective Co-Determination in Industry	31
Citizenry Capable of Direct Participation in Policy-Making	25
Responsive Political Elite	25
Freedom from Want, Distress	24
Referenda on Important Policy Issues	21
An Army for Internal Security	18
Direct Popular Participation in Policy-Making	18
Non-Discrimination against Extremists	7
Only Moderate Differences in Income	5

* proportion of total agreeing that the item is essential
  to a democracy and is present in the Federal Republic

Source: See Table 3

Likewise, the 55 per cent of the adult population who identify democracy with increasing economic equality and worker or employee involvement in the industrial enterprise (co-determination) is not satisfied that this has been realised in West Germany. Note, however, that the proportion of the population that has this conception of democracy is far smaller than that which thinks of democracy in liberal or procedural terms: individual liberty, free elections, competitive parties, freedom of religion. 'Procedural Democrats' are quite content with the accomplishments of the Second Republic. Those who want democracy expanded (Substantive Democrats), however, are far from satisfied. This gap between the ideal and the real affords one explanation for the emergence of 'citizen action group' movements in recent years and their demand for the institution of referenda on major policy issues, most notably of course, nuclear power.

By combining the responses to the two questions, the contemporary image of political democracy held by the population and the extent of its realisation in the Federal Republic can be ascertained. We suggest that a consensus on a particular value, norm or condition is present when the respondent perceives that the condition is both important for any democracy and is actually present in the Federal Republic. The consensus or congruence between the ideal and the actual political democracy for twenty items used in 1978 is presented in Table 4. Clearly the liberal or procedural conception of democracy is the most widely shared in the Federal Republic today: political competition or choice (several competing parties), freedom of speech, press and movement (the latter especially salient because of East Germany and the Wall), free elections, and 'one man, one vote'. On all of these items there is a high degree of agreement that they are important to a political democracy and can be found in the Federal Republic.

When democracy, however, is conceived in terms of substantive policy outputs, especially of a socio-economic character, and as a system with widespread and direct popular participation, the degree of consensus drops sharply (Table 4). Only 45 per cent of the population believes that in a democracy the freedom to choose an occupation is important and that such a condition exists in the Federal Republic. Co-determination in industry, freedom from want, referenda, and direct popular participation in policy-making are identified with democracy in the Federal Republic by less than a third of the population. Tolerance of political extremists and the absence of large income differences have consensus levels of less than ten per cent.

On two items there is a strong consensus, but in a negative direction. That is, about two-thirds of the adult population does not believe that the army in a democracy has a role in internal security and 57 per cent of the total sample does not perceive the *Bundeswehr* playing such a role in the Federal Republic. A similar proportion (65 per cent) takes a very hard line towards members of extremist political parties. In an 'ideal' democracy supporters of extremist parties should expect to be 'disadvantaged' and 60 per cent perceive this to be the case in the Federal Republic.

The ideological position of the respondents relates to their evaluation of what is needed for an ideal democracy and what is actually present in the Federal Republic most significantly in five areas: (1) The army as an internal security force. While 75 per cent of the 'left' group reject this as a characteristic of a democracy, 59 per cent of those on the right and 68 per cent of those in the middle made this judgment; (2) Industrial co-determination. About two-thirds of the 'left' regarded workers' participation in corporate enterprises as an essential condition of a democracy as compared to 49 per cent of the right group and 54 per cent in the centre; (3) Tolerance or non-discrimination of those in extremist political parties. While 55 per cent of the left took the position that members of extremist parties should not be automatically discriminated against, only 28 per cent of the right and 33 per cent of the centre shared this view. These responses probably reflect the influence of the radicals in public service or *Berufsverbot* controversy. The acceptance or tolerance of political non-conformity, that is of those outside the spectrum of the 'system' parties (CDU/CSU, FDP and SPD), is still not a salient feature of the political culture. The treatment of the four million foreign workers and their dependents could indicate that this also extends to social non-conformity as well; (4) Economic or income differences: about half of the left respondents, as compared to 29 per cent on the right and 35 per cent of the centre group accept the notion that in a democracy 'the income differences should not be too large'. The relatively low level of support among the left for this item again indicates the extent to which the dominant conception of democracy in the Federal Republic is still liberal and procedural rather than radical or substantive; (5) Freedom to choose an occupation. This item could also be interpreted as a surrogate for social mobility. Almost 60 per cent of the left respondents do not believe that Germans have the right to freely choose their occupation as compared to 43 per cent on the right and 48 per cent of the centre group. The importance of education as a requisite for such a free choice and the still significant class bias in the educational system are factors which perhaps underlie these responses.

THE FEDERAL REPUBLIC AND THE 'LEGITIMACY CRISIS'

The theorists of the legitimacy crisis start from the assumption of increased system (economic) output (a 'strengthening of productive forces') which 'heightens the power of the system'.[13] Yet this change in performance can produce a change in values in the direction of greater demands for socio-economic equality. These demands, in turn, if sufficiently broad in scope can constitute a new challenge to the legitimacy of the 'democratic' state which had previously been responding to other goal values such as individual accumulation and private property rather than to the real interests of the mass of the citizenry.

As the scope of state activity increases, the need for popular participation, which in a democratic system legitimises this activity, also increases. Theorists such as Jürgen Habermas, see this development as a 'legitimacy crisis' of modern democracies in that the state, in spite of this need for greater popular participation as the basis for legitimation, is still controlled by the dominant economic interests. The modern capitalist state is thus confronted with a dilemma: to deal with the problems of modern society it must have popular participation, and indeed consideration of this participatory input is the only rational way for the state to deal with its policy tasks. Yet for the state to pursue this 'most rational' course brings it into conflict with the existing capitalist socio-economic structures. This contradiction between the state as an agent of the ruling class and its need for democratic legitimation through popular participation can only be ultimately resolved through the transformation of the class structure of advanced capitalist societies.

The representative institutions of liberal republics (including the Federal Republic), largely nineteenth century in origin, are insufficient to meet this growing need of the modern state for legitimation. There is thus a legitimacy 'deficit' that can be resolved only through an enlargement of participatory channels. Political participation as the communication of policy and personnel preferences by the governed to decision-makers is seen as the only rational way to arrive at solutions to political problems. Yet the modern democratic state's need to overcome the legitimacy deficit by encouraging participation places it in growing conflict with the established socio-economic elites of modern capitalist societies, who have controlled this political system. The position of the state as the agent of the dominant social class is thus threatened by this need to increase participation. Again, the modern democratic state can manage this legitimacy deficit and rationally channel increased participation only if its class structures are changed.

This prognosis is based on the inability of the modern state to control a private economy for whose problems — recession, unemployment, inequality — it is held politically responsible. The state's problems vis-à-vis capitalism are seen as steadily increasing. It needs a high investment level to create sufficient jobs to avoid the politically negative consequences of unemployment. But a continually high investment level also brings inflation and the rise of the multi-national capitalist enterprise which reduces its control capability. At the same time, a strong sense of nationalism which could 'absorb' some of the discontent produced by the business cycle is, according to the theory, decreasing.

When addressing the specific situation in the Federal Republic, Habermas has conceded that 'while there are several of these symptoms present . . . their effects on the political system have been minimal'.[14] He has suggested that policies toward the employment of political 'radicals' in the public service (Radikalenerlass) and their implementation by some states (Länder) have so restricted the free expression of political opinions and the proper socialisation of young people that the legitimacy crisis remains latent.[15]

In spite of their frequent expressions of commitment to an empirical examination of their theories, the work of Habermas, Offe and other 'critical theorists' is not amenable to empirical testing. Habermas, for example, consistently takes a pre-empirical stance toward the theory stressing that although it must be tested, it cannot be as yet, concentrating in the meantime on 'more important arguments and counter arguments'.[16] He concedes that: 'It is not easy to determine empirically the . . . conditions under which the possible crisis tendencies actually set in and prevail.

The empirical indicators we have at our disposal are as yet inadequate'. What those empirical indicators could be are also not specified. He develops no quantitative indicators of a 'legitimacy crisis', he does not even suggest what such indicators might look like. The political form such a legitimacy crisis might take is also not specified: A drop in voting turnout? The emergence of new 'anti-system' parties? An increase in political protest demonstrations? A decline in support for basic democratic norms and values? Political violence? On the rare occasions when Habermas or Offe are specific, their empirical referents or 'examples' reveal a naïve and simplistic conception of political issues in modern industrial societies. Offe's equation of the 1935 Wagner Act in the United States with the 1966 West German Grand Coalition, with both cited as examples of ruling class adaptation to a crisis, is an example of this type of reasoning.[17]

PARTICIPATION AND CITIZEN INFLUENCE

Recent surveys, however, provide some means to make at least a provisional examination of the legitimacy crisis theory in the contemporary Federal Republic. While support for basic institutions and values is consistent with

TABLE 5

CITIZEN INFLUENCE, 1975-78

Q. Do you have the feeling, that a person as a citizen has an influence on the decisions of the federal government, or is one powerless?

	1975 %	1976 %	1978 %
Citizen has no influence, is powerless	55	54	48
Citizen has influence	23	29	30
Is sufficient	13	19	19
Insufficient	8	8	9
Undecided	2	2	2
Undecided	22	17	22
Total	100	100	100

Source: Institut für Demoskopie, Survey Nos.1250, 2178, 3061

'stable, legitimate democracy', the Federal Republic's citizenry in the late 1970s was by no means content with their political system. Between 1975 and 1978 national samples were asked the question, 'Do you have the feeling that a person as a citizen has an influence on the decisions of the federal government, or is one powerless?' As the data in Table 5 show, roughly half of the adult population felt that they had little influence as citizens on the policies of the Federal government. Roughly a third of the respondents believed that the citizen does have influence, but most of this group also added that this influence is 'insufficient'. Thus less than 10 per cent were satisfied with citizen influence on the policies of the Federal government. Yet in terms of democratic values, attitudes, support for political institutions, general satisfaction with the way democracy is functioning and confidence that the present system can successfully deal with future policy problems the system is stable and legitimate.

The relatively high proportion of respondents who feel they have no influence on what the government in Bonn does is consistent with the support for more citizen influence in decision-making. As we have seen the incongruence between what *should* characterise a democracy and what the Federal Republic actually *is* is greatest in the area of citizen participation. Most West Germans also want their deputies to act in accordance with the 'majority' of their constituents rather than according to their own 'judgments', much less the dictates of the party leadership.[18]

This general sense that the views of citizens are not sufficiently considered in the policy process appears to be a phenomenon common to several other advanced industrialised societies.[19] In the German case, however, it does not relate to major loss of support for basic democratic values, norms and institutions or demands for major system change. On a ten-item 'system support' scale drawn from a 1978 survey, the average support level for those who thought that the average citizen did have some influence in the policy process was 80 per cent as compared to 65 per cent for those respondents who perceived citizens as 'powerless' to influence policy-makers. Thus a generalised sense of inefficacy or powerlessness does relate to a lower level of support for the democratic system, although a solid majority of the 'powerless' still endorse the representative, republican order. In 1976 while about half of the adult population felt 'powerless' to influence governmental decisions, fully 80 per cent of another sample surveyed in the same year were 'very' or 'fairly' satisfied with the way democracy was functioning in the Federal Republic.

This type of dissatisfaction cannot, as yet, be regarded as the type of critical orientation which produces a legitimacy crisis. For system legitimacy to be challenged, the expressions of discontent and criticism, according to the recent analysis by Lane, must (1) be directed at the *system as a whole* and not at specific policies, procedures or personalities; (2) challenge the existing *rationales or values* underlying the system; (3) persist over some *long duration*; (4) be structurally rooted in some *socio-economic* or *cultural group* which has been systematically deprived, and (5) be

FIGURE 1

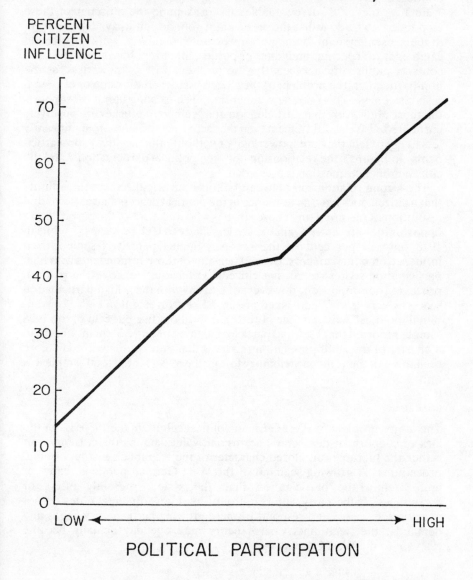

CITIZEN INFLUENCE
AND POLITICAL PARTICIPATION, 1978

related to a sense of *personal discontent* which can be related to system performance ('people content with their own lives do not act out their beliefs in system inadequacy.')[21] None of these conditions or requisites for a legitimacy crisis are present in the Federal Republic. Even the sense of personal satisfaction with life is high (67 per cent in 1978) and there is only a weak relationship between satisfaction with life and support for the present political order.[22]

Finally, the 1978 survey enables us to examine the attitudes of those respondents who do utilise the participatory opportunities available to them in the present system. If the citizen who votes regularly, works in election campaigns for specific candidates or parties, attends political meetings, and contacts public officials feels that he or she is just as 'powerless' as the non-participant, the problem of the citizen-system relationship or of system responsiveness takes on a new dimension. The existing literature supports the thesis, however, that participation and feelings of efficacy are positively correlated.[23] We should expect then that active participants are significantly less likely to feel they are 'powerless' or without influence than non-participants. In Figure 1 the relationship between political participation[24] and the citizen influence question is presented.

The strong relationship between political participation and the attitude that a citizen does have an influence in the political process suggests a partial resolution of the problem. Those citizens who make use of the participatory opportunities presently available are less likely to feel 'powerless'. While in 1978 only 14 per cent of the non-participants perceived some citizen influence on policy-makers, over 70 per cent of those respondents with high participation scores stated that citizens do have influence in the political process. The proportion, however, of citizens with these high participation scores is very low. When asked about their involvement in eight 'conventional' political activities (see note 24), only about five per cent of the 1978 sample reported that they had participated in six or more of them. Less than a quarter of the adult population reported that they were involved in more than three of the eight participatory forms; the mean for the total sample was only 2.26.

CONCLUSION

The major problem of West German political culture in the 1980s is not the lack of support for democratic norms and values among the citizenry, but rather the hierarchical, closed character of the Republic's institutions and procedures. A growing segment of the West German public is ready for more democratic participation than the system presently offers or encourages. If the party, interest groups, and governmental elites do not over time perceive and respond to these growing participatory needs and demands, the 'legitimacy crisis' theory may one day actually become relevant to the West German case.

NOTES

1. For representative examples see B. Schaffner, *Fatherland: A Study of Authoritarianism in the German Family*, New York: Columbia University Press, 1948; D. Rodnick, *Post-War Germans*, New Haven: Yale University Press, 1948; H. V. Dicks, 'Some Psychological Studies of German Character', in T. H. Pear, (ed.), *Psychological Factors of Peace and War*, New York: Philosophical Library, 1950.
2. S. Verba, 'Germany: The Remaking of Political Culture', in L. W. Pye, S. Verba (eds.), *Political Culture and Political Development*, Princeton, New Jersey: Princeton University Press, 1965, p. 137.
3. For a general overview see D. P. Conradt, 'Changing German Political Culture', in G. Almond and S. Verba (eds.), *The Civil Culture Revisited*, Boston: Little-Brown, 1980, pp. 212-72 and the work cited therein. See also K. L. Baker, R. Dalton and K. Hildebrandt, *German Politics in Transition*, Cambridge, Mass.: Harvard University Press, 1981, for an analysis which links changes in political culture to developments in the party system and voting behaviour, and F. D. Weil, 'On the Condition of Liberalism in West Germany Since World War II', Ph.D. Dissertation, Sociology Department, Harvard University, 1980.
4. G. R. Boynton, G. Loewenberg, 'The Decay of Support for Monarchy and the Hitler Regime in the Federal Republic of Germany', *British Journal of Political Science*, Oct. 1974, p. 465.
5. For data on other institutions and values see D. P. Conradt, 'West Germany: A Remade Political Culture?', *Comparative Political Studies*, 7, No. 2, July 1974, pp. 230-6; G. R. Boynton, G. Loewenberg, 'The Development of Public Support for Parliament in Germany, 1951-59', *British Journal of Political Science*, April 1973, pp. 169-89; R. K. Allerbeck, *Demokratisierung und sozialer Wandel in der BRD. Sekundäranalyse von Umfragon 1953-74*, Opladen; Westdeutscher Verlag, 1976.
6. D. Devine, *The Political Culture of the United States*, Boston: Little-Brown, 1972, pp. 88, 116-19.
7. Devine, p. 118.
8. Conradt, 'West Germany: A Remade Political Culture?'.
9. For an extensive discussion with supporting data of these factors see Conradt, 'Changing German Political Culture', pp. 256-63.
10. Institut für Demoskopie, Survey No. 1093.
11. A 1975 survey found that 11 per cent of the adult population had participated in some type of citizen initiative group. Among respondents under the age of 50, this proportion rose to 15 per cent and 29 per cent of those with an academic educational background (*Abitur* or University) stated that they were involved in one or more of these organisations. Participation in political demonstrations was also strongly related to age and education. While only 9 per cent of the total sample had ever demonstrated, 19 per cent of those under 30 and 20 per cent of the academically-educated stated that they had used demonstrations as a means of political expression. Among the 50 and over age group, only 4 per cent had ever demonstrated. Given the rising educational levels in the Federal Republic, the implications of these findings are readily apparent. EMNID, *Informationen*, 27, No. 4, 1975, pp. 7, A22.
12. Two items, 'Obedience of the laws by all' and 'A Federal **President** who is the Head of State' were discarded after an exploratory factor analysis found no significant relationship between them and the other items.
13. Jürgen Habermas, *Legitimation Crisis*, Boston: Beacon Press, 1975.
14. Jürgen Habermas, 'Legitimationsprobleme im modernen Staat', *Politische Vierteljanresschrift*, Sonderheft 7, 1976, pp. 53-4.
15. Ibid.
16. Habermas, *Legitimation Crisis*, p. 33.
17. Claus Offe, *Strukturprobleme des kapitalistischen Staates*, Frankfurt: Suhrkamp Verlag, 1972, p. 96.
18. Institut für Demoskopie, Survey No. 3061.
19. See James D. Wright, *The Dissent of the Governed*, New York: Academic Press, 1976, and Ronald Inglehart, 'Political Dissatisfaction and Mass Support for Social Change in

Advanced Industrial Society', *Comparative Political Studies*, 10, No. 3, Oct, 1977, p. 462.

20. The scale was composed of three items tapping attitudes toward the parliament (the need for the institution, its work and the responsiveness of deputies), two questions dealing with the constitution, one question each on freedom of political expression in the Federal Republic and the need for a competitive party system, one item about Hitler, and two questions on democracy as a desirable form of government for the Federal Republic.

21. Robert E. Lane, 'The Legitimacy Bias: Conservative Man in Market and State', in Bogdan Denitch (ed.), *Legitimation of Regimes*, Beverly Hills and London: Sage Publications, 1979, p. 63. (my emphasis)

22. Institut für Demoskopie, Survey No. 3061.

23. See S. Verba, N. Nie, J. Kim, *Participation and Political Equality*, Cambridge: Cambridge University Press, 1978.

24. The political participation scale was computed from questions about the respondents' voting turnout, political conversations, campaign activity, efforts to convince or persuade others about political issues, general and specific levels of political knowledge, attendance at political meetings and rallies, and political party membership.

The Politics of Economic Management in West Germany

K. H. F. Dyson

The politics of economic management in West Germany appears somewhat obscure to many foreign observers of the German political scene. This obscurity derives in part from the sheer complexity of a system of economic management that comprises a variety of autonomous actors and in part from a different language of political economy from that which is to be found in the English-speaking world. The perseverance of a lack of interest in Germany's economic management is nevertheless remarkable. Although Helmut Schmidt made management of economic policy the criterion of his own formidable political reputation at home and abroad, political scientists have preferred to give more attention to such topics as parties and elections, politics and law and the public administration. As far as the chancellor was concerned, the 'model Germany' which he presented to the electorate in 1976 was primarily an economic model. He was at pains to emphasise that the benefits of the impressive *Sozialstaat* depended on a secure economic basis.

There has been a selective, politically motivated interest abroad in the system of economic management that presides over and guides the major and most respected industrial economy in Western Europe. Neo-liberals like the French Prime Minister Raymond Barre and the leadership of the British Conservative Party have sought to justify redesign of methods of economic management by reference to the German model. This article will explore the politics of economic management in the 1970s in a narrative fashion and offer an analysis of the character of the system of economic management and of the language of political economy in the Federal Republic.

PLANNING AND ECONOMIC MANAGEMENT

West Germany *has* a politics of planning. Within the SPD a body of technocratic and left-wing opinion has favoured an improvement of 'the steering capacity' of the state over social and economic development. From 1969 to 1972 this planning euphoria focused on the attempt of the Chancellery planners under Horse Ehmke to develop a sophisticated information system for the planning of government's business and a long-term planning with reference to the major functions of government.[1] Lack of administrative support and decline of political interest in so ambitious and time-consuming an endeavour led to the demise of comprehensive political planning in 1972. Thereafter, as we shall see, SPD enthusiasm concentrated on the new Research and Technology Ministry of Ehmke, on the concept of an active, long-term structural policy for the economy that could bypass the

conservativism of the federal Economics Ministry and would supplement
the global fiscal measures which deal with the major economic aggregates.

The oil crisis of 1973 generated a heightened sense of the social and
economic restrictions on integrated state action and a greater awareness of
threats in politics and of the need for a more selective planning which would
serve as an instrument of crisis management.[2] A highly industrialised
economy like that of West Germany in which exports accounted for 27 per
cent of GNP (1978) was especially vulnerable to changes in the international
economy. As a consequence SPD policy makers believed that research and
technology, structural adaptation and labour-market policies would be
central to economic management in the 1980s. Under Ehmke and later Hans
Matthöfer and Volker Hauff, the Research Ministry became the major
spokesman in Bonn for the concept of planning in economic management.

Under Schmidt's chancellorship the importance of departmental and
subject-matter planning for areas like defence and transportation was
recognised and indeed encouraged. However, in the Chancellery and in the
classical economics ministries of Economics and Finance there was growing
disillusionment with the value of planning in the global economic management of a market economy. It had been generally agreed that future projec-
tions of the development of economic aggregates, rational analyses of
economic policy options and a 'positive' coordination of economic actors
with reference to the goals of economic policy were essential to economic
stabilisation. The Council of Economic Advisers (*Sachverständi-
genrat*) had been created in 1963 to ensure that economic policy measures
were designed to achieve the general goals of economic policy; under SPD
Economics Minister Karl Schiller prognoses had become a major instrument
of economic policy as government sought to enlighten the various economic
actors about the assumptions underlying its policy measures and about the
consequences of their own behaviour for growth, employment and price
stability; and between 1967 and 1969 a variety of planning institutions like
the *Konjunkturrat* (Counter-Cyclical Advisory Council), the *Finanzplanungsrat* (Financial Planning Council) and the joint federal/state
committee for the planning of regional economic structure were created to
coordinate public-sector action.

The economic uncertainties and disappointments of the 1970s led,
however, to a decline of faith in the power and accuracy of economic analysis
that had sustained planning euphoria. As we shall see, the limitations of
macro-planning of economic aggregates were underlined by the events of
the 1970s. The Council of Economic Advisers did not possess clearly defined
and ranked goals against which it could provide the objective and non-
controversial measure of government policy that had been expected of it;
prognoses proved all too often erroneous and threatened to destabilise
economic conduct by overestimating growth as in 1977; and the diffusion of
responsibilities in expenditure planning and in regional planning did not
facilitate rational priority setting. (For example, changes in the formula for
distribution of finance in regional planning required a prohibitive three-
quarters majority that enabled the greater number of states to starve industrial problem regions like the Ruhr of the increased aid that they needed to

adapt their excessively narrow economic structures.)[3] When the planning of global economic management was confronted by such obstacles and difficulties, the attractions of an even more detailed planning of economic sectors were few and limited to the *Jusos* (Young Socialists) and SPD technocrats, neither of whom enjoyed great influence.

Both planning of fiscal policy and planning of structural policy were important political themes in the 1970s. However, under conditions of economic uncertainty, interest in the planning of global economic management declined in favour of the short-term adaptability required by crisis management; and planning of structural policy did not become as central to economic management as many SPD policy makers had hoped. Planning was never likely to become the central theme in economic management because, unlike in France, the term did not fit readily into the consistent and elegant body of economic theory that has so dominated economic policy throughout the life of the Federal Republic. The historical background of the social market economy was the desire to re-establish the idea of a distinction between state and society after the experience of the 'total state' of the Third Reich. The state's simple purpose was to provide the basic economic order, the moral framework of economic policy, within which the economic process could unfold automatically. Its functions were to ensure economic stability by safeguarding the currency and to maintain competition and participation in the economic process by policies for small firms, anti-monopoly policy and incentives for saving and shareholding. State intervention was to encourage rather than to substitute for market forces. *Ad hoc* interventions in the economic process were to be avoided in order to secure the autonomy of economic activity as the chief function of civil society. The net result of the doctrine of the social market economy was a depoliticisation of economic decision-making, a restriction of the scope of political rule by market decision and an autonomous central bank to reduce the influence of politicking on currency management.

Faced by the continuing electoral success of the parties which advocated the social market economy in the 1950s, the SPD underwent a difficult process of conversion away from policies of nationalisation and economic planning that was to provide the basis for a remarkable consensus about economic policy in the 1960s and 1970s. The SPD's famous *Bad Godesberg* Programme of 1959 did not display much enthusiasm for economic planning:

> Free competition and the free initiative of entrepreneurs are important elements of Social Democratic economic policy . . . the Social Democratic Party is in favour of the free market wherever real competition exists. But whenever markets are dominated by individuals or groups, various measures are required to preserve the freedom of the economy. As much competition as possible — as much planning as necessary.

Ministers, Policies and Institutions

In contrast to Willy Brandt his predecessor, who presided over an economic debate with whose technical fiscal and monetary details he was unfamiliar,

Schmidt acted as an economic supremo. Schmidt's first declaration of policy in 1974 pledged his government to concentration. Concentration meant for Schmidt priority to an economic management that would create stability and opportunities for growth. He worked in close cooperation with his FDP Economics Ministers (Hans Friderichs and from late 1977 Graf Otto Lambsdorff) and gave active and detailed support to the budgetary discipline that was imposed by his successors as SPD Finance Ministers (Hans Apel and Hans Matthöfer, who tended to appear as his State Secretaries).

To the irritation of some cabinet colleagues and of the parliamentary party an economic-policy cabinet dominated the formulation of government economic policy. Its members were the Chancellor, Hans-Dietrich Genscher (as leader of the FDP), the Economics, Finance and Labour Ministers, and the President of the Bundesbank. In addition, Schmidt drew on an informal circle of elite advisers who were drawn from the worlds of banking and industry.[4] He pursued a strategy of continuous close personal contact with leading figures throughout the economy. The purpose was not just to gain a detailed grasp of a constantly changing economic situation and to acquire a sense of the possible but also to bring to bear on elite decision-makers a global perspective. Schmidt conceived of politics as an activity concerned with safeguarding and improving the economic basis of the state in order to prevent the re-emergence of the sort of material and moral evils that had haunted recent German history.[5] Hence he practised a business-like approach to politics, one which emphasised the importance of technical knowledge to practical problem-solving and of discipline. Ministers were encouraged to specialise in their own particular tasks and general theoretical discussions in cabinet were discouraged. Under Schmidt's chancellorship the characteristics of political leadership were economic experience and expertise; emphasis on international economic statesmanship with Germany playing a leading role in the Western economic summits; skills of crisis management rather than long-term strategic visions; a sense of the possible; and contacts and cooperation with those possessing economic and financial power in business (over investment policy), banking (over interest rate and exchange rate policies) and organised labour (over wages and technological change).

Schmidt's political style was functional to the effective management of government business under conditions of impending economic crisis and was difficult to dislodge in the context of the political and economic pressures that accompanied recession. Nevertheless, it was associated with problems of identity and vitality for the SPD. A gap emerged between SPD party policy and a government policy that was presided over by a highly popular chancellor on whom the party seemed dependent for electoral success. Within the SPD there was a less rosy view of the record of the government. By the late 1970s the mayor of Hamburg (Schmidt's home state) was speaking of a 'spiritual deficit' as resignation spread through the SPD. Volker Hauff, the Federal Research Minister, emphasised the need to motivate through goals and values other than economic ones. In November 1977 the SPD districts of Lower Rhine, South Bavaria and South Hesse attacked 'the lack of direction' and 'neglect of programmatic work' of the party. They were joined in the next year by Bremen, Hamburg and Schleswig-Holstein. Loss of young voters to the 'green' parties in local and state elections were seen as symptomatic of these failures. Party intellectuals like Peter Glotz and Erhard Eppler sought to reactivate party discussion from outside Bonn. Indeed the post-1974 phenomenon of a reversal of the flight of able SPD politicians and officials from state capitals to Bonn that had occurred since 1969 was to be explained in part by the frustration of the discipline of power in Bonn. The absence of an offensive reform strategy in line with SPD party policy could of course be understood in structural terms rather than solely in terms of Schmidt's 'limited' political conception and 'authoritatian' style. The SPD had to govern in coalition with the Liberals, FDP, which provided two successive powerful Economics Ministers who were seen as close to the employers' interests and whose influence was a source of irritation to both the SPD and the unions.

Moreover, the consolidation of the CDU/CSU (Christian Democratic Union/Christian Social Union) majority in the Bundesrat meant a dual majority at the federal level. The upper chamber of state governments could veto any legislation that affected the territorial, financial or administrative interests of the states. For example, before the election of 1976 the CDU/CSU threatened Apel's budgetary strategy by blocking his proposal for an increase of the value-added tax. In the arbitration committee of Bundestag and Bundesrat representatives various reforms, like the 1975 tax reform, were so amended that their specifically SPD content was heavily reduced. Of course, the SPD Bundestag party was not without influence: for example, it contained influential lobbies for coal (one of whose members was Adolf Schmidt, chairman of *IG Bergbau*), the Saar and the Weser.

West German policy style in economic management emphasised dialogue in order to generate confidence and stable, realistic expectations and to foster a global perspective, both internationally and at home, and expertise (*Sachlichkeit*) in order to ensure the relevance and objectivity of that dialogue. A sense that these two qualities were lacking in so powerful a partner as the United States after 1976 shocked West German political leadership and played a part in the deteriorating US/German relations of the late 1970s. Dialogue in a spirit of objectivity was the animating spirit of the collaborative 'power-sharing' that characterised German economic policy-making and could function because of the widespread political agreement on the character of the economic order.

The language of German political economy displayed some interesting features. Whereas the English-language term 'economic system' suggested a close association with the idea of equilibrium, the German term *Wirtschaftsordnung* (economic order) manifested a characteristically German connection between law and economy and the role of legal cate-gories in economic debate. This connection found its best expression in the related term *Wirtschaftsverfassung* (economic constitution). *Wirt-schaftsverfassung* referred to the legal basis of the economic system, to the constitutional provisions, legislation, regulations and court judgements which related to the organisation and functioning of the economy. The importance of law in economic policy did not just reside in the extent to which issues like lock-outs, co-determination and the implementation of the nuclear programme were transferred to the courts for legal resolution. As is generally true of politics in a Roman Law country, legal categories were part of the texture of political life. The term economic order suggested a requirement to relate conduct in a rationalist manner to economic 'first principles', to those of the social market economy. Second, an effective functioning of the economic order was seen to depend on an acknowledgement of interdependence, in other words on a spirit of social partnership (*Sozialpartnerschaft*). In addition, the term 'stability' expressed a fundamental principle of the social market economy that was the precondition of attainment of specific goals of economic policy: a stable structure of relative prices was essential to investment in real growth and permanent employment. Social partnership and stability have been central terms in the German language of political economy: the first supported neo-corporatist ideas of collaboration in economic policy, the second was associated with the monetarist view of inflation.

At the heart of classic neo-liberal thought about the social market economy was the idea of an independent, neutral force that could take a detached view and create the objective conditions for stability. This idea found its expression in the law of 1957 which established the Bundesbank and laid down its statutory requirement to safeguard the currency. Its autonomous exercise of this key function was only to be understood against the recent historical background of two disastrous hyper-inflations. However, the 1960s saw the growth of Keynesian thought, its political expression by the SPD Economic Minister Schiller after 1966, and its embodiment in the new policy instruments that were created by the law on stability and growth of 1967. Besides facilitating deficit budgeting to counteract the sort of recession that had been experienced in 1966/7, new instruments of collaboration were established: the *Konjunkturrat* and the *Finanzplanungsrat* to coordinate the economic policy assumptions and spending plans of federal, state and local authorities; and *Konzertierte Aktion* (concerted action) to coordinate the assumptions of public authorities, trade unions and employers with reference to the attainment of the so-called 'magic square' of goals that were laid down in the new law (price stability, high level of employment and external balance with continuous economic growth).

The purpose of these new instruments was enlightenment. Continuous mutual information would enable rational and objective decisions in terms of the public interest so that an effective 'global steering' of macro-economic aggregates could be achieved with a minimum of direct government intervention in individual markets. As we shall see, after 1972 under Schmidt's direction there was a shift back towards monetary policy as stabilisation returned to top priority. Whilst the Bundesbank acquired a leading role in economic policy, Schmidt took a detailed interest in its activities and enjoyed notably close personal relations with its successive presidents — Klasen, Emminger and his former state Secretary Pöhl. Nevertheless, the central characteristic of German economic policy remained a flexible 'strategy of the middle way' that embraced Keynesian and monetarist elements and rejected a dogmatic approach that could threaten the social consensus which was seen as the key condition of an effective economic policy. There was tension between both elements, but each was derived from, or rationalised with reference to, the larger concept of the social market economy.

The system of economic policy-making was well adapted to a dispersal of the heavy load of responsibility that is involved in the management of a modern economy. A complex system that relied so heavily on the maintenance of distinct spheres of action and delegation of decision was heavily dependent on cooperative dialogue for its effective functioning. As this division of labour combined with the presence of competing party interests and ideologies, the system could be expected to generate some intense politicking.[6] Even so, the system was held together by a basic concept, the social market economy, and by a common language of political economy that emphasised collaboration.

One element of the economic policy-making system was government policy for long-term improvement of conditions for growth: for example, identifying bottlenecks (like energy) and easing structural adjustment by stimulating innovation (as in micro-electronics). SPD ministers saw an active structural policy as one of their major contributions. In particular, the creation of the Research and Technology Ministry in 1972 expressed a recognition of the importance of state support in the development and introduction of new technologies. Technocratically-minded SPD ministers like Horst Ehmke and Volker Hauff pursued the idea of modernisation of the economy through an active, anticipatory technology policy. The activities of this new 'structural ministry' aroused suspicions: of imperialism as its able expert staff extended their interests into the sectoral and environmental concerns of FDP Economics and Interior Ministers; and of favouritism as 80 per cent of its assistance went to fifteen groups of firms (notably to Siemens). This area of expenditure became a major priority when Matthöfer shifted from the Research to the Finance Ministry.

A second element of the system of economic policy-making was the encouragement of responsible collective bargaining. The importance of attitudes in both sides of industry to effective economic management was well understood, and social partnership, particularly in the form of *Konzertierte Aktion*, was undoubtedly helped by SPD participation in government. However, *Konzertierte Aktion* did not arrive at binding decisions and was primarily an occasion for the government to present 'orientation' data to the unions and employers so that they would be better informed about the consequences of their prospective policies. In fact, wage agreements kept within government figures only during recession periods like 1967/8 and 1975/6.[7] The trade unions resented the narrow scope of its subject matter, and their withdrawal in 1977 was eventually the cause of its collapse. Nevertheless, there was a continuing recognition that the principle of *Tarifautonomie*, of autonomy of price and wage determination from public regulation, was dependent on some measure of social partnership, of collaboration with reference to the public interest.[8] If *Tarifautonomie* was a stronger theme in West Germany than in that other haven of neo-corporatist politics, Austria, and suggested the danger of centralisation of economic decision-making, social partnership was more firmly established than in Britain.

Thirdly, in line with the government's determination that monetary policy should carry the main burden of stabilisation, the Bundesbank assumed the key role in the fight against inflation. For the purpose of enlightenment of the *Tarifpartner* Schmidt encouraged the Bundesbank to publish annually its monetary target. As the central bank was not subject to the directives of the government when exercising its power to safeguard the currency, there was scope for conflict between the two centres of economic decision-making. However, both institutions sought to work closely together.[9] On the one hand, the bank looked to the government to provide a consensus for policy and recognised the importance for the success of its monetary policy of the government's decisions on exchange rate policy and the size and financing of its deficit. On the other, the government realised that the bank's authority gave it considerable room for manoeuvre to safeguard what it saw as the longer-term requirements of stability against political expediency. The Bundesbank was criticised primarily for doing its job too well: for prolonging and deepening the 1973/4 recession, for throttling recovery in 1976 and for threatening economic expansion again in 1979 by restrictive monetary measures. These measures were the consequence in part of repeated failure to achieve monetary targets and in part of the inflow of 'hot' money. Two new constraints to central bank policy emerged from the mid 1970s: the rapid growth of the budget deficit and the mark's role as the world's second reserve currency. The Bundesbank was noticeably sceptical about Schmidt's major initiative to bring an element of stability into the world's currency markets, the European Monetary System which came into operation in March 1979. The central bank not only persuaded the chancellor to reduce the number of participants in the system but also reserved for itself the right to suspend interventions in currency markets unilaterally if support of the EMS threatened its duty to safeguard the currency.

A fourth element which cannot be ignored in an account of German economic management is the universal banking system which, as we shall see, has meant a large role for bankers in industry and the emergence of an industrial-banking oligarchy. Government was insulated to a greater degree than in Britain from the complex and detailed problems of monitoring and responding to the problems of major companies. The banks served as an 'early-warning' system which identified weaknesses in industry and on occasion mounted rescue operations.[10]

Finally, regular expert reports were issued by the five economic research institutes and notably by the Council of Economic Advisers and had a marked impact on the level of intellectual sophistication in economic argument.[11] Their role was to provide neutral, authoritative advice about the measures which were needed to achieve the goals of economic policy outlined in the law of 1967.

The overall picture is one of a variety of economic actors whose autonomous activities are perceived to be interdependent. For example, the stabilisation policies of the Bundesbank are seen as essential to the effectiveness of the long-term structural policies of the government, whilst the effectiveness of stabilisation is viewed as dependent on cooperation and consent. The system continued to operate without polarisation owing to the conversion of the SPD and its *Bad Godesberg* programme of 1959 to the concept of the social market economy and owing to the style of political leadership that was pursued by the SPD chancellor. In the next section the strains to which this policy-making system was subjected will be examined.[12]

The Politics of Economic Management, 1973-80

The oil crisis brought an abrupt halt to the political success of Brandt only a few months after an epic electoral victory which had returned the SPD back to power, for the first time as the largest party in the Bundestag. One of his difficulties was to achieve cooperation between two powerful and sophisticated economics ministers, Friderichs (FDP) who was a newcomer to Bonn and Schmidt who had succeeded Schiller as Economics and Finance Minister in summer 1972. As a consequence of difficult coalition negotiations in late 1972 the Economics and Finance Ministries were once again separated. Their cooperation was essential not just on grounds of administrative rationality but also in order to maintain the SPD/FDP coalition. The fact that the major instruments of economic policy were in the hands of Finance Minister Schmidt served rather to exacerbate the rivalry. Both ministers were agreed on the need for a severe deflationary programme in May 1973 and for tight monetary and credit restrictions by the Bundesbank. However, when at the end of 1973 both wanted to give a boost to the economy, they disagreed about how best to achieve this. Friderichs emphasised the importance of a continuation of the highly restrictive monetary policy; Schmidt reflected anxieties within the SPD when he argued that a policy of very high interest rates was likely to undo the effects of any measures that were designed to stimulate employment. The dispute was tactical rather than strategic and typical of later disputes within the coalition government. Successive SPD Finance Ministers, who were responsible for relations with the Bundesbank, worried about the tactical problems of coordinating the central bank's monetary policy with government's fiscal policy, especially when they perceived the need for reflation.

Symptomatic of Schmidt's conversion to the importance of monetary policy was the appointment in November 1973 of Dieter Hiss, an economic expert who had previously been responsible for monetary and credit policy, as the head of the *Grundsatzabteilung* (central policy division) of the Finance Ministry. Until the stabilisation measures of February and May 1973, monetarists had criticised Schmidt for facilitating an economic boom that was destined to lead anyway to a sharp, painful stop. An inflow of short-term capital after July 1972 had exacerbated the Bundesbank's difficulties of controlling the money supply. The oil crisis occurred against a background of frivolous expansion in areas like construction and of excessive indebtedness of investors. However, the mark's floating free of the dollar in April 1973 handed effective management of exchange rate to the Bundesbank which was then in a better position to insulate the economy from international financial disturbances. In 1974 the Bundestag elected a Chancellor who was not only economically sophisticated and preoccupied with economic crisis management but also converted by experience to stabilisation as the key to growth and employment.

Many of the disputes about economic policy within the coalition between 1974 and 1976 reflected the uncertainty about the implications of the oil crisis. At first, contradictory data clouded the government's view and even suggested that the crisis might not be a dramatic one. In early 1974 the major effects on employment were in construction, textiles, clothing and shoes. Great uncertainty hung over the car industry which experienced short-time working followed by redundancies later in the year. An export boom helped to offset some of the recessionary consequences of the sharp fall in domestic demand. The zero growth of 1974 was sustained by a 12 per cent expansion of exports at constant prices, an expansion whose effects were most notable in chemicals, electronics and steel (where productivity records were achieved).[13] Despite a record level of bankruptcies, the highest level of unemployment in July 1974 since 1960 and pressure from the car and construction industries for help, the government determined to defer further reflationary measures till 1975 (when the planned tax reform was expected to stimulate demand). Meanwhile economic uncertainty and fear for jobs were relied on to erode inflationary expectations. Bonn built up an economic policy reserve with the Bundesbank that could eventually be used for reflation. It pursued a dual economic strategy of general deflation which aimed to keep inflation below the 'critical' point of 10 per cent and specific aid to certain sectors like energy (but not the construction industry because of excess capacity).

The timing of a reflationary package posed serious political problems. On the one hand, Bonn's economic strategists and the Bundesbank saw such a package as dependent on evidence that collective bargaining was oriented to stabilisation. An early reflation could generate inflationary expectations in the 1975 pay round. On the other hand, mounting unemployment threatened to produce a sharp deterioration of relations between the SPD and the unions.[14] Also, an important state election was pending in North-Rhine Westphalia in spring 1975. Loss of this key state to the CDU would be disastrous for the SPD's morale and would give the opposition a veto over future domestic policy through domination of the Bundesrat. As the recession produced over one million unemployed in the winter of 1974/5 and began to hit skilled workers in, for example, machine tools, the mood of gloom within the SPD deepened. The extent of the economic downturn had been underestimated. In December 1974, despite the opposition of the Council of Economic Advisers, the government introduced a reflationary package. Its chief feature was a 7.5 per cent investment grant which was to last till 30 June 1975. Once again party political profile was at stake in the design of the programme. Rivalry continued between the new Finance Minister Apel and Friderichs, who was strongly supported by the FDP's powerful economics spokesman in the Bundestag, Lambsdorff. Pointing to the poor rates of return in industry (half those of the United States) and the rising proportion of wages in national income, Friderichs wanted assistance to industrial investment. Apel, who feared that there was little prospect of a revival of industrial investment in the near future, favoured public investment especially in urban transportation (to help the Ruhr). The case for aid to industrial investment won the day. The specifically SPD part of the package was a wage subsidy which was to be financed out of the economic policy reserve and to be paid to employers who took on the unemployed or cancelled planned redundancies.

The first signs of recovery from the worst period in West Germany's economic history appeared just in time to help the SPD/FDP back to power in North-Rhine Westphalia. Nevertheless, recovery was slow, in large part because the Bundesbank delayed in reducing interest rates. Although recovery continued through 1976 and helped the federal government to win, albeit with a much reduced majority, the election of that year, the recession proved more difficult to reverse than that of 1966/7. As early as 1974 the Kiel Institute for International Economics had stressed that the economy was not just experiencing a cyclical downturn. A structural crisis was affecting various sectors like textiles, shoes, clothing and leather goods and would spread. Industry had to face new competition from the Eastern bloc and the Far East where producers enjoyed the advantages of low unit labour costs and state aid. This structural crisis had been exacerbated by an excessively low exchange rate for the mark in the 1950s and 1960s. Undervaluation had encouraged uncompetitive industries, indeed an overexpansion of the industrial basis that made the German economy very vulnerable to the newly-industrialising countries.

In addition to disappointment about the pace and unevenness of recovery, an economic strategy that was oriented to stabilisation had serious political costs for the SPD and led to the jibe that Schmidt was the best Chancellor that the CDU had had. One of the notable failures of SPD reform occurred when Friderichs vetoed Education Minister Helmut Rohde's proposals for a reform of vocational training. This reform sought to increase state supervision of training schemes and examinations and to encourage apprenticeships by a compulsory levy on industry. To the irritation of the SPD, Schmidt adopted a conservative position for fear of adverse effects on the climate of investment and for reasons of appeasing a coalition partner who might raise further difficulties about codetermination legislation. He risked the resignation of an Education Minister who had particularly close contacts to the unions.

Poor industrial investment, a very slow drop in unemployment after 1975 and the failure to create jobs even in such areas of expansion as electronics led the government to decide on a four-year public investment programme in 1976. To the gratification of the SPD, 16 billion marks were allocated to infrastructural projects, especially for highways and environmental protection. However, the effects of this programme on unemployment were expected to be marginal. The recovery lost its impetus early in 1977. The scepticism of bankers and industrialists about economic prospects with continuing investment fatigue proved better founded than the optimism of most economic research institutes which had been forecasting 7-8 per cent growth for 1977. A revival of orders for investment goods and machine tools in 1976 had been due to an expansion of overseas orders. Domestically, there was continuing uncertainty about the adequacy of profits with which to finance investment, and in some sectors overcapacity was so great that higher demand was unlikely to generate new investment. By summer 1977 it was clear that the government's forecast of 5 per cent growth could not be realised and that there would be serious consequences for employment and for budgetary and social policies. In August the Economics Minister issued a crisis prognosis of 5 per cent unemployment (the previous high had been 4.7 per cent in 1975) and warned of a new recession.

The economic debate of autumn 1977 displayed a new uncertainty and an even greater disagreement about the likely effects of alternative measures. Despite the guidance of economics supremo Schmidt the Economics, Finance and Labour Ministers found difficulty in agreeing on an integrated economic strategy based on clearly ordered priorities and a rational analysis of options. They pursued a package of politically symmetrical measures. Friderichs, who was backed by the opinion of the Council of Economic Advisers, emphasised the psychological value of general tax cuts and of assistance for industrial investment. In particular, it was necessary to increase the share of profits in national income. From 1970 to 1977 profits had increased by 69 per cent, wages by 109 per cent. SPD ministers wanted tax reductions for workers and/or higher public expenditure. On the one hand, FDP ministers were sceptical of the value of another public investment programme because of the difficulties that had arisen in the implementation of the 1976 programme. On the other, SPD ministers doubted the economic value of general tax cuts and worried about the social justice and threats to consensus of an 'employers' policy'. Only a small proportion of the 14 billion marks released by the 1975 tax reform had gone into consumption; savings rose to a record level in that year. Schmidt pressed for tax relief at the bottom of the scale on grounds of both social justice and the lower savings propensity of poorer paid workers. Friderichs fought for generous depreciation allowances for industry. Accordingly, the compromise package emphasised tax changes to benefit both employers and workers. A major casualty was Apel's determination to make reduction of the budget deficit his top priority.

Early 1978 was a time of great tribulation for the government. Painful issues like unemployment, pensions and internal security in the wake of terrorist attacks were creating an identity crisis within the SPD. SPD opponents of the anti-terrorist legislation in the Bundestag were symptomatic of this disillusionment. There was also a crisis in the relationship of the unions to the government: over the abortive scheme for vocational education to deal with youth unemployment, over tax cuts which appeared to favour profits, over the break with indexed pensions and over the failure of wage restraints to generate jobs. Strikes and the falling value of the dollar depressed expectations in industry. The two major strikes of early 1978 by the metalworkers in Baden-Würtemberg and by the printers served to underline the existence of a structural crisis in the economy.[15] The falling value of the dollar meant a changed international context and a new vulnerability of the German economy. It led to a new turbulence in currency markets, cheaper imports that threatened German producers and danger to exports which since 1973 had saved the economy from even deeper recession.

A central feature of economic debate after 1973 had been uncertainty about what was likely to happen (there was a diminishing faith in prognoses) and about what could be done. Uncertainty was at its height in late 1977 and early 1978, particularly with respect to the prognosis for growth (which had only just been half realised in 1977). Between 1973 and spring 1978 there had been nine economic recovery programmes and an unprecedented growth of public debt to deal with the recession. Despite, and perhaps because of, the breakdown of *Konzertierte Aktion* in 1977 the pressures for wage restraint from employers, economic experts and the Bundesbank were considerable and often unrealistic. For example, in its report for 1978 the Council of Economic Advisers pressed for wage rises of not more than 3 per cent if investment was not to be further depressed. In the face of such uncertainty, of falling orders from home and abroad and of a forecast of two million unemployed by 1985 from the German Economics Institute (DWI) of Berlin the unions were 'disciplined'. Notwithstanding its troubled start the 1978 wage round (with an average increase of 5.7 per cent) proved the cheapest to industry of any previous round in the 1970s. The wage costs of industry were extremely stable in 1978 and 1979. Beginning in 1977, an especially high increase in profits reversed the earlier trend to an increase of the percentage of wages in national income. In addition, in 1978-9 public authorities, notably the federal government and the Bundesbank, combined to give the economy its biggest stimulus since 1973: eight billion marks of tax cuts, followed by another ten billion in 1979, a planned increase of federal, state and local authority spending by up to 10 per cent, and a record low level of interest rates. As a consequence the economy began to pick up quickly in 1978-9, and a new optimism spread even to such sectors as construction.

By early 1979 the economy was performing at its best since 1973. For the first time during this troubled period (indeed since 1971) an investment goods boom occurred. In contrast to earlier recoveries, that of 1978-9 was the product of a domestic revival rather than of an export-led boom. During the 1970s profits had been used to reduce debts to banks, to purchase high-yielding government bills or to rationalise work in order to reduce labour costs. By the late 1970s the age of plant was encouraging investment on a new scale. After a *continuous* fall from a high of 7 per cent in 1974, price inflation reached a record low of 2.1 per cent in 1978; and in the summer of 1979 unemployment dropped below 800,000. As a consequence of union restraint in line with the expectations of the federal government wage inflation dropped (from 6.9 per cent in 1977, to 5.7 per cent in 1978 and 4.8 per cent in 1979). The pressure on prices from wages fell markedly.

With the second major oil crisis of 1979 oil prices more than doubled between the end of 1978 and the beginning of 1980. This new crisis threatened to send inflation back towards at least 5 per cent in 1980 (election year) and to reduce growth and increase unemployment. The world recession that was likely to follow jeopardised exports. Unionists who had pursued moderate claims and pensioners were likely to pose problems in election year. The federal government took two initiatives, one of which was abortive. Research Minister Hauff produced a rigorous energy-saving programme which was blocked in cabinet by the Economics Minister Lambsdorff who opposed such governmental intervention. More successfully, Schmidt sought to impress on union leaders that the oil price rise represented a permanent resource transfer, a tribute to OPEC that could not be recovered by higher wage demands and redistributive struggles. Economic recovery depended on 'reasonable' pay demands. The receptiveness of union leaders to this exercise in economic education was one reason why the German economy reacted more efficiently to the second oil crisis than in 1973.

In addition, political emphasis was once again placed on stabilisation by the Bundesbank's policy of dear money. There were political anxieties in Bonn about the effects of a policy of high interest rates on growth and employment in election year. However, anxieties about the political effects of rising inflation were even greater. Fears of a repeat of 1974/5 did not in fact materialise. Despite the new uncertainty economic activity continued to be brisk. Capital utilisation in manufacturing and construction was higher than at any time since 1973. In the winter of 1979-80 unemployment did not deteriorate in cyclical terms. The major reason for rising inflation was a 27 per cent increase in import prices between 1979 and 1980. One important effect of this increase of import prices was an end to the large balance of payments surplus that had so irritated other deficit countries and led earlier to pressures on Germany to reflate more strongly. After a sharp rise in 1973/4, the surplus had in fact fallen till 1978 when it rose to the second highest figure since 1949. In 1979 the balance of payments went into deficit for the first time since 1965. The reason for this turnaround was a sharp decline of the surplus on the balance of trade, a decline which reflected higher prices for oil and the vigorous revival of the economy. Overall, however, the economy and the system of economic management continued to display a remarkable degree of adaptability and resilience.

The Problem of State Finances

The major development in economic management was the huge increase in the size of the public debt. In 1980 it was already higher than the federal budget and, according to the financial plan, debt servicing would account for almost one quarter of total federal expenditure in 1981 and become the largest item in the budget. The decisive change came in 1974/5 when the debt was more than trebled in order to finance reflationary programmes at a time of falling tax revenue with recession and the tax reform. A higher debt was incurred in the 1974 budget than in the first four years of the government combined. Indeed public debt had declined from 7.2 per cent of GNP in 1962 (under a CDU/CSU/FDP government) to 5.8 per cent in 1973. As the 1980 election approached, the politics of the budget revolved around two alternatives: either to concentrate on reducing the debt as the Bundesbank wanted (in which case tax cuts would become the major electoral issue) or to make tax cuts as the FDP wanted (in which case the public debt would be the major electoral issue). SPD Finance Minister Matthöfer preferred to give priority to the problem of the public debt which threatened to seriously reduce future room for budgetary manoeuvre. Eventually it was agreed to prepare a programme of tax cuts which would take effect after the election in 1981. As a corollary Schmidt and Matthöfer sought to educate the SPD before the election about the limited scope for new expenditure commitments especially in the context of a more volatile international situation to which a vulnerable West Germany has responded with an enlarged aid programme, higher defence spending and increased contributions to the EEC.

A further problem of economic management was that of realising expenditure programmes in the interests of economic recovery. By 1978 some 25 billion marks of public investment were blocked: airport developments at Düsseldorf and Frankfurt by citizen-action groups, road construction by long procedures of approval, purification plants by complicated legal provisions and the nuclear programme by the courts.[16] In addition, and to the irritation of the federal government, the state governments and local authorities were not cooperating fully with federal reflationary measures. They were holding back their expenditures, not taking up federal aid and building up reserves. Their abiding suspicion of budget deficits led to criticism of their lack of economic sophistication especially from Keynesians. The problem was especially great at the local authority level which accounted for two-thirds of public investment. Their contribution to economic management was negative; local authorities increased expenditure during booms and reduced them during recession. Federal reflationary programmes were in danger of doing little more than make up for mistakes at the state and local authority levels. In 1977 only eight out of 14 billion marks that had been allocated to federal reflationary programmes *up till 1975* had been spent. A long, complex process of official approval extending from local authorities, district administrations, state governments to the federal government and then back again meant that use of the sixteen billion marks provided by the four-year investment programme of 1976 would not begin till late 1978. The *Konjunkturrat* and the *Finanzplanungsrat* did not prove effective forums for a coordinated fiscal policy in the interests of economic management. Success of federal expenditure programmes was very much in the hands of state governments and local authorities.

As might be expected of SPD/FDP governments, the state's share of GNP rose from 37.9 per cent in 1969 to 47.3 per cent in 1979. However, the recession revealed in sharper focus the problems of the *Sozialstaat*. On the one hand, shortfalls in tax revenue disclosed the burden of social service expenditure and forced an expansion of public debt. On the other, the SPD left-wing and CDU social reformers like Heinrich Geissler criticised the failure of the *Sozialstaat* to channel resources to those most in need (like the mentally handicapped) whilst farmers and the self-employed benefited not only from great tax privileges but also from social expenditure (for example, child benefits). In particular, the social budget of the Agriculture Ministry had grown sharply in the 1970s; the federal government was subsidising very generous pensions for farmers to the tune of 78 per cent. Public-service pensions were also very much more generous than those for employees in the private sector. *Beamte* and farmers (especially the better-off) represented the two groups most favoured by the *Sozialstaat*. Transfer payments appeared not only to be having perverse effects as far as the criterion of need was concerned but also to have grown so large over time that they had become more important for the citizen than the more visible results of collective bargaining. Social policy had come to represent a distribution of political power that was easier to ignore than to tackle. The *Beamtenbund* and the *Bauernverband* had their respective spokesmen in the Interior and Agriculture Ministries. Although the Social and Labour Minister remained responsible for the classic core of social policy (pensions, health and unemployment insurance), he was no longer the determining voice. When cuts in social expenditure (for example, pensions) were being considered, the heavy subsidies to *Beamte* and farmers remained politically immune.

Against this background Herbert Wehner, the powerful chairman of the SPD in the Bundestag, spoke of the need for a 'social policy offensive' in time for the 1980 election. Already the chancellor had been personally embarrassed in 1976/7 by his failure to keep to his election promise on pensions. The legislative period 1976-80 was haunted by the recurrent problem of financing pensions. By 1977 the value of pensions was higher than ever before. The standard pension was 63.3 per cent of net income in employment and had grown at an annual average of 10 per cent since 1972, a rate much higher than that of wage rises. However, higher unemployment and lower growth reduced contributions. In 1977 the principle of index-linked pensions was broken for the first time since 1957. Extra money had also to be found to fulfil the requirement of the Federal Constitutional Court that by 1984 there should be an equal treatment of men and women in pension law. The issue of pensions caused bitter dispute between SPD and FDP (the Chancellor tended to side with Lambsdorff's reluctance to return to dynamic pensions and favour financial realism) and between the government and the unions which preferred increased contributions to loss of dynamic pensions. In the end the social policy offensive of the SPD was abortive. The attempt of the Wehner Commission to reform pension policy in order to assist the 40 per cent of employees who lived off normal pension insurance failed when Schmidt and Matthöfer sought to avoid promises of any expensive social reforms in an election year when political attention would focus on tax cuts and the public debt.

CONCLUSIONS

The West German government's policy response to the threat of economic recession that had been generated by changes in the international economy in the 1970s was conditioned by the differentiated and liberal institutional structure of the economy at home. In particular, and as a response to distrust of state economic power after the experience of the Third Reich, much reliance was placed on two institutions: the central bank for the attainment of economic stability, and the big commercial banks as the major focus of relationships with industry for assisting the adaptation of industry to changes in the market. State and bank power was matched to privately formulated and competitive market strategy, oriented to the requirements of industrial efficiency and product development. Domestically, the commercial banks, as market-oriented institutions themselves, ensured that the strategies and structures of industry were sensitive to the working of the market in which they developed their own particular expertise. Internationally, the German government and banks sought to breathe new life into transnational institutions and arrangements in order to ensure stabilisation of the international economy and to open or maintain access to foreign markets. In other words, German economic policy did not consciously seek to impose the state's will on the market and to insulate firms from the market's constraints. The differentiated character of the economic policy-making system was the counterpart of the focus on sensitivity to market in domestic policy and on the constraints of interdependence and the need for dialogue and adaptation in international economic policy.

The government's economic policy was based on the premise that the problems of stability and growth had economic causes and could not be effectively tackled, and indeed were likely to be aggravated by addressing their political symptoms. This premise was supported by government's insulation from the political pressures of industry by the commercial banks in the field of industrial policy and by the central bank's insulation from reflationary political pressures in the realm of currency management. The banks acted as major initiators and organisers of industrial activity so that industrial policy remained somewhat screened from the general arena of politics. Outside the SPD left-wing and technocrats, the conception of an activist, entrepreneurial role for the state had little support, except when the structural problems of industry were perceived to be too great for the banks to handle alone (as in such cases as the Ruhr coal industry in the 1960s and the Saar steel industry and the shipbuilding industry in the 1970s). The premise of the economic cause of industrial problems was widely shared; distributional struggles, which involved the exercise of power in the economic system, were constrained by the primacy that was attached by actors within industry itself to the attainment of the economic goals of stability and growth.

An economic policy-making system as differentiated as that of West Germany suggests considerable limitations on party government in economic policy-making. The formulation of economic policy displayed a curious ambiguity. One characteristic of the system of economic management was the pervasiveness of party identification not only amongst senior officials in the economic ministries but also as a criterion in appointments to the council of the Bundesbank, most notably, Karl Otto Pöhl (SPD), a former journalist, State Secretary in Bonn's Finance Ministry and confidant of Schmidt, who in 1979 became president of the Bundesbank. More generally, the growing importance of partisans in positions of authority suggested the *Parteienstaat* (party state) character of the Federal Republic.[18] Successive economic policy programmes were designed with great attention to party political symmetry — aid to the lower-paid to meet SPD concern about social justice and aid to the employers to meet FDP concern for the logic of the social market economy. Electoral considerations also influenced economic policy formulation. The attempt of the coalition parties to adopt distinctive profiles before an election, as in 1979-80, could exacerbate problems of making policy for energy, pensions, taxation and the public debt. Public subsidies were often designed to attract voters or at least to appease party feeling. Expenditure on agriculture — particularly on social policies for farmers — was greatly expanded by an FDP Agriculture Minister. The Ruhr aid programme was launched in time for the local authority and state elections of 1979 and 1980 in North-Rhine Westphalia, whilst a new and generous programme of aid to the shipping industry appeared before the Schleswig-Holstein election of 1979.

To the sensitive observer, the balance of party political power was clearly significant for the evolution of economic policy. The term consensus, when applied to German economic policy, is liable to detract attention from differing party political perspectives. For instance, within the social-liberal coalition SPD ministers like Ehrenberg tended to prefer the Keynesian response of a sharp injection of demand in order to offset recessionary tendencies; by contrast Friderichs and later Lambsdorff sought to concentrate on a longer-term improvement of the conditions of supply in the name of competitiveness. Furthermore, SPD politicians, including Schmidt, held a more instrumental conception of the market economy. The term social market economy did not even appear in the SPD's election programme of 1980. As in its framework programme OR'85 the party emphasised an 'active, anticipatory structural policy' that was centred on the Research Ministry. The disputes between Hauff's 'SPD ministry' and Lambsdorff's 'market economy ministry' over energy and structural policy surfaced in the 1980 election campaign, in which Lambsdorff came to personify the principles of the market economic order. Following the FDP's electoral success in increasing its share of the vote in 1980 from 7.9 per cent to 10.6% (whilst the SPD stabilised its share) the balance of party political power in economic policy was altered. Within the coalition government FDP ministers emphasised the central role of the Bundesbank in the attainment of economic stability in the context of new problems of external balance and the need for priority of tax cuts over public expenditure in fiscal measures. It was increasingly difficult for the Chancellor to maintain a sense of party political symmetry in these altered circumstances. The SPD was alarmed by the government's apparent greater willingness to sacrifice employment to more pressing requirements of economic stability.

At the same time, professional public-service values remained paramount in economic policy-making and were safeguarded by the growing percentage of public officials in the membership of the major parties. The government was not notably constrained by detailed alternative economic policies of the coalition parties although its economic ministers offered contrasting perspectives. This situation was not fundamentally changed by the SPD's new medium-term programme 1975-1985. The parties hesitated to be very specific in the face of their self-conception as 'catch-all' parties

(*Volksparteien*) which deliberately opened themselves to attract a maximum of support and of the prevailing conception of social partnership which emphasised cooperation.[19] Schmidt sacrificed SPD party policy not only to the exigencies of coalition (as over vocational education and co-determination) and the need (as with the 1975 tax reform) to get the agreement of the Bundesrat but also to his view of the autonomy and priority of government. He was assisted by SPD Finance Ministers like Apel and Matthöfer who were progressive technocrats and backed Schmidt's attempt to educate party and country into the logic of economic argument.

There was also the autonomous role of the Bundesbank which, as in its controversial restrictive measures of January 1979, was prepared to withstand criticism from Bonn. The Bundesbank's policy leadership stemmed from a combination of intellectual and legal authority that confirmed its strategic importance. Its authority flowed from the perception at political and administrative levels of the priority of stabilisation and of the significance of monetary policy to stabilisation and from the legal authority of the central bank to act to safeguard the currency.

Another source of expertise in economic policy-making was provided by interest groups. Certain interests had notably close cooperative relations with government ministries that overrode party considerations—the nuclear industry with the Research Ministry, the oil industry with the Economics Ministry and the *Beamtenbund* with the Interior Ministry. In particular, the Federal Association of German Banks and the Federation of German Industry (BDI) had intimate contacts with the Economics and Finance Ministries. The head of the currency policy division of the Finance Ministry had previously been on the payroll of the banks' association, whilst the director-general of the BDI for many years was Fritz Neef, former State Secretary in the Economics Ministry (he was replaced by a former State Secretary in the Defence Ministry). Interests were also able to offer their expertise and exert their influence in parliament. In the Bundestag 70.3 per cent of the members of the committee on labour and social policy were union members and 77.7 per cent of the members of the agriculture committee were farmers.

The dictates of party policy were sacrificed to the need to tie together a loosely structured, yet clearly identifiable system of economic policy-making through negotiation and accommodation. Partisan arguments were firmly presented and argued in the context of a perceived interdependence which suggested the value of mutual forebearance. An economic expertise that paid great attention to the logic of the economic order carried a great deal of influence in the deliberations of interests as well as of the government and Bundesbank. Accordingly, economic problem-solving took on a technically rational character. It was pervaded by a functional rather than ideological spirit that subordinated specific goals to the larger requirements of an effective functioning of the whole economy. The nature of German economic argument is only to be understood against the background of an intellectual tradition of political economy that has given key place to the concept of the state.[20] This tradition has fostered public-regarding attitudes. a deep sense of interdependency and social responsibility even in the exercise of private economic power. No longer is the concept of the state simply identified with a public bureaucracy which seeks to realise certain inherent public purposes in the face of political opposition and market constraints. It is used to imply a shared responsibility for maintaining a particular moral framework for economic activity.

Generalisations about the future of Germany's economic policy arrangements must inevitably be tentative and provisional. In the 1970s, as in the two previous decades, West Germany's economic policy arrangements were tied together by shared assumptions. These assumptions are rooted in historical experiences of inflation and of the political and economic dislocation which inflation can induce. Consequently, there has been a cultural support for the central bank's stabilisation policies and for union wage restraint, both of which have supported each other. There are, nevertheless, threats to the harmony and stability of the economic policy-making system, threats which already surfaced in the 1970s. Problems of cooperation could be aggravated, for example, by changes within the system of collective bargaining as a result of intransigence of the employers or of rank-and-file dissent within the unions; by the effects of a change in political power on the climate of industrial relations; or by a perception that the central bank's overreaction was producing unbearable costs in terms of growth and unemployment. Perhaps even more significantly, in the longer run it is possible that anti-inflationary cultural attitudes will erode in importance as time, political security and experience of new economic problems displace the value that has been attached to price stability in German economic calculations.

NOTES

1. For details see K. H. F. Dyson, 'Improving Policy-making in Bonn', *Journal of Management Studies*, May 1975, pp. 157-74.
2. F.W. Scharpf, *Krisenpolitik*, Friedrich-Ebert-Stiftung, Bonn-Bad Godesberg.
3. For a discussion of the political problems of the Ruhr see K. H. F. Dyson's chapter on West Germany in A. Cox (ed.), *Policy, Politics and Economic Recession in Western Europe*, London: Macmillan, 1981.
4. Members of this circle included bankers like Jürgen Ponto (a terrorist victim of 1977) of the Dresdner Bank and Wilfried Guth of the Deutsche Bank and industrialists like Berthold Beitz (Krupp), Herbert Grünewald (Bayer), Hans Merkle (Bosch) and Bernhard Plettner (Siemens). The influence of bankers was not new; Adenauer had relied on the advice of Hermann Abs (Deutsche Bank) and Robert Pferdmenges. In the 1970s Ponto emerged as a successor of Abs, arranging huge international credits and reportedly being favoured by Schmidt in 1974 as the new Finance Minister. He held appointments on the supervisory boards of such powerful corporations as Krupp (Dresdner Bank became once again its chief financier), Thyssen, Daimler-Benz, Metallgesellschaft and Hapag-Lloyd.
    On Schmidt's conception of political leadership see Peter Glotz, *Die Innenausstattung der Macht, Politisches Tagebuch 1976-1978*, Munich: Steinhausen, 1980.
6. The intense politicking in industrial relations in the 1970s and the theory and practice of social partnership are discussed by Dyson in Cox (ed.), op. cit.
7. G. Lehmbruch and W. Lang, 'Die Konzertierte Aktion', *Der Bürger im Staat*, September 1977, p. 207.

8. Hanns-Martin Schleyer, *Unternehmerpolitik*.
9. For a useful discussion see H. Bockelmann, 'The Role of the Bundesbank', address to ASGP conference, Liverpool, 1979.
10. For example, the banks mounted major rescue operations for the ailing Krupp empire in 1967 (in effect Krupp passed into their hands) and for the electronics giant AEG in the 1970s. A discussion of the universal banking system, of the industrial power of the banks and of the AEG rescue operation is contained in Dyson, op. cit.
11. The Council of Economic Advisers, the so-called 'five wise men', dates from legislation of 1963. It was established as an authoritative institution whose members were appointed for five years by the Federal President. The yearly reports of the Council were expected to assist an objectification (*Versachlichung*) of wages policy. In contrast to its American equivalent, the Council's function was to advise all those responsible for economic policy decisions and not just the federal government. Its reports are submitted to the Bundestag and the Bundesrat and the government is legally obliged to present a reply. By and large the Council has adopted a critical view of government policy and served to stimulate a more sophisticated economic discussion. As with another economic institution, the Bundesbank, its self-assurance and prestige derive from a reputation as a neutral and objective actor which stands above particular interests. The Council's best known recommendation was for *Konzertierte Aktion*.
12. The detailed development of the German economy is discussed in Dyson, op. cit.
13. On German exports see Dyson, ibid.
14. On unemployment as a political issue see Dyson, ibid.
15. These strikes and the relations of government and unions are discussed by Dyson, ibid.
16. On the importance of the nuclear issue see Dyson, ibid. The best general discussion is contained in H. Kitschelt, *Kernenergiepolitik*, Frankfurt: Campus, 1980.
17. The role of parties in economic policy is also discussed in Dyson, ibid.
18. On the concept of the 'party state' and its practical expression in the penetration of party members into the major public institutions see K.H.F. Dyson, *Party State and Bureaucracy in West Germany*, Beverly Hills: Sage, 1977. For details about the parties and the Bundesbank see K.H.F. Dyson, 'The Ambiguous Politics of West Germany', *European Journal of Political Research*, No. 7, 1979, pp. 388-90.
19. For an excellent general discussion of the parties' impact on public policy see W. E. Paterson, 'Problems of Party Government in West Germany: A British Perspective' in Döring H., and Smith G. (eds) *Party Government and Political Culture in Western Germany*, London: Macmillan, 1981.
20. The implications of the continental European state tradition for political economy are discussed in K. H. F. Dyson, *The State Tradition in Western Europe*, Oxford: Martin Robertson, 1980.

The Federal Republic — A Conservative Revisionist

Jonathan Story

Chancellor Helmut Schmidt's presence at the summit conference in Guadeloupe, in January 1979, alongside the leaders of the United States, France and the United Kingdom, appeared as substantiating evidence of Germany's emergence as the preponderant economic and diplomatic power in western and central Europe. Yet it may be equally argued that the essential condition of the West German predicament is not dominance so much as dependence in a world of sovereign states. Political consensus on the functioning of the constitution reinforces the Federal Republic as the European Community's foremost exporter, industrialist and banker; but the continuing integration of the German into the European and world economy accentuates the Federal Republic's dependence on the cooperation of other governments. Cooperation is always partial, burdened by the past, the fact of Germany's division and the continuous evolution in relations between the great powers.[1] The most that can be done is for the West German authorities to draw on an understandable pride to preserve what has been accomplished in the last thirty years in the Federal Republic, and to seek to pre-empt unfavourable developments by timely actions, and reinsurance arrangements. West Germany's paradox, then, is to be conservative by disposition and interest but revisionist by dint of its industrial pre-eminence, national claims and geographic centrality in Europe. West Germany needs the European Community, but cannot create it in its own image; it has sought American military protection, but cannot live easily with the dollar.

THE ROOTS OF THE GERMAN REVIVAL

Since the setting up of the Federal Republic in 1949, German export performances have rested on a formidable production system. The currency reform of 1948 and foreign demand for German goods in the Korean war helped to set to work the industrial system built up during the war.[2] Federal government policies, also, were geared to stimulating investment, and curtailing domestic consumption. Furthermore, the international context for a national expansion of German industrial capacity could hardly have been more favourable. Marshall Aid totalling 4.4 billion dollars[3], an undervalued currency, and American championing of a freeing of European trade enabled German producers, at first reluctant, to redirect production to western markets. No tariffs were erected between the two Germanies, inter-German trade being regulated according to the 'interzonal' trade agreement of 1951. This status of inter-German trade was recognised in the General Agreement on Tariffs and Trade, and later in the protocol appended to the Rome Treaty, setting up the European Community. The West German economy grew at an annual average of 8 per cent in the 1950s, investment rates attained 25 per cent of GNP, income from entrepreneurship averaged 40 per cent of national income, labour costs — held down by the abundant supply of unemployed labour and immigration from eastern Europe — remained low, and concentration trends gathered pace. By 1958, the German industrial production index based on 1950 stood at 209.

Conditions in the 1960s became less favourable for German business. Full employment was attained in 1959, and the construction of the Berlin Wall by the East German authorities in 1961 ended the exodus of skilled labour to the West. Women entered the labour force, and workers were imported from the Mediterranean countries as labour shortages shifted the balance of influence away from capital as a factor of production to labour. Unions pressed their claims in tighter labour markets, and the proportion of national income which was taken by employees rose to 57 per cent. Though gross fixed capital formation remained at an annual average of about 25 per cent over the decade, growth rates in GNP declined to an average of 5 per cent.[4] Corporate investment strategies became more capital intensive, and greater recourse was taken to external sources of financing. German industrial corporations thus became more sensitive to the monetary policies of the Bundesbank, which had been set up in 1957 with a statutory mandate to maintain price stability and co-operate with the government in the elaboration of economic policies. At the same time, a growing consensus among political elites on the desirability of corporate concentration to meet foreign competition — particularly American — allied with an ineffective Federal Office of Cartels, opened the authorities in Bonn to demands for government handouts. West Germany's membership in NATO, American pressures to increase the purchase of US arms, and labour requests for more public expenditure on welfare, culminated, therefore, with a redefinition of central government's role in macro-economic management in 1966-67.

The Ministry of Economics' powers were extended in the 1960s with the slow introduction of Keynesian fiscal policies. Planning in the French manner was rejected for a toolkit of fiscal fine-tuning, the first element of which was set in place in 1963 with the nomination of the five economists to a Council of Experts with a brief to report to the government on a yearly basis. The import of inflationary pressures into West Germany, linked to the Johnson administration's inflationary financing of the 'Great Society' and the Vietnam war,[5] and the related difficulties in coordinating policies between the Bundesbank and the Ministry of Economics, helped precipitate the recession of 1966-1967. The fall of the Erhard government, and the creation of the Grand Coalition between Christian Democrats and Social Democrats, paved the way for the Federal Republic's partial compliance with Western demands — expressed in the Organisation for Economic Cooperation and Development (OECD) annual studies on West Germany — for more emphasis on deficit spending. The Stability and Growth Act provided the Ministry of Economics with an extensive set of policy instruments, placing the relations between business associations, trade unions, the federal and *Land* ministries and the Bundesbank on a more formal basis.

Federal and *Land* governments were to coordinate fiscal policies more closely in order to contribute 'in the framework of a market economy to achieving simultaneously, a high degree of employment and external equilibrium, together with a steady and adequate economic growth'. This was to be achieved by government action, virtually free of parliamentary scrutiny, and by 'concerted action' between government, employers associations and trade unions on income policies.[6]

Bonn's *Liberaleordnungspolitik*, implying a state limited to maintaining the conditions necessary for market competition and price stability, became increasingly difficult to reconcile with the strains in relations between France and the United States over the Atlantic alliance, the international financial system, trade and agricultural policies and relations with developing countries. In 1967, the Federal Republic emphatically opted for priority in relations with the United States, with devastating long-term effects on world monetary stability. Agreement on military offset arrangements was reached, with the Bundesbank confirming Washington in its intention not to convert dollar holdings into gold as the French were doing. Germany's obligations were to be met by the Bundesbank's purchase of medium-term United States securities, as a way of reducing German inflationary pressures under conditions of fixed exchange rates and payments surpluses. The counterpart to America's military protection was thus Germany's acceptance of a de facto world dollar standard. The subsequent financial upheavals have been ascribed by Robert Triffin to America's diplomatic success in ending the convertibility of dollar into gold, leading to an enormous increase in international liquidity.[7] Triffin calculated that United States government indebtedness in the form of Treasury securities, and bank liabilities to foreigners, doubled from 78 billion dollars end 1969 to 144 billion dollars end 1972. International foreign exchange reserves doubled over the same period, and private bank foreign lending and liabilities rose from 121 billion dollars in 1969 to 217 end 1972.

This explosion in liquidity led, not just to the generalised adoption of floating rates in March 1973 and to the five-fold increase of oil prices in 1973-1974, but to the subsequent 'recycling' of funds to countries in balance of payments deficits, to the need for western banks and corporations to promote open markets in the western world and industrialisation in the 'developing' world for the repayment of debts, and to the opportunities for western governments to finance deficits by increasing debts on international capital markets. In the 1970s, this was the price which many Western and Eastern European governments had to pay to preserve the political and social stability which German exporters, among others, required.

The Federal government nonetheless moved slowly and reluctantly to floating exchange rates. Fixed exchange rates, sanctioned by the Bretton Woods agreements of 1944, helped to sustain the price competitiveness of West German exports. Trade associations were active in bringing pressure on the Ministries of Finance and Economics to retain the undervaluation of the DM. The Christian Democrats, too, feared that floating exchange rates would jeopardise the price arrangements on farm products recently reached with other member states in the European Community. But the continued inflow of short-term capital led the Bundesbank in October 1969 to adjust the parity rate upwards. 'The revaluation of the DM was designed to check as quickly as possible, internal economic activity and the domestic price rise.'[8] At the subsequent Hague summit, Chancellor Brandt joined with President Pompidou in making proposals for a European monetary union, based on fixed exchange rates in the European Community, one of the main planks of the new government's *Westpolitik*. The move was made partly to allay French fears of an independent German foreign policy towards Moscow and the eastern bloc countries, and partly to secure the SPD's Free Democrat partner the support of the domestic farm lobby.[9] But the Germans insisted from the start of the negotiations leading to the launching of the Werner Plan on monetary union, that monetary policy should be based on harmonisation of economic policies between member states. No agreement could be reached with Paris, while the Federal Reserve embarked on an expansionary monetary course in 1970. The Bundesbank allowed the DM to float up in May 1971; in August, President Nixon announced the end of the dollar's convertibility into gold and imposed a 10 per cent surcharge on imports, seeming to threaten the whole trading and financial system on which German prosperity depended. In December, the DM was again pegged up against the dollar. The following year, the European Community's meagre efforts to narrow the band of fluctuations between member currencies was overshadowed by the Nixon administration's pre-election boom, leading a synchronised boom in the rest of the industrialised world, dragging the German economy through the sudden expansion of foreign demand for German exports into an inflationary growth. In March 1973, the final decision was taken to 'float' the DM, by withdrawing Bundesbank interventions on foreign exchange markets.

As long as the Federal Republic adhered to fixed exchange rates, by pegging the DM to the dollar, none of the domestic institutional innovations, nor the attempts to maintain exchange rate parities in the European Community, met with much success. The trend to a decline in the share of national income going to entrepreneurship continued; labour markets remained tight, leading to a further inflow of Mediterranean labour; 'concerted action' between government, management and unions failed to improve industrial relations.[10] Growth rates after the 1966-1967 recession became more erratic, with very high rates of growth in 1968 and 1969, accompanied by high profits for enterprises and an unprecedented wave of strikes led by the unions, whose members had considered that their cooperation under 'concerted action' had been sold to the employers' benefit. Domestic prices rose to about Community levels, as the Bundesbank attempted to mop up short-term capital inflows on the exchange markets; foreign exchange reserves rose from over 7 billion to 27.4 billion dollars between 1969 and 1973[11], when the Ministry of Economics effectively lost control to the Bundesbank over exchange rate policy, which it had acquired under the 1967 Act. By floating the DM free of the dollar, the West German economy was partially isolated from the world financial upheavals of the subsequent years. But, equally, the DM became a 'polar currency',[12] to which the Scandinavian, Benelux, Austrian and Swiss currencies were tied in movements against the dollar, and against the British pound sterling, the French franc and the Italian lira in western Europe. The DM became the major alternative asset, besides the Swiss franc, the Japanese yen (and gold) to the United States dollar: its value was thus a function of domestic German *and* American monetary policies.

While West Germany moved to a direct correlation between the DM exchange rate and domestic American monetary policy, West German trade and industry was becoming increasingly bound into European markets. Between 1950 and 1969, the Federal Republic's accumulated trade surplus amounted to DM 180 billions.[13] This surplus by the 1970s was accounted for by the heavy concentration on capital goods, with 55 per cent of total exports, intermediary goods representing 25 per cent and consumer goods only 10 per cent.[14] Machinery and transport equipment accounted for about 46 per cent of exports. Geographically, German exports had shifted away from the developing world to industrial countries, which absorbed 83 per cent of total exports in 1970, as against 76 per cent in 1955. In particular, Western European markets had increased their importance for German producers, taking 70.6 per cent of the total. The European Community took 46.7 per cent of the total exports, as against 35.2 per cent in 1955. In 1970, the United States was still just ahead of France as the Federal Republic's main export market.

The combination of free-floating and domestic stabilisation measures in early 1973 enabled the Bundesbank to regain control over monetary policy. Nominal interest rates rose sharply, unemployment moved up, and West German growth rates declined to zero for that year. The export surplus expanded. Geographically, the West German surplus with the Community of the Nine increased from DM 0.8 billion in 1972, to DM 8.5 billion in 1973, and DM 17.3 billion in 1974. The surplus rose with Austria, Switzerland, the Scandinavian countries, as well as with the United States and the Soviet bloc. France had to detach the franc from the DM in January 1974, and again in 1976. A similar pattern showed in the composition of German exports. The net surplus in industrial exports (defined as the net of categories 5-9, SITC) rose from DM 45.1 billion in 1970 to 54.9 billion in 1972, to 73.8 in 1973 and 107.8 billion in 1974. Eighty-six per cent of this net surplus came from two categories — manufactured goods, and machinery and transport equipment. It was from this strong external position that West Germany faced the oil price rises of early 1974. It was also the base from which Herr Schmidt, succeeding Brandt to the Chancellorship in May 1974, sought to set the tone for a more assertive German policy in the Atlantic alliance and in Western Europe.

WEST GERMANY'S EXPORT PERFORMANCE: 1974-1978

The Federal Republic's emergence as the European Community's foremost exporter elicited a foreign and domestic response: West German trade surpluses became a significant symbol in domestic political debates on economic policies in Western Europe. The evolution of Socialist and Communist parties in Western Europe re-inforced the pessimistic evaluations by German corporations of business prospects. Not only did international markets appear threatened; they tended to assess their relative competitiveness pessimistically. Such calculations are derived from considerations of the movements of effective exchange rates and of domestic indicators such as changes in relative prices and costs.[15] However the calculations are made, the results point to a deterioration in Germany's international price competitiveness, whether measured in exchange rates or unit labour costs. First, the effective exchange rate of the DM against the currencies of Germany's main trading partners rose by 28 per cent between 1973 and 1978. Secondly, unit labour costs measured in a common currency reveal that only Japan, Switzerland and The Netherlands experienced a faster growth than Germany. Nonetheless, the accumulated trade surplus (cif imports and fob exports) between 1974 and 1978 amounted to DM 201.7 billion. In 1978, West Germany was in surplus with western industrialised countries, the Soviet bloc and OPEC member states. Deficits were recorded with The Netherlands, Italy and Japan.

The significance of Germany's pivotal position in the European economies may be briefly summarised. Firstly, West Germany dominates the European market space and derives its principal earnings from Western Europe. Secondly, the composition of German exports and imports points to the degree of industrialisation, and the role of West Germany as Europe's workshop.

West Germany may be said to dominate the European market in three senses. Firstly, nearly three-quarters of West German trade is European. Between 1973 and 1978, the European Community of the Nine absorbed about 45 per cent of total West German exports, and accounted for about 49 per cent of total West German imports. Austria, Switzerland and Sweden absorbed 12.6 per cent of West German exports over the same period, and accounted for 8.8 per cent of German imports. Other Western European countries in the OECD accounted for a further 15 to 20 per cent of West German commercial exchanges, in addition to which the proportion of West German trade with the Soviet Union and with Eastern Europe remained at around 5 to 6 per cent of the German total. Secondly, over the decade, the European continent, East and West, accounted for about 95 per cent of the accumulated trade surplus of West Germany, with the European Community — particularly France and Britain — taking about 23 per cent; Austria, Sweden and Switzerland taking another 40 per cent; the Mediterranean countries absorbing about 20 per cent, and eastern Europe 10 per cent.[16] Thirdly, West German trade patterns shifted from an Atlantic orientation, to a North-South emphasis. The United States accounted by 1978 for 7 per cent of West German imports and exports. Japan — America's single largest trading partner — accounted for only 1 to 2 per cent of West German exports and imports. The most notable increase in German trade came with OPEC and the developing countries, which together took 22 per cent of German exports as against 10.8 per cent in 1970. The German export drive on OPEC markets after the 1974 oil price increases resulted in an accumulated trade surplus of over DM 10 billion between 1976 and 1978.

West Germany became the workshop of Europe, as an analysis of trade content indicates. A net importer of food, raw materials and mineral fuels, West Germany remained strongly in deficit in these categories, despite an improvement in agricultural trade. The deficit for these categories, amounting to 316 billion DM between 1973 and 1978, was compensated by an accumulated surplus over the same period of 513 billion DM for categories 5-9 (chemicals, manufactured goods, machinery and transport, miscellaneous manufactured articles and other commodities). This accumulated trade surplus came from the 715 billion DM imports, and the accumulated total of 1,228 billion DM of industrial good exports. The major part of this huge export effort derived from manufactured goods (306 billion DM) and machinery and transport (669.7 billion DM). The accumulated net surplus from these two categories exceeded the accumulated deficit of all German food, raw materials and mineral fuels over the period. No other Western European country approximated that performance.

Despite the pride of German businessmen in their successes, they remained far from optimistic about their future. One complaint concerned the growing penetration of the domestic markets by foreign competitors, reflecting the relative deterioration in German international price competitiveness. Imports of chemicals, manufactured goods, machinery and transport and manufactured articles all rose faster in proportion to GNP than exports in the same categories. Between 1974 to 1978, the ratio of the growth of all import categories to the rate of growth in GNP was positive. By the end of 1978, total imports as a percentage of GNP had risen to 19 per cent, as compared to 15.8 per cent in 1973. But the volume effect of import trade was offset by an improvement in the terms of trade resulting from the international price trends in raw materials and mineral fuels, and in the appreciation of the DM. In 1978, the ratio of the growth in exports to growth in GNP was slightly higher than that for imports. As a result the trade surplus actually increased to DM 41.2 billion, the second highest surplus in Germany's post-war record. West German foreign exchange reserves reached DM 100 billion, in 1978, underscoring the concern of other countries in Western Europe, particularly France, of the form and means of the redistribution of the trade surplus and the foreign exchange reserves through the other categories of the balance of payments. Over the period 1973-78, three developments hindered that redistribution taking place.

In the first place, the Federal Republic's trade surplus was insufficiently offset by outflows under the services account, leaving the current account in permanent surplus between 1973 and 1978. The net deficit on invisible earnings, which had increased markedly from 1969 to 1975, levelled off in that year. Four reasons are adduced. First, the outflow of remittances from foreign workers in West Germany to their countries of origin along the Mediterranean basin declined, reflecting the lower number of foreign workers in West Germany and the tendency of those who stayed to spend a larger proportion of their earnings in their country of adoption. Secondly, as West German agriculture moved nearer to self-sufficiency, net transfers through the federal budget to the Common Agricultural Fund of the European Community fell off. Third, West German businesses benefited by a rapid increase in net earnings on interest and dividends from the rapid increase in private investment abroad in the 1970s. As the DM became attractive in 1978 to foreign central banks, growing returns were earned on interest-bearing foreign official currency reserves. Finally, West Germany continued to benefit by the steady increase in foreign exchange receipts from the allied troops in Germany.

The second development emphasised the significance to West German macro-economic policies of the continued link between the DM exchange rate and domestic American monetary policy. In January 1976, the redefinition of the International Monetary Fund's Articles of Agreement consecrated the dollar standard, on the basis of 'fixed but flexible' exchange rates. Implicitly, the acceptability of this new standard depended on the dollar retaining a fairly consistent value in relation to other currencies. In this respect, the Republican administration of President Ford initially had adhered to the contractionary monetary policy followed by the Federal Reserve. American price levels declined, unemployment levels rose, and the trade balance moved to surplus. But fears in Washington of playing into the hands of Western European Communist parties by subjecting France, Italy and Spain to a triple trade surplus from the United States, the Federal Republic and the oil exporting countries, coupled with a pre-election fiscal expansion by the administration to ward off the challenge from the Democrats. Carter's victory in the autumn of 1976 led to a further easing of fiscal and monetary conditions in the United States, an aggravation of the current deficit, and a massive demand for the DM as an international reserve currency, to heavy inflows into the West German money supply, and to a pronounced deterioration in relations between Bonn and Washington. Between the second quarter of 1977, and the first quarter of 1978 the Bundesbank absorbed 7.6 billion dollars into foreign exchange reserves.[17]

The third development reflected the growing importance of the banking institutions for German policy. In 1976, the net outflow of long-term capital was sharply reduced by long-term movements by banks reflecting the confidence of portfolio managers in the DM relative to the dollar. Similarly, short-term capital inflows by banks moved strongly positive. The OECD, referring to the year 1978, makes the following comment: 'This discrepancy between international capital transactions of the bank and non-bank private sector is even more pronounced if long and short-term capital flows are aggregated. Total net imports of DM 14.9 billion by the banking sector contrast with the DM 8.6 billion net capital export by the non-bank sector'.[18] Thus, the combination of German trade surpluses, and United States macro-economic policies, precipitated a steady capital flight into the DM and into the German banking system. In the short term, the Federal Republic's trade surplus with Western European neighbours rose; their external position in the short term was alleviated by the decline in price of dollar-denominated oil products. In the longer term, the inflows to the German money supply contributed to the upsurge of economic activity in 1979, at the time that oil producing countries decided to compensate for the decline in the dollar's purchasing power by a renewed series of price rises.

Thus, the events of 1977-78 were not a straight repetition of the early 1970s. In the first place, official and private dollar and Eurodollar holdings had expanded with the growth of 'offshore' markets in London, Luxembourg and elsewhere from 217 billion dollars in December 1972 to 658 billion in December 1977.[19] Secondly, the Bundesbank and the Supervisory Office in Berlin feared that the activities of German bank subsidiaries in these locations, particularly Luxembourg, complicated their task of supervising domestic monetary and credit conditions. Thirdly, as the Carter administration's boom got under way in America, private and central bank dollar holders unloaded, pulling the DM into the role of an international reserve currency. Fourthly, German acceptance of American dollar policy had been a way of buying defence services against the Warsaw Pact; floating free of the dollar in March 1973 had made that goal compatible with the domestic requirement for monetary stability. But President Carter's human rights campaign in Eastern Europe, his handling of German-American defence relations, and the breakdown of arms limitation talks in 1977 with the Soviet Union's decision to go ahead with the installation of SS-20s, all implied that the benefits to Germany supplied by American defence were decreasing. Finally, the inflows into the German money supply, and the growth of the DM as a reserve currency, and alternative asset to the dollar, suggested that the costs of the financial relationship with the United States were rising. The year 1977 marked not so much the emergence of the Federal Republic as a 'Gaullist' force in Europe,[20] as a shift away from the special relationship with the United States.

WEST GERMAN STRUKTURPOLITIK: 1968-1978

While the financial underpinnings of the Federal Republic's foreign and defence policies were becoming shakier, the DM's revaluation against other currencies precipitated industrial change in the Federal Republic. According to figures from the European Community Statistical Office, the share of industry (including construction) in national product in 1975, amounted to nearly 51 per cent compared to 41 per cent for France and Britain. The sector employed over 11 million people, while gross fixed capital investment in that year amounted to 31 per cent of the total of the European Community — 29 per cent more than new investment in France and 19 per cent of the new investment in Britain. In terms of manufacturing, the figures are rather less impressive, but nonetheless tell a similar story of West Germany as Western Europe's foremost industrial power. West German manufacturing employed 7.8 million people in 1974, whose average productivity was only slightly superior to the French manufacturing labour force.[21] But West German manufacturing accounted for 27 per cent of total exports in manufacturing and machinery in Western Europe, while the West German economy absorbed 19 per cent of Western European imports in the same categories. Manufacturing and machinery, as has been mentioned, formed the core of the German surplus.

Over the whole period, slower average growth in GNP accompanied some significant modifications in the structure of the German economy. Continuities in past patterns were evident with the continued decline in the total labour force. Agriculture dropped from 8.5 per cent in 1970, to 6.5 per cent in 1978. Farming accounted for only 3.2 per cent of GNP. Services continued to expand their share, with transport and communications remaining stable. The main change came in industry: German industry had increased its proportion of the total labour force to 48 per cent, and of GNP to 53 per cent by 1970. By 1978, 1.5 million employees had been dropped, and industry's total share of the labour force had decreased to 45 per cent. Its share of GNP fell to 50 per cent.

The relative ease with which the change was accomplished is generally ascribed to the timely adoption in the 1960s of appropriate industrial policies. The immediate cause for a more active government policy towards industry was the experience of 1965-1966, when the Erhard government had distributed electoral largesse, regardless of the budgetary and macro-economic implications. Furthermore, the Kennedy Round of trade negotiations with the Americans and Japanese, and the demands of developing countries in UNCTAD for access to developed country markets, pointed to the desirability of greater coherence in government attitudes and policies towards businesses. The Law on Stability and Growth of 1967 set the general framework, with the Principles of the Federal Government's Sectoral and Regional Policy, published in 1968, presenting 'only a special aspect of the general economic policy aimed at maintaining full employment, stable prices, balanced foreign trade and satisfactory growth'.[22] Government intervention was only justified when whole sectors faced long-term difficulties of adjustment to changing conditions: entrepreneurs and managers were to retain responsibility for the necessary adaptation; the government was to help business through the provision of business information, training facilities, soft credit, to smaller enterprises and employment bureaus. Special but temporary aid was to be provided for sectors undergoing rapid change.

A more active industrial policy required a more developed institutional setting. Since the 1950s, the Ministry of Economics formed the nucleus around which policies affecting industries had been formed. The Ministry had two divisions, one responsible for industrial affairs dealing with mining, energy, steel, and the second division with all the rest. This system was modified in 1972 with the creation of the Ministry of Technology and Research, with a special brief to promote 'high technology' industries. The federal system was brought more into play with the provision of central government assistance to the regions. The Federal and *Land* authorities have developed a common plan covering 60 per cent of the territory, composed of 21 'action' areas containing 'crucial' localities.[23] The *Länder* have in some cases developed their own industrial policies, involving the provision of tax incentives, subsidies, loans, etc., or have been willing instruments of central government 'restructuring' policies. The Kiel Institute has calculated that by 1974, industrial assistance in the Federal Republic amounted to 5.6 per cent of GNP. Only 15 per cent of that sum went to manufacturing.[24]

This relatively modest government contribution to West German manufacturing may be ascribed to a continuity by the SPD-FDP coalition of past policies. Though the Federal Republic had inherited a substantial position in the economy from the Weimar Republic and the Third Reich, successive governments were at pains not to pursue a *dirigiste* industrial policy. In the 1970s, the Federal government reckoned to hold up to 80 per cent of the shares in some 600 concerns, ranging from energy utilities to heavy industrial concerns, including chemicals, steel, shipbuilding and cars.[25] The weight of the public sector compares readily with that of France in the national economy: it accounts on average for about 16 per cent of gross fixed capital formation, and employs 9.2 per cent of all salaried workers. The six-state *Konzerne* represent alone, 10 per cent of investment in the capital sector, and employ 350,000 people, of which two-thirds are accounted for by Volkswagen, and by the energy group, VEBA.[26] In addition, the *Land* and municipal administrations may exert considerable influence on private business through the public banking sector, which accounts for about 75 per cent of total turnover of the sector as a whole. But the authorities have preferred in general to delegate industrial decisions to business enterprises, to enforce the anti-Cartel laws leniently and to provide for a favourable legal, fiscal and social system within which businesses may prosper.[27] Despite high unemployment, unions have had to rest satisfied with demand management policies and the Co-Determination Law of 1976.

Continuity in West German industrial policy contrasted with change in foreign policy, with Chancellor Brandt's opening to Moscow and Eastern Europe. Ideological rivalry between the two Germanies was stimulated, and projected into the domestic politics of the Federal Republic's Western trade partners.[28] The West German debate, conforming to the predilections of the economic research institutes, tended to take the international political context for granted, or only mentioned it as one 'factor' among others. The focus was more on the implications to the German economy of exchange rate changes, on the declining productivity of capital, or on the international division of labour.[29] The exchange rate arguments, associated with the 'structuralists' in the Bundesbank, held that the DM's undervaluation since the currency reforms of the late 1940s had led to an over-industrialisation of the West German economy, to an artificial stimulus to exports and to a shielding of domestic producers from international competition. Factors of production had been attracted into sectors which were increasingly open to competition from lower cost importing countries. An appropriate policy for the West German government was therefore to encourage German companies to move to the production of more sophisticated products through capital intensive investments, more skilled workforces and research and development. Expansionary budgetary policies would not lead to an increase in investment and to a durable increase in employment. The Federal Republic had therefore to become accustomed to lower rates of economic growth, until the 'structural transformation' of industry had been accomplished: unemployment was a temporary cost, mitigated by social security.

A contrary argument, prevalent on the left of the SPD and among trade unions, saw the upward movement of the DM, combined with lower growth and unemployment, as designed to loosen the labour market, reconstitute profits, and facilitate foreign direct investment by German corporations abroad. An alternative way of reconstituting profits would have been for government to boost domestic consumption, and thereby alleviate the external constraint imposed on West Germany's trade partners by the trade surplus, allowing labour to reconstitute its share in national income and jeopardising the upward movement of the DM that was necessary to attract reluctant German investors abroad. For the 'structuralists', Germany would have abandoned the virtues of 'structural adjustment' for the vices of France, Italy and Britain. Given the political impediments in the way of budgetary stimuli, German Marxist and 'structuralist' analyses could thus agree that industrial change in Germany was related to the process of global industrialisation. But whereas the latter emphasised competitive conditions in a world of states as precipitating the internationalisation of German corporations, the former stressed the existence of a vast pool of manpower in the developing world, and the ready transferability of technology.[30]

The one common denominator in the West German debate on industrial policy has been the acceptance of limited policy options for the Federal authorities. German business enterprises and banks have been left to make their own policies. In turn, a modest government contribution to industrial policy has been possible because of the peculiar relations between West German business enterprises and banks. The universal banking system, where banks act as commercial and investment bankers, as stockholders and as major participants on the capital markets, has created a web of reciprocal influence and advice between the banks and their clients. A collective policy for German industry, it has been argued, is elaborated through 'coordination by banker'.[31] The phenomenon has deep roots in German history. After the Franco-Prussian war of 1870, banks were allotted a crucial role in transforming the new Germany's scant savings into long-term loans. Their influence was extended after both world wars when outstanding credits were converted into bank-held shares and bonds to foster reconstruction. As major shareholders in their own right, and through the exercise of proxy rights for shares in deposit from customers, the banks may wield a determining power on company supervisory boards. Their coordinating functions derive from overlapping shareholdings and interlocking directorships that facilitate the flow of information between banks concerning the problems and prospects of German businesses. The system is said to provide German businesses with ready access to funds and advice, but equally it is said to restrict competition through insider dealings, and through the encouragement to concentration between businesses. Large corporations seek high levels of self-financing to preserve their managerial prerogatives, while smaller companies have scant alternatives to absorption by larger ones as the stock markets, too, are dominated by bankers.[32]

Government policy as defined in the late 1960s was clearly compatible with the interests of the German industrial-banking élites. The government set out actively to eliminate 'obstacles to such mergers and cooperative projects as make economic sense in view of technical progress and free competition'. The Cartel Office was no longer 'to prosecute agreements that do not considerably restrict functional competition'.[33] This emphasis was modified to the extent that government initiatives were taken in favour of small and medium size businesses[34] but the policy nonetheless represented official endorsement of a trend suspected by a growing number of West Germans as placing unacceptable power in fewer and fewer hands at the expense of the country's representative institutions. In 1973, the Cartel Office's powers to preserve and to protect competition were duly strengthened. But between 1973 and 1977 only 2 out of 773 mergers reported were prohibited,[35] the comprehension of the Ministry of Economics and many loopholes in the legal system providing corporations with numerous escape routes.

A series of enquiries into the role of the banks on foreign exchange markets, and in the process of competition was sparked by the Herstatt and Hessische *Landesbank* failures. The Monopoly Commission Report of 1976 studied the structure of bank credit, the relations of banks to corporations and the banking market. The Report proposed a reduction of the banks' rights to hold equity to five per cent, by contrast to their extensive rights under the existing system.[36] Voting rights were to be restricted accordingly; whereas presently a 25.1 per cent holding provides banks with blocking powers over managerial decisions. The banks argued that their power was being exercised on behalf of small shareholders, and in the national interest. Their actions lent some credence to the hypothesis. The Deutshe Bank, for instance, acquired and disposed of the Flick family's holding in Daimler-Benz, to resist the Shah's takeover bid; foreign banks' participation in West German markets have been limited to 2 per cent of the aggregate volume of banking business[37]; heavy bank lending to the steel, mechanical engineering or metal production sectors was cited as evidence of the banks' social responsibility in helping industrial sectors in difficulty to redeploy their resources. Furthermore, the leading banks have cooperated closely with the Bundesbank over domestic monetary and foreign exchange policies; regular meetings are held in the Capital Market Committee to decide the total volume of new issues per month on the DM bond markets. The Bundesbank insists that lead managers of DM issues should be German banks: foreign loans to Eastern Europe, Scandinavia or Mediterranean countries therefore have a strongly political colouring. Equally, the Bundesbank's practice of controlling the revaluation of the DM by purchasing foreign currency to hold the DM down has increased the importance of Bundesbank control over the German banks, to mop up the additional liquidity entering the system. Their holding of medium and long-term government paper also facilitated the government's non-inflationary financing of the general government deficit.

Whatever the degree of conflict or cooperation within German elites, an underlying consensus on the thrust of German industrial policy is discernible through the patterns of domestic and foreign investment. Steel-based industries in West Germany have been developed to sustain a competitive export sector, while foreign investment has been undertaken in particular by the chemical and electro-mechanical sectors.[38] Only after 1973 did West Germany become a net exporter of capital. By 1975, the total recorded foreign direct investment since 1952 amounted to about DM 42 billion.[39] Of this investment, 70 per cent had gone to the developed countries, with the

European Community accounting for 34 per cent of the total, and the United States nearly 13 per cent. The remaining 30 per cent went to 'developing countries'. Motives for outward investment included the search for lower wage costs, the development of raw materials, the avoidance of currency fluctuations, the pre-emption of import restrictions, or on account of the transferability of technology. A marginal amount was 'redeployed' to serve the domestic German market. An overwhelming motive, however, is German corporate concern for 'political stability'. A few examples may suffice. Of total foreign direct investment to 'developing countries', 59 per cent went to the Canary Islands, Spain, Brazil, Israel, Iran and South Africa. After the Shah's fall, direct investment to developing countries fell to 14 per cent of the total. As for investment to the United States, a Swiss executive has been quoted as saying that German corporations 'fear the big Russian bear and want an independent base where they can survive'.[40]

The expansion of West German foreign direct investment in the past decade took place against a background of rapid expansion of German banks abroad.[41] A number of reasons have been adduced for this development. Firstly, West German industry has enjoyed an expanding share of world trade, so that an increasing portion of German banking business has become international. Secondly, the growth of off-shore capital markets, and the importance of capital flows have heightened the importance of commercial banks at the expense of the central banks in the management of international money. German banks are thus able to escape domestic supervision only to enter world markets under the control of no central bank, and characterised by 'savage' competition.[42] ' Thirdly, domestic banking resources have become dearer as savers have switched from sight to time deposits, encouraging German banks to look outside traditional markets for new sources of funds. In 1979, ten German banks with international activities, owed between 25 to 40 per cent of profits and balance sheet assets to international operations. Exposure to risk has grown accordingly, as has the psychological importance to German banks of the Bundesbank, and its foreign exchange reserves, as a lender of last resort. Finally, the revaluation of the DM in the 1970s, and its emergence in 1978 as the second world trading currency after the dollar, has both strengthened the comparative balance sheets of German banks against foreign banks with resources tied up in less buoyant currencies, and has promoted them as key participants in the evolution of international monetary affairs. In turn, the Bundesbank has had to accept as a consequence of its own policies in 1967, and 1973, the emergence of the DM as an international reserve currency, no longer under its own control.

The ease of West Germany's adaptation to the international conditions of the 1970s was thus, in economic terms, relatively smooth. Industrial policy was conceived in the ideological context of the *Liberaleordnungspolitik*, and adapted to the Federal Republic's constitutional realities. The government declined to take the dirigiste path, with important exceptions among the *Länder*. But even there, the openness of the economy and the multiplicity of agencies ensured that responsibilities in the system as a whole for wages, profits and risk was delegated. The clue to

German industrial policy remained the dense network of relations between business enterprises and banking institutions. This placed maximum weight on the famed consensus between managers and workforces in post-war German society. It assumed government dependence on industries or banks to continue providing services and goods. It facilitated the continued credibility of the separation between the realms of economic matters and political affairs. But the provision of these goods and services became more than ever related to the pattern of international exchanges, and the Federal government's efforts to set the framework for the economic process, more than ever a matter of international diplomacy.

MODEL GERMANY: 1974-1979

The success of German economic diplomacy depended, evidently, on the cooperation of other governments, responsive to their own particular domestic conditions and international contexts. Western attitudes towards the Federal Republic varied from one extreme of admiration for keeping inflationary and unemployment increases to a minimum, to another as an archetypical mercantilist power forcing its major trading partners to align their national economic policies on priorities set in Bonn. The two paradigms echoed the debates among economists about the relative virtues of 'monetarism' or 'Keynesianism'. On the one hand, 'monetarists', represented among conservative and liberal parties in Western Europe, discerned the successes of the Federal Republic in the Bundesbank's close control over the monetary base. Disturbances in the German economy derived from the inflationary policies of its major trading partners. On the other hand, the 'Keynesians' in the Federal Republic and abroad linked the Federal Republic's stabilisation policies to the expansion of the trade surplus, and to the reluctance of the major trading partners in Western Europe to aggravate the recessionary impact of oil price increases by stabilisation policies of their own. In the one, the Federal Republic appeared as a victim of the rest of the industrial world's excesses. Germany therefore served as a 'model' to emulate. In the other, the Federal Republic was a major source of the industrialised world's discomforture. It should be brought to act as a 'loco-motive' pulling other economies out of recession by expansionary policies of its own.

What in fact were German performaces in terms of unemployment, inflation and fiscal and monetary policies in the years after 1973? In the first two years following the stabilisation measures of 1973, GNP growth declined to zero, and then to -2.6 per cent. Unemployment rates rose to over one million; restrictions were placed on immigration from Mediter-ranean countries; over 671,000 foreign workers had withdrawn from the labour force by 1978. Earlier measures taken by the SPD-FDP government, involving the setting up of a Federal Office, dividing the Republic into 146 official labour districts to facilitate the flow of information on labour market conditions, seemed inadequate. The debate on unemployment conse-quently split along party political lines, with the Social Democrats and trade unions being moved onto the defensive during the boom of 1976, when the labour force contracted by a further 235,000. The 'structuralists', who questioned the effectiveness of traditional reflationary policies, appeared to have won their case. School-leaving age was prolonged; maternity leave was lengthened; early retirement was encouraged. The Christian Democrats, Free Democrats and industrial associations tended to argue that such temporary measures had to be accompanied by a reduction in the share of national income going to the state in the form of wage taxes and social security payments. It was not so much the efforts of the Bundesbank to maintain price stability that aggravated the unemployment problem — the argument ran — as the financial burden on businesses of public welfare policies that acted as a barrier to the reduction of unemployment.

Consumer prices, rising 7 per cent in 1974, moved down in the following two years. First, the Bundesbank's abandonment of intervention on foreign exchange markets to hold down the DM eased the task of control over the domestic money supply. The upward movement of the DM also served to hold down imported commodity prices. Secondly, domestic markets remained open and competitive, even though the trend towards concentration continued. Above all, the SPD-FDP coalition succeeded in pushing through the Worker's Codetermination Law of 1976. This, together with a higher rate of unemployment and the expansion in the supply of welfare services, may have accounted for the trade unions' restraint in pressing wage demands. The unions continued their traditional policies in cooperating with management to compensate for real wage increases by productivity improvements.

As unemployment rates rose and inflation rates declined, the Federal Republic came under pressure from Western European governments and from the United States to reduce the trade surplus by stimulating domestic aggregate demand. German 'Keynesians' thus found external allies, while responding to domestic criticisms on the rapid growth of public sector debt from 19 per cent of GNP in 1974 to 27 per cent in 1977, that high savings rates by households, and low demand for funds by business enterprises, enabled the deficits to be financed in a non-inflationary manner. Furthermore, as the banking sector, which might in different conditions have been more a vocal opponent of deficit spending, came to hold a growing share of government revenues, the banks developed a vested interest in the continuation of the policies: the distribution of income from taxpayers to government debt holders integrated the banking system closer into the state apparatus, possibly reducing the inertia in the system to a reduction of the general government's activities in the economy.

Government debt might have risen more steeply, but for the passage in August 1975 of the 'Law to Improve the Structure of the Budget'. The opposition parties, strongly entrenched in the Bundesrat, invoked the constitutional constraints on the federal government to prevent a recurrence of that year's federal deficit, amounting to 5.8 per cent of GNP. The deficit was said to stimulate inflationary expectations, discouraging investment. Article 115 of the Basic Law was cited, whereby the net borrowing requirement of the Federal (and *Land*) governments was not to exceed capital outlays, unless there were sound reasons for government action to avoid a 'disturbance of macroeconomic balance in the economy'. The Bundesrat's influence was all the greater as the federal authorities have to refer to it for about 85 per cent of total revenues. In the following year, the contraction in public sector borrowing accompanied a rise in aggregate demand. But, the 'Model Germany, to which Chancellor Schmidt referred in the autumn 1976 federal election, was a good deal more restrictionist than it might have been, had the Social Demoncrats had a free hand. Equally, the Federal Republic's ability to accede to American and British request for reflation was severely curtailed.

When the deficit countries in Western Europe were joined by the United States under the incoming Carter administration to press for German reflation, conflict with the Federal Republic was inevitable. The Bundesbank, with its commitment to price stability, was a jealous guardian of the monetary context within which the government elaborated fiscal policies; the opposition parties were well entrenched in the Bundesrat; and the SPD's partner, the FDP, was reluctant to back union demands for reflation. The liberal electorate showed signs of discontent over the rise in tax levels, federal deficits and government intervention in market processes. Nonetheless, Chancellor Schmidt was able to override domestic resistance to reflation in 1977, as the Federal Republic's contribution to western economic policy coordination. At the London summit in May 1977, Schmidt agreed to set the German economy on course for a growth rate of 4.5 per cent for the coming year: the Bundesbank lowered interest rates; the government initiated a medium-term investment programme; taxes were cut, and regional and local authorities were exhorted to imitate the federal authorities in raising expenditures. The measures began to take effect towards the end of 1977. In June 1978, the Germans agreed to the 'concerted action' programme adopted by the OECD Ministers, and confirmed at the Bonn summit. The Programme to 'Strengthen Demand and Improve Growth', involving stimulatory measures amounting to DM 16 billion, obtained parliamentary approval, after the FDP had insisted on placing the emphasis on tax cuts. The measures were an important factor behind the rapid expansion of the German economy in 1979, a reduction in unemployment levels and an increase in investment in machinery and equipment.

The Federal Republic entered the second 'oil shock' at a high level of economic activity, also, on account of an unwanted monetary expansion. From October 1977, dollars were shifted into DM, as the Carter boom got under way and the United States trade deficit expanded. In December, the Bundesbank decided to reduce domestic interest rates further; to discourage speculative inflows by raising compulsory reserve requirements, and to activate swap arrangements with the United States Treasury. Interventions in foreign exchange markets were increased to hold down the DM. But leakages into the money supply obliged the authorities to allow monetary growth to exceed targets. Only when the inadequacy of technical measures to check the downward move of the dollar became apparent, did the German authorities come to admit a changed international context for Germany at the end of the 1970s. The election of Carter to office served to highlight the dubious wisdom of Germany's leading too heavily on the

United States in monetary matters. Revaluation of the DM jeopardised German exports markets in Europe; drove up labour costs; precipitated foreign investment by German corporations; complicated domestic monetary management, and ran counter to government fiscal measures to boost aggregate demand. Devaluation of the dollar reflected the re-ordering of American priorities from foreign to domestic concerns. Furthermore, there was little that the German authorities, by contrast to March 1973, could do alone: stabilisation would have run counter to the London summit commitment, and in any case would have precipitated an expansion of the trade surplus, and a further flight into the DM, at a time when conservative governments in Paris and Rome were seeking to fend off the Euro-Communist parties' bid for power.

The German diplomatic offensive in 1978 to revert to a more stable exchange rate regime, and to break the trend to the DM's use as an international reserve currency therefore opened in unfavourable circumstances. The struggle with the United States proved uneven. If Carter's expansionary domestic policies were dependent on the willingness of foreign central banks, particularly the German, to hold dollars, the Bundesbank alone had little alternative to holding them other than allowing the DM to move up, or allow domestic prices to rise to European levels. Hence, the German decision to combine with the Saudis, the Swiss and the Japanese in pressing domestic restraint on the United States. A sharp turn for the worse on foreign exchange markets in April 1978 provided the occasion: following a letter from King Khalid to President Carter warning that Saudi-Arabia could not continue to resist demands in OPEC to raise the dollar price of oil products if the United States currency continued to devalue, Schmidt, in a speech at Hamburg accused the United States of failing to meet its responsibilities to the international economy. Foreign central banks, he argued, could not continue to absorb the excess liquidity from the United States balance of payments.[43] The United States Treasury response was to offer foreign holders a guarantee for their dollar holdings, and when central banks proved unmoved, to invite the Germans to intervene on foreign exchange markets with the DM thereby taking pressure off the dollar. By 1978, the DM had become in any event the second world reserve currency, irrespective of the desires of the Federal authorities;[44] central banks in the Commonwealth, Latin America and South-East Asia opted for the DM. Thus, the United States measures of 1 November, 1978, under a joint Treasury and Federal Reserve initiative, amounted to a confirmation of a trend the German authorities were unable to avoid: in return, for a domestic stabilisation in the United States, the German authorities had to acquiesce in the confirmation of the DM's role as an international reserve currency. The announcement of the sale in German, and other capital markets, of up to 10 billion dollars worth of Treasury securities, denominated in foreign currencies, initiated a new regime of controlled exchange rates, with the DM as a major participant. The world was launched on a multiple currency system.

German efforts to promote control over international currency markets fared no better. America and Germany proved either unwilling or unable to control the outcome of their policies. The United States authorities opposed the international surveillance of domestic monetary affairs, implicit in the German-backed proposals for a new international reserve asset to absorb the world's supply of dollars. On the other hand, the United States shared the German authorities' general concerns at the way that Euromarket operations complicate domestic monetary policy, or pull their commercial banks into risky loans. Both have sought to reform bank accounting procedures, to provide more information on the activities of foreign subsidiaries. Neither has succeeded in extending supervision over international currency markets. Too many centres compete for the custom of international banks, and too many governments or corporations have become dependent on access to the markets for regulations to be agreed on, or to stand a chance of being introduced simultaneously everywhere. Furthermore, the trend to a borrowers market eases loan terms for borrowing developing countries, and on the European continent. Thus, 83 per cent of COMECON gross debts were held by commercial banks in 1979.[45] Tighter lending conditions following the fall of the Shah, the rise in oil prices, and the upward movement of interest rates in the United States, spilled over rapidly into internal conditions in eastern bloc countries, aggravating in particular the Polish government's financial difficulties.

German perceptions and interests diverged, too, from American ones. The German authorities remain wedded to their commitment to domestic monetary stability, and to Germany's limited ability to play a leading role in world affairs. At the IMF conference in Belgrade in 1979, Finance Minister Matthoefer stated that: 'Germany is a medium-size country that does not want to take over a leading position in world monetary affairs. The United States must handle this.'[46] The statement may be seen in counterpoint to an American proposal for the Federal Republic as a 'bigemonial partner',[47] in promoting liberal trade policies between industrialised countries and developing countries, or in contrast to the reluctant German acceptance of the DM as a reserve currency. It also holds a number of implicit assumptions, examined in the following sections. Firstly, German modesty in rejecting a world role on a par with the United States is another way of saying that Germany can only aspire to act together with countries of similar size in the European Community, particularly with France. Secondly, Germany's geographic and strategic military situation prevents it from adopting the style of a major monetary power in world affairs. Loans to COMECON countries are inherently risky: they may be praised or criticised either as subsidies to, or interference in communist government policies. Finally, the German authorities have in mind the problems confronting Britain as a medium-size country that ran a reserve currency, under fixed exchange rates, but sacrificed domestic objectives to external balance. The shift to a current account deficit in 1979 made the analogy plausible.

GERMAN CONTINENTAL ECONOMIC DIPLOMACY: 1977-1980

At the height of the Federal Republic's attempt to resist American and British pressure to reflate and revalue, Bonn launched a continental policy to preserve stability in the region, involving a German option for continuity in power of Communist parties in Eastern Europe, and an opposition to their coming to power in Western Europe. The shift towards alliance with France from 1977 on amounted to a recognition of the fact that the Federal Republic was first and foremost a West European state, with its main trading partners and political peers in the European Community. The new convergence with French policies was signalled in February 1977, on the occasion of one of the regular summit meetings between the French and German heads of government. President Giscard d'Estaing stated that the 'Franco-German entente constitutes the cornerstone of all progress in the construction of Europe'.[48] Chancellor Schmidt, in reply, rendered homage to the President and to his predecessor, General de Gaulle, declaring that the Federal Republic desired a strong France. The meeting had been preceded by Giscard d'Estaing's efforts since 1974 to reconcile closer French cooperation with the Federal Republic, and dependence on the Gaullist party in the National Assembly. But the failure in 1976 of Franco-German coordination of economic policies, coupled with the commitment to comply with the Rome Treaty in direct elections to the European Parliamentary Assembly, had contributed to Giscard d'Estaing's replacement of Jacques Chirac, the Gaullist leader, by Raymond Barre, a former vice-President of the European Commission. Barre, much appreciated in Bonn, left no doubt about his intentions of fashioning French economic policy on *Modell Deutschland*, as the German Social Democrats' election manifesto in 1976 described the results of their seven year's tenure. Thus in February 1977 Schmidt and Giscard d'Estaing stated the hope that the Community might 'renew in 1978 progress towards economic and monetary union (which we consider) an 'obligatory passageway on the road towards the union of Europe'.[49] The two governments would make proposals to the European Council on the better harmonisation of economic policies.

In the following months, the European Commission picked up the various threads of economic and monetary policy from earlier plans for monetary union. Discussions had come to focus on the relative rates of inflation among member countries in the European Community, and the appropriate methods for achieving monetary integration and national economic stability. This included the 'All Saints Day Manifesto', published in *The Economist* in November 1975, for an indexed parallel currency; the Tindemans Report proposing formal acceptance of a 'two-tier' Community; general disillusion on the continent over floating exchange rates; and recognition that too rapid an alignment of domestic inflation on German rates would increase unemployment, and provide political grist for Socialist or Communist party mills. Commission President Jenkin's proposals at Florence in October, linking progress to economic and monetary union, enlargement and European Parliamentary Assembly elections thus met with some reserve in Bonn, and little was done to embarrass President Giscard d'Estaing until the French general elections of March 1978. Immediately afterwards, intense consultations with Paris were initiated, and despite the apathy in many capitals, Schmidt and Giscard d'Estaing agreed on an ambitious plan presented to the other heads of government at Bremen early in July. Both overrode domestic opposition, Schmidt from the ministries in Bonn, the Bundesbank, the banks and economic institutes, and Giscard d'Estaing from the Gaullist, Socialist and Communist parties. In September, the French government presented to the National Assembly its new macro-economic and industrial policies, overtly modelled on West Germany.[50] The same month, Schmidt declared the political importance of the monetary proposals, and admitted that the transition from fixed to floating rates had weakened the European Community.

After lengthy negotiations between member governments, the European Monetary System (EMS) was agreed to in its final form at the European Council at Paris in March 1979. The EMS is distinguished from the earlier 'snake' in a number of respects. Firstly, the European Currency Unit (ECU), an artificial currency defined in terms of fixed quantities of Community monies, is to function as a *numéraire*, a means of settlement among central banks and as an 'indicator of divergence' between Community currencies. This system is the result of a compromise between the Federal Republic, where the Bundesbank feared that the EMS would endorse inflation in its own currency, and weaker currency countries, which did not wish to repeat the experience of the snake, and assume most of the onus of adjustment against the DM. Finally, a European Monetary Cooperation Fund was to replace the existing arrangements, and to be transformed eventually into the European Community central bank. During the transition stage until March 1981, — postponed until 1983 — the Fund receives in deposit 20 per cent of member countries' gold and dollar reserves on a temporary 'swap' basis. In return, central banks receive ECUS. At the time of the EMS introduction, the Community governments anticipated the creation of about 13 billion dollars of ECUs with gold postulated at 150 dollars an ounce. But by 1980, the gold price was over 600 dollars, leading to a total rise in ECUs created by gold's dollar price, of 50 billion dollars.

At the time, the German authorities' objectives in setting up the EMS were many and contradictory. In the first place, the EMS was one thrust in the diplomatic offensive resulting in the stabilisation of the dollar in November 1978. The Bundesbank's tardy conversion to the EMS was advanced by the speculative inflow into the DM in October, resulting in an expansion of German foreign currency reserves from 39.3 billion dollars to 48.4 billion in the fourth quarter of the year.[51] The dollar's strength since then has helped stabilise rates in the Community. To that extent, the EMS exercise was successful. Secondly, the EMS formed part of the German authorities' efforts to reduce the risks inherent to national *numéraires*. As it came into effect after the fact, the EMS had no influence at all on the DM's emergence as an international reserve currency. Indeed, the attempt to disguise the DM's role in Europe under the ECU in the EMS deprived the Germans of the leverage that they had managed to exert over the smaller countries associated with the DM in the snake. The ample funds available to member countries through the ECU 'swap' provide little incentive to prompt corrective action in the way of price stability. The 'elements of degeneration' in the Common Market since the end of the Bretton Woods system to which Schmidt referred in an article to the

Financial Times in January 1979 [52], have not disappeared. Thirdly, the Germans have not been able to arrange a concerted push in the Community for greater control over Eurocurrency markets. The rise in oil prices in 1979 and 1980 has not eased matters: the Federal Republic in 1980 moved to current account deficit, eased regulations on capital inflows, and has come to share weaker currency countries' ambivalent attitudes to the markets both as source of funds and as sources of destabilisation. Finally, Schmidt's objective in setting up a 'zone of stability' in Europe was to facilitate 'the smooth development of prices, costs, exchange rates, investment, employment and markets'.[53] In Germany, domestic price levels have risen slightly, costs have increased less than abroad, entailing a small real devaluation of the DM in the EMS; investment, especially in machinery and equipment, rose in 1979, along with a tightening of the labour markets; export shares were maintained.[54] But the international crisis has accelerated at such a speed that the strategy of little steps implicit in the EMS is in danger of being blown away in a gale of currency instability, social upheavals and war in non-European regions, and in eastern Europe.

The German government also considered the EMS as an application of the Tindemans Report proposal, where the 'stronger' currency countries would set the pace for the weaker.[55] France, after the March 1978 election results, was the only partner. Subsequently, Giscard d'Estaing accentuated his European policies over the EMS, Community industrial and commercial measures and the European Parliamentary Assembly. Domestic reforms were initiated with a view to reducing the state's functions, and a massive propaganda barrage mounted to modify the prevalent norm of a state-defined as opposed to a market-formed economy. The theme of the 'German model' came to dominate French political debate. The debate was summarised in an article series, entitled 'Twenty Years of German Success', published by *Le Monde*, on the occasion of the European Council meeting at Paris in March, 1979.[56] Two themes, both for domestic French consumption, were to the fore. Both betrayed the mixture of admiration and fear of Germany in France that had burst into the open in late 1977, at the height of the drama over the kidnapping and murder of Herr Schleyer, the industrialist. One held that Germany was riding the world crisis better than France due to prompt government response to changed international conditions in the early 1970s, to an innovative and export-oriented industry, to sound labour relations, responsible management and supportive, but not interventionist government policy. Trade surpluses, in short, were the external manifestation of German virtues. The other theme, included in the assumption of Germany as a rising economic *and* political power, reflected the fear that a wavering American leadership in Western defence was precipitating a rapprochement between Bonn and Moscow. Alain Cotta, the French economist, writing in the winter number of *La Revue Française de Gestion*, on the subject of the 'German model', hinted darkly that Germany's integration into the world economy, and its development as a 'strong' currency country, would enable it 'to constitute one of those economic and political poles around which new privileged zones could be constituted, introducing some novelties into the functioning of the world economy, subjected until recently to the Pact of Yalta'.[57]

While the French government was developing its policy towards the Federal Republic on the Community and in domestic economic policies, the Soviet Union opened a 'charm campaign' towards Bonn. The campaign underlined the dual aspect of Moscow's relations with Bonn as threat and partner. The Soviet Union is a direct military threat, in terms of conventional arms and nuclear fire power. It is a partner in terms of détente and trade. Moscow holds the key to inner-German relations. In context, the campaign's immediate objective was to establish common ground with Bonn on the East-West balance; to pre-empt encirclement by a Sino-Japanese-American alliance in the East, and a German-American, or Franco-German alliance in the West; to secure the continuation of German industrial and financial cooperation within a context of détente; or to forego growing ties between Easton European countries, particularly Poland and Hungary, with the Federal Republic, through the reinforcement of relations between Moscow and Bonn.[58] In May 1978, Brezhnev made a state visit to the Federal Republic, the first since 1973. A 25-year treaty of economic cooperation was signed, as a framework for the development of commercial, industrial and technological relations in a 10-year phase, renewable for three five-year periods. German business circles greeted the treaty with scepticism, in view of the modest development of Eastern business. But the treaty's significance as a symbol of Bonn's long-term commitment to a policy of détente in Europe was underlined with its updating on the occasion of Schmidt's visit to Moscow in July 1980, after the invasion of Afghanistan, as the political crisis in Eastern Europe was becoming manifest, and despite the United Stated administration's call for allied sanctions against the Soviet Union. The new agreeement consits of an 11-page section, defining the area of bilateral cooperation, and four annexes specifying which products or techniques are of particular relevance.[59]

The Federal Republic's attachment to détente with Moscow may be seen as the counterpart in the East to its relations with Paris in the West. The development of economic exchanges forms one of the German industrialists' underlying tenets on European integration, as it is of the SPD-FDP government's *Ostpolitik*: relations are defined between states in a network of treaties, and sustained through exchanges and reciprocal obligations. In eastern policy, favourable conditions are thus preserved for an eventual settlement of the German problem. Contradictions are omnipresent. Firstly, the Federal Republic and the Soviet Union are not comparable entities in political and military terms, though their economies are compatible. According to OECD Series A Trade Statistics, Germany remained in surplus with Eastern Europe between 1974 and 1979 as an exporter particularly of finished products; but its surplus declined with COMECON, reflecting a deficit as an importer of energy products from the Soviet Union, especially natural gas.[60] Secondly, this decision signalled not only Bonn's intention to pursue détente with the Soviet Union, but its recognition of the importance of Eastern European and Russian energy sources as a long-term alternative to Middle East supplies, and as the best method of promoting COMECON exports. The original strategy on trade and détente — the promotion of manufactured exports from COMECON — had run into problems of disposal of Eastern European products, related to quality, competition from non-European suppliers, or Community protection in agriculture, textiles etc. Such a commitment to interdependence by Germans and Russians assumes a continued American military check on Russian military power, and a willingness by the Soviet Union to cooperate with the Federal Republic in the development of COMECON in those areas of politics and economic affairs, where Germany is strongest.

A third, and related point, is that the Eastern European regimes, particularly East Germany — which, as Herr Honecker frequently points out, is wide open to political, ideological and economic competition from the Federal Republic — have failed to develop a counter-model to that of the Federal Republic; the East German regime's legitimacy rests on the Communist Party's claims to monopoly power in the supposed interests of workers; that monopoly power is being seriously challenged in Poland by workers themselves; the Hungarians have moved uneasily to a partial decentralisation of decision-making. The Federal Republic has not even to propose internal reforms in Eastern Europe to be accused by the East Germans, the Czechs and Moscow to be sustaining 'anti-socialist elements'. The Federal Republic remains a handy scape-goat. But fourthly, it is also an indispensable source of finance. COMECON debts in hard currencies have expanded from 11.8 billion dollars in 1973 to 58.5 billion in 1978, at an annual average rate of 38 per cent, compared to 23 per cent of total developing country debts.[61] A substantial part, particularly in official export credits, is held by West German authorities and banks. Furthermore, the trade agreements of 1978 and 1980 are government-backed long-term financing instruments, in addition to the benefits derived by the Soviet Union as a major gold exporter from the decline of the dollar, and the rise of the DM. Objectively, to use a Marxist term, the Soviet Union benefited by the vagaries of the dollar since 1971, and particularly since 1976. Indeed, one may add, caustically, that the Soviet Union has only to invade a peripheral country, such as Afghanistan, to increase the returns on its own gold sales to world markets: all contributes to the financing of German-Soviet trade.

The continental dimension, then, of German economic diplomacy and predicaments, points to a more significant development than may emerge by selective examination of 'German models'. The 'German mode' is all things to all men. To the British and American governments, its interpretation served as an argument in favour of 'reflation' and revaluation. To the French government, it provided the *raison d'être* for change in domestic and Community policies. For Moscow, the Federal Republic is an economic partner, and ideological competitor, in view of the political failures of Communist regimes. Above all, though, the debates on Germany point not so much to the emergence of Germany as a power — as an economic dwarf transmogrified into political giant — but of the German problem. The coincidence in timing between the deterioration in American-German relations over the related issues of the dollar and the defence, the effort to establish a 'zone of stability' in the Community with France, and the development of relations between Bonn and Moscow, was interpreted, particularly in Washington, as evidence of a lessening German commitment to the Western alliance. The analysis is erroneous. The confluence of events around the Federal Republic in 1977 and 1978 points rather to the declining security by Germany in a bipolar world, built up since the defeat of the Axis powers in 1945. What has re-emerged is the central problem for Europe since Bismark: the European state system, and Germany's position in it.[62] The ambiguities of the one penetrate the ambiguities of the other, indeed are accentuated by the continued involvement of the two great powers and the evolution in global economic relations.

CONCLUSION

The Federal Republic's economic performances rest first and foremost on a political consensus about the functioning of the Constitution. Participation at many levels in policy is assured through political parties, interests and associations, the law courts and the media, or the federal nature of the constitution itself. The political process lacks any clear pole of reference, such as the Presidency in France; its intractibility is furthered by fragmentation, and overlapping responsibilities between ministries, legislatures, Bund and *Länder*. Ideological debate has been contained within the ample bounds of *Liberaleordnungspolitik*. The theory posits the state as setting the rules, while the economic process provides the requisite goods and services. Its acceptance, along with the Atlantic alliance and European integration, derives dialectical significance in the context of Germany's division and the monopoly claim on power by the Communist Party of the Soviet Union. Above all, it was preserved, with minor institutional modifications and theoretical adjustments, through the period of economic change initiated by the DM's revaluation, lower rates of growth, the trend to industrial concentration in an ever more open economy, and the interpenetration of public and private financial mechanisms as government debt expanded. In the 1970s, with conditions in the Federal Republic more than ever dependent on the evolution of world politics and competitive patterns, the German government was pulled into international economic diplomacy in a global context.

Chancellor Schmidt, succeeding Brandt in 1974, brought a national liberal frame of reference to the new global diplomacy. National interests in 'the struggle for the world product' informed the wrangling about 'tariff headings, preferences and counterpreferences, the purpose and extent of protectionist measures'.[63] But, equally, the dialectics of the two Germanies sharpened by Ostpolitik and détente was projected through Socialist and Communist parties or unions' rivalries into the domestic politics of the Federal Republic's Western European trade partners. Divergent political conditions between 1973 and 1978 pre-empted any convergence in economic policies and performances on German norms, while prompting the United States, first under Presidents Nixon and Ford, to seek in the Federal Republic a 'bigemonial' partner in European and world affairs, and then under President Carter to urge the Federal Republic to reflate and revalue to sustain, among other objectives, the conservative governments in France and Italy. The western debates over the 'German model' between 'Keynesians' and 'monetarists' were essentially over different policies to preserve the Western European order. Schmidt, in this context, had little difficulty in overriding domestic resistance to the reflationary package agreed on at the London summit in May 1977. But when the United States administration talked the dollar down, and the DM up, the German government opted for a return to a Bretton Woods in Europe with France, and on negotiated terms. The Germans were far from getting their own way: the EMS eased the burden of adjustment on deficit countries; it failed to break the emergence of the DM as an international reserve currency, or to reduce inflationary pressures in the European Community. But it did provide a common European framework for policy, within which Giscard d'Estaing was able to promote policy changes in France long desired in the Federal Republic.

The Federal Republic's preponderance as the European Community's foremost exporter, industrialist and banker implied an inevitable priority in policy to the Continent. The priority was by inclination and perception more towards the United States, initially. The decision in 1973 to float the DM freely, and to stabilise the domestic economy, led to an expansion of the trade surplus in Europe, and to a confirmation of previous trends in German trade patterns. The growing outflows on services, overshadowed temporarily by the export surplus, contributed by 1977 to the easing of financial constraints on Mediterranean countries. Foreign direct investment, exceeding inflows after 1973, went first to the European Community, to the developing countries along the Mediterranean, to the United States and to a few 'stable' developing countries in the Third World. Hence, when in 1977 the costs of over-dependence in monetary matters on the United States rose while the military benefits of alliance became less tangible, the German government complemented its diplomatic shift to consolidate the alliance with France, with an overture to the Soviet Union to preserve détente, and not to aggravate the difficulties of Communist regimes in Eastern Europe. But whereas political and economic processes in the European Community reflect domestic German norms, West German relations with COMECON are riddled with contradictions. In particular, the Federal Republic has sought to preserve détente in Europe from the deterioration in world political conditions by proceeding with the Soviet Union in the areas of trade, investment and finance. But it is precisely in these areas that the Soviet Union and Eastern European governments are least competitive, or feel least secure, and where the temptation to compensate through bluster, military threat or financial leverage over the creditor, is greatest.

As a member of the Atlantic alliance, the Federal Republic eased the way to a dollar standard in 1967 by agreeing not to join de Gaulle in converting dollars into gold. Considerations of 'high' policy prevailed over the more mundane aspects of 'low' policy. Subsequently, the decision to float the DM free of the dollar in 1973 reconciled temporarily the dual policy objectives of receiving United States defence services, on terms acceptable to the United States, and of maintaining domestic price stability. But the DM become a 'polar currency' in Europe, and an alternative asset to dollars — along with the Yen, the Swiss franc and gold. The DM exchange rate was correlated to United States monetary policies. German banks were pulled abroad by the development of the Eurocurrency markets, the growth of foreign direct investment by German corporations as the DM moved up, and the slowing down in growth of domestic sources of funds. The Bundesbank had to accept, grudgingly, a severe limitation on control over the operations of foreign subsidiaries of German banks. The DM became an international reserve currency: the opinion of foreign central bankers on German domestic policies is now of direct relevance to German policy-makers. The German authorities have made partial and unsuccessful efforts with others to regulate Eurocurrency markets. They succeeded, with the Japanese and the Swiss, in November 1978, in nudging the United States towards restrictive policies. But being committed to more stable exchange rates in the EMS, and in relation to the dollar, German adjustment to the 1979-1980 wave of oil price increases has been borne on domestic prices and costs. German interest rates have rippled up with American as the economy has turned down. The Germans were unable to follow the Japanese in growing through the oil price increases of 1979-1980, allowing the exchange rate to take the burden of adjustment through downward floating, and recovering by an intensely price competitive export drive. By 1980s, the Germans were looking to the Japanese model, like the French had to the German.

The Federal Republic, then, is torn between the partially overlapping, partially conflicting pressures of its economic integration into the European Community, on the one hand, and its dependence on global trade, payments and capital flows, on the other. At the same time, it has sought to organise cooperation between its neighbours to East and West. Successes have been recorded through a complementarity between German diplomacy and domestic political stability. Preservation of the domestic consensus is thus the governments' 'ardent obligation' in all areas of policy. In the past, this has been done by single-minded adherence to an easily understood set of principles in foreign and economic policy. Decisions have been made with a view to maintaining balance between the elements of policy, to deflecting burdens on to others wherever possible, or to reconciling opposites in international relations. This defensive and conservative policy has contributed to the slow transformation of the post-war order, in which Germany achieved security and peace. That order is crumbling, and the capacity of the Federal Republic to isolate the domestic system from external disruptions has been sharply reduced.

In economic policy terms, this vulnerability is expressed in the theme of Germany's catching the 'English disease'. In 1980, the Federal Republic could not ride out the rise in oil prices as in 1973-1974 on the back of an export surplus: oil-producing country markets have shrunk, and European and Japanese exporters have increased their share of German markets. In August, the trade account moved to deficit. Given the outflow on services, the current account moved into deficit in 1979 to the tune of DM 9 billion, in 1980 of DM 30 billion, and in 1981, of an estimated 20 billion. The foreign exchange reserves began to melt like snow in the sun.

The authorities faced a choice, therefore, between devaluation and a rise in indebtedness. The first option of devaluation has the advantage, given favourable elasticities, of promising a worsening of the deficit in the short-term, and a recovery through price competition on exports in the longer-term. But, domestically, the authorities fear that a devaluation of the DM would feed directly through into domestic price levels, already rising at an average of 5 per cent in 1980. Externally, they feel obliged as members of the EMS to consult with partners on parity changes. France, running a huge trade deficit with the Federal Republic, has no interest in allowing the DM to move down too far against the franc. Indeed, in October, the Banque de France intervened on exchange markets to support the DM. The other policy option, then, has been to finance German government and external deficits by debt financing. Government bonds have been issued on the agreement of the Capital Markets Committee, confirming the role of the DM as an international reserve currency. As the authorities would have to switch to borrowing in foreign currencies, if the DM came under pressure, they face two possibilities: the first is to reduce the sources of debt, particularly in government finances. Given the state of the labour markets, with unemployment again over the one million mark, the SPD is unlikely to countenance too severe a reduction in government expenditures. In any case, the Bund cannot control *Länder* governments. The second option is not to increase the debt, and to keep the DM an attractive asset for foreign borrowers. This implies a priority to price stability under fixed exchange rates, a competitive rise in interest rates against British and American rates, and a readiness to accept higher rates of unemployment. With the anticipated change in union leadership, the fragile consensus between labour and capital may suffer. Furthermore, the need to firm up interest rates against American contributes, firstly, to keeping upward pressure on the dollar, and raising the dollar oil bills of Germany and of Germany's customers. Secondly, high interest rates help tighten the loan conditions for developing countries. Some form of 'recycling' may be arranged between Saudi Arabia and Turkey; but the same cannot be said so readily of Poland and other Eastern European governments, also hit by the world crisis.

Thus, the Federal Republic's fiction of a separation between 'politics' and 'economics' is no longer tenable. It was credible in the 1950s and 1960s, when the political power present at the creation of the Federal Republic could maintain a low profile, and allow the 'economic process' to run of its own accord. In the 1970s, Germany had to take over many of the tasks less willingly assumed by the United States. It became more visible. But that did not mean that Germany was an 'emerging power', but rather that the German problem and the European state system was re-emerging as the central feature of European affairs. In 1977 and 1978, the Federal Republic developed an active diplomacy to try to preserve the European order, equated with integration in the West and détente with the East, most compatible with its own requirements. It cannot be said to have succeeded. In 1980, the election to office of a reputedly more determined President in the United States has led to a realignment of the Federal Republic, together with France and Britain, to the United States. But there can be no returning to the point of departure. Germany's predicament is first and foremost European. It must therefore seek to preserve the peace, without appeasing, to preserve the domestic consensus without jeopardising it. In these conditions, the standard economic analysis, with its recourse to special factors, exogenous variables, residuals and interventions, is out of place. Perhaps the questionmark over Germany is whether contraction of the British condition, if not of the British disease, is compatible with the domestic consensus and with Germany's predicament as epicentre of the bipolar world.

NOTES

1. Anne-Marie Le Gloannec, 'La montée en puissance de la République Fédérale d'Allemagne', *Revue Française de Science Politique*, No. 2, April 1980, pp. 291-305.
2. H. C. Wallrich, *Mainspring of the German Revival*, New Haven: Yale University, 1955, p. 7.
3. Ibid., p. 155.
4. J. François-Poncet, *L'Allemagne Occidentale,* Paris, Editions Sirey, 1970, pp. 97-100.
5. Harold Van B. Cleveland, W. M. Bruce Brittain, *The Great Inflation: A Monetarist View*, Washington: CIR Report, 1976, pp. 36-40. The argument in its financial implications is accepted by myself as sound. The authors, however, gloss over the political and military aspects of German-American financial relations, and content themselves with the view of the 'inevitability of floating' the DM versus the dollar.
6. George M. Küster, 'Germany', in Raymond Vernon, ed., *Big Business and the State — Changing Relations in Western Europe*, Cambridge, Mass,: Harvard University Press, 1974, pp. 68-72.
7. Robert Triffin, 'The International Role and Fate of the Dollar', *Foreign Affairs*, Winter 1978/79, pp. 269-86.
8. Deutsche Bundesbank, Annual Report for the Year of 1969, p. 7.
9. See Edward L. Morse, 'European Monetary Union and American Foreign Economic Policy', in Wolfram Hanreider, *The United States and Western Europe*, Cambridge: Winthrop Publishers, 1974, pp. 187-200. Also Loukas Tsoukalis, *The Politics and Economics of European Monetary Integration*, London: Allen and Unwin, 1979.
10. For the period, 1968-1973, Frank Vogl, *German Business After the Economic Miracle*, London: Macmillan, 1973.
11. International Financial Statistics, (IFS).
12. Brendan Brown, *The Dollar-DM Axis: On Currency Power*, New York: St. Martin's Press, 1979.
13. Figures from Bernard Keizer, 'Les choix de la Republique Federale d'Allemangne' *Economie et Statistique*, No 102, July/Aug. 1978, p. 42.
14. OECD, Economic Surveys, 1978 and 1979, Statistical Annex.
15. OECD, Economic Survey, *Germany*, 1979, pp. 19-22.
16. Calculations on imports and exports by region: 1972-1978, in OECD Surveys, *Germany*, 1978, 1979.
17. IFS.
18. OECD Economic Surveys, *Germany*, 1979, p. 29.
19. Triffin, 'The International Role and Fate of the Dollar', p. 271.
20. Fritz Stern, 'Germany in a Semi-Gaullist Europe', *Foreign Affairs*, Spring 1980, pp. 867-86.
21. EEC Industrial Statistics.
22. *The Industrial Policies of 14 Member Countries*, OECD, Paris, 1971, pp. 11-48.
23. 'Common Plan for Regional Development', *International Herald Tribune*, April 1979 (Special Supplement).

24. Frank Wolter, 'Industrial Policy in the Federal Republic of Germany', unpublished paper delivered at INSEAD, March 1979.
25. 'Bonn, An Unwilling Industrialist', *Financial Times*, 4 Jan. 1979.
26. 'Le poids des entreprises publiques', *Le Moniteur de Commerce International*, 20 March, 1978.
27. For a contrary view, H.O. Eglau, *Erste Garnitur: Die Mächtigen der Deutschen Wirtschaft*, Düsseldorf: Econ Verlag, 1980.
28. Anne-Marie Le Gloannec, 'La RDA et l'EuroCommunisme', *Revue Française de Science Politique*, No 1, Feb. 1979, pp. 19-32.
29. Bernard Keizer, 'Les choix de la République Fédérale d'Allemagne', *Economie et Statistique*, No 102, July/Aug. 1978, pp. 33-53; Hans-Hinrich Glismann, Ernst-Jürgen Horn, 'Problèmes de conjoncture et de croissance dans une économie ouverte', *Economie et Statistique*, No. 97, Feb. 1978; Folker Fröbel, Jürgen Heinrichs, Otto Kreye, 'Die Neue Internationale Arbeitsteilung: Ursachen, Erscheinungsformen, Auswirkungen', *Gewerkschaftiche Monathefte*, Köln, No. 1, 1978.
30. Fröbel, Heinrichs, Kreye, *Die neue Internationale Arbeitsteilung, Strukturelle Arbeitslosigkeit in den Industrieländern und die Industrialiserung der Entwichlungs Länder*, Hamburg: Rowohlt, 1977; Kurt Lanz, 'Le tour du monde de chimie', Presses Universitaires de France, 1979.
31. Andrew Schonfield, *Modern Capitalism: The Changing Balance of Public and Private Power*, 1965, OUP, London, p. 253.
32. 'West Germany', in J. M. Samuels, R.E.V. Groves, C. S. Goddard, *Company Finance in Europe*, The Institute of Chartered Accountants, London: 1975, pp. 56-94.
33. 'Germany', *Industrial Policies of 14 Member Countries*, OECD, Paris, p. 25.
34. 'Le Modèle Allemand, Dossier', *Revue Française de Gestion*, No. 18, Nov.-Dec. 1978, pp. 31-41.
35. 'Competition Bows out to regulation in the EEC', *Financial Times*, 11 May, 1977.
36. 'Bank authorities seek greater accountability', *International Herald Tribune*, April 1979.
37. 'Limited Scope for Foreign Banks', *Financial Times*, 8 March, 1978.
38. Bernard de Montmorillon, 'Comportement national et international de quelques groupes industriels allemands', Le Modèle Allemand, *Revue Française de Gestion* Nov.-Dec. pp. 13-22.
39. UNIDO Working Paper on Structural Changes, No. 5, Nov. 1978, 'Industrial Redeployment Tendencies and Opportunities in the Federal Republic of Germany'.
40. *The Economist*, Oct., 1980, 'The New Wave', p. 13.
41. Jean-Louis Laurrens, 'Stratégie internationale des banques allemandes', *Revue Française de Gestion*, No. 18, Nov.-Dec., 1978, pp. 23-30.
42. Ibid., p. 30.
43. *Frankfurter Allgemeine Zeitung*, 28 April, 1978.
44. *Financial Times*, 29 July, 1979.
45. *International Currency Review*, Vol. 12, No. 5, p. 31.
46. *Financial Times*, 29 July, 1979.
47. C. Fred Bergsten, 'Die amerikanische Europa-Politik angesichts der Stagnation des Gemeinsamen Marktes. Ein Plädoyer für Konzentration auf die Bundesrepublik', *Europa Archiv*, Folge 4, 1974, pp. 115-22.
48. Maurice Delarue, 'Paris et Bonn resserrent leur coopération', *Le Monde*, 5 Feb. 1977.
49. *Le Monde*, 6-7 Feb. 1977.
50. Rapport Economique et Financier: Comptes Prévisionnels pour l'année 1978, *Ministére de l'Economie*, July/Aug. 1978.
51. IFS.
52. Helmut Schmidt, 'Europe on the threshold of a big step forward', *Financial Times*, 2 Jan. 1979.
53. Ibid.
54. OECD Economic Survey, *Germany*, 1980.
55. Manfred Lahnstein, 'Uber die Wahrungsunion zur Wirtschaftsunion', Europa Archiv, Folge 9, 1978, pp. 263-70.
56. *Le Monde*, 12-17 March, 1979.

57. Alain Cotta, 'La France et l'exemple allemand', in *Revue Française de Gestion*, No. 18, Nov./Dec. 1978, p. 9.
58. See Chancellor Schmidt's speech to the Polish Institute for International Affairs, *Europa Archiv*, 25 Jan., 1978, pp. 24-32.
59. *Financial Times*, 2 July, 1980.
60. These figures, I owe to an unpublished INSEAD paper, by Michael Kennedy, 'The Structure and Implications of East-West Trade', June 1980.
61. *International Currency Review*, Volume 12, No. 5, p. 30.
62. David P. Calleo, *The German Problem Reconsidered*, Cambridge: Cambridge University Press, 1978.
63. Helmut Schmidt, 'The struggle for the world product', *Foreign Affairs*, April 1974, p. 440.

Dimensions of West German Foreign Policy

Roger Morgan*

As the 1970s gave way to the 1980s, the central paradox of the Federal Republic's international position became clearer than ever. On the one hand, the strength of an economy relatively unscathed by the world recession, and the internal stability of a society ruled without serious challenge by Schmidt's social-liberal coalition, facilitated the Federal Republic's continued ascent into a position of considerable power and influence, both potential and actual. On the other hand, despite all the expectations and apprehensions of the Federal Republic's partners abroad (expectations that Germany should share more burdens, apprehensions that German power might become dangerous), the all-too-familiar constraints on German freedom of action continued to limit what the Federal Republic could actually do: the continuing division of Germany and the exposed position of Berlin meant that *Aussenpolitik* was still heavily conditioned by *Deutschlandpolitik*; the Federal Republic's non-nuclear status necessitated a cautious role in NATO's strategic planning; and the (partly self-imposed) constraints on economic expansionism curbed any idea of the German economy being reflated as a 'locomotive' to pull the Western world out of recession.[1]

By the time of the 1980 election campaign, the old argument about whether the economic giant was or was not a political dwarf had been settled: in the world scene of the Carter presidency, the breakdown of détente after Afghanistan, and the Thatcher government's wrangling over the Community budget, the Federal Republic clearly *was* a political giant, and the most puzzling questions were then of how the giant's power actually could or could not be used, and in what circumstances.

FOREIGN POLICY ISSUES IN THE ELECTION

The general German mood of late 1980 — the feeling that the country was now so big that it was intimately concerned with all the central issues of world politics and economics, but that the precise modalities of its involvement were not clearly defined — is well captured in the text of parallel questionnaires which *Der Spiegel* submitted to the two candidates for the chancellorship shortly before 5 October, and also in their answers. As one would expect in an article which appeared a week before polling day, most of the 38 questions are concerned with either personal matters or domestic political issues, but the five questions on foreign policy (including one

*Research for this essay was supported by a grant from the Ford Foundation.

essentially on *Deutschlandpolitik*) shed a significant light on what the influential *Spiegel* thought its readers wanted to hear from the two candidates, and on what these in turn wanted to say.

In answer to the first foreign policy question, whether the Eastern treaties of the 1970s offer a basis for better relations with the Soviet bloc in future, Schmidt's response is a stout defence of his government's *Ostpolitik*, based on neighbourly treaty-relations with the East European peoples and their governments, and stressing the need, 'not merely to respect the existing treaties in a legal sense', but also 'constantly to fill them with life and reality'.[2] Strauss's answer — significantly, the answer which the majority of German voters refused to support — is that Brandt's Eastern treaties were 'falsely conceived, atrociously negotiated, badly formulated and thus open to contradictory interpretations', and that the so-called 'policy of détente' had failed. While respecting the existence of the treaties, Strauss would follow Adenauer's principle of extreme caution in dealing with the Russians, 'coolly, free from illusions, vigilantly, on the basis of historical wisdom and political experience'.

To the second question, what the candidates would do to repair apparent strains in Germany's relationship with the United States, Schmidt's answer is that the Bonn-Washington relationship is 'in order', that 'occasional differences of opinion' are perfectly normal, and that 'the Americans need reliable, but also critical, German partners, who speak their minds freely and are not timid about representing the national interests of the Germans'. Strauss, in contrast, asserts that the SPD is stirring up 'anti-American feelings' in Germany, and that the SPD's 'Moscow faction' is threatening to take the Federal Republic out of NATO. Strauss adds the further argument that neutralist tendencies in the SPD even threaten to take the country out of the European Community as well, which would mean 'putting ourselves at the mercy of Moscow'.

The third question asks for the candidate's assessment of the prospects for new disarmament talks, as proposed by Brezhnev. Schmidt's answer is a cautious reaffirmation of the need for the reduction of nuclear weapons in Europe by both sides, on a balanced basis, so that the security of Germany is maintained and that a nuclear arms race is avoided. Strauss's reply to the question, in contrast, is a vehement attack on Brezhnev's proposals as a trick designed to hinder NATO's efforts to catch up the Russian lead in medium-range missiles: he attacks Schmidt for having accepted, on his June visit to Moscow, the Soviet proposal that nuclear systems in Western Europe should be the subject of East-West negotiations, and, by doing so, for sowing the seeds of discord in the alliance.

Der Spiegel's fourth question suggests that a German chancellor may be expected to play a diplomatic role on a broader scene than that of the Atlantic alliance: 'Given the uncertainties of détente in Europe, do you regard it as desirable to engage in a closer dialogue with the People's Republic of China, or should we hold back from such attempts at rapprochment?' Schmidt's reply is a statesmanlike rejection of the idea of 'playing off one Communist great power against the other': the Federal Republic's normal diplomatic and economic relations with China should be maintained, but playing about with a so-called 'Chinese card' is to be avoided. Strauss's reply opens up much grander perspectives: Europe cannot be seen as an 'island of détente' while the Soviet Union crushes the independence of Afghanistan, and 'Since the return of the Peoples' Republic of China from its self-chosen isolation to the stage of world politics, German *Ostpolitik* cannot end in Moscow . . . China too must be brought into our calculations on this point.' The bi-polar world of Yalta is no more, argues Strauss, since 'China as a great power in the Far East, as a future world power, and as an economic partner has brought about a new relationship of forces. In view of this 'friendly relations with the largest people in the world . . . are an imperative of *Realpolitik*' and therefore Schmidt's impolite treatment of the Chinese head of government in Bonn was a typical example of 'the kind of error he makes'.

The fifth and last question concerned with external policy reverts from *Aussenpolitik* to *Deutschlandpolitik:* how soon after being elected would the rival candidates visit the GDR's Chairman Honecker, and what results would they expect from such a meeting? Schmidt rather curtly states that his proposed 1980 meeting with Honecker had to be postponed for reasons (i.e. Afghanistan and Poland) which would be clear to all Germans, and declares that a meeting should take place, 'when Herr Honecker and I regard the moment as favourable for a conversation, which will certainly not be about maximum demands by one side on the other, but about a composing of interests, which brings advantages to the Germans in both states'. Strauss, in contrast, forswears any idea of meeting Honecker unless East Berlin is ready to remove the automatic shooting-installations on the frontier of the two Germanies, and to end the standing orders to the East German border guards to shoot all refugees. Further West German economic and financial help to the GDR must depend, he argues, on 'free access to Berlin, free movement for visitors between the parts of Germany and, in a reasonable time, the dismantling of the Wall and the death-areas' (i.e. on the border). Strauss finally claims that as he is 'no socialist illusionist', he sees more clearly than his opponent that the key to inner-German relations lies not in East Berlin but in Moscow.

Der Spiegel's rapid survey of foreign policy issues facing Germany provides, precisely because the questions are both chosen and answered with electoral considerations in mind, an indication of which themes are uppermost in the public consciousness. The answers bring out, in the first place, the contradictory nature of German feelings about East-West détente: on the one hand the awareness of growing insecurity in the context of a general crumbling of détente, and on the other hand a determination that East-West economic transactions, and negotiations on arms control, should continue despite everything. Another theme which reverberates throughout the questionnaire is the awareness of Germany's influence on the world scene: the Federal Republic is seen as a major international actor, able and obliged to conduct relations of a substantial kind with the two superpowers and also with the rising power of China. Whether the policy advocated is the restrained one of firm but prudent assertion of German national interests (as for Schmidt) or the more venturesome one of exploring

common interests with China (as for Strauss), the Federal Republic's status
as an international power with policy options is uncontested.

And yet, underlying this consciousness of power and influence, the
vulnerability stemming from Germany's division is constantly present: in the
discussion of whether the new Chancellor should meet his East German
counterpart (and if so, to discuss what agenda), and in the repeated references to the way in which this predicament requires careful handling of
relations with Moscow.

As significant as the themes which are stressed, though in a different way,
are those which are mentioned only briefly, or not at all. The Federal
Republic's role in the European Community, for instance, receives no
attention apart from Strauss's passing suggestion that the SPD might be
tempted to take Germany out of the EEC. In fact the 1980 election
campaign, like the campaign for the directly-elected European Parliament
in 1979, confirmed that most West Germans regard their country's membership of the Community as of self-evident advantage to them, but that no
German party now wishes to propose significant new developments in EEC
policies, and thus incur political controversies with Germany's partners
and/or additional expense for the German taxpayers.

A more surprising omission, perhaps, is any reference to the Federal
Republic's growing role in the United Nations: even in a brief pre-electoral
survey, the Chancellor might have been expected to make something of the
fact that, although it had been a member of the UN for less than ten years, his
country, had achieved the rank of a Security Council member, had played a
prominent part in many UN conferences on economic and development
questions, and had in 1980 seen the German Permanent Representative in
New York (Rüdiger von Wechmar) elected President of the General
Assembly.

The *Spiegel* exchange also omits (whether for lack of space or because of
the controversial nature of the issue) any references to German arms sales to
the Third World, to the possibility of a military role for the Federal Republic
outside the NATO area (e.g. a naval presence in the Persian Gulf), or to a
more active political involvement in proposing solutions to the problems of
the Middle East, Southern Africa, or other troubled areas.

It is also noteworthy, though again hardly surprising, that neither *Der
Spiegel* nor the two candidates thought it necessary in the context of the
questionnaire to set out any considerations on Germany's position in the
world economy: there is no reference to the Federal Republic's leading role
in the annual summit meetings of the seven main non-Communist industrial
countries, to the influence and responsibility in world economic management which stems from Germany's economic strength, or to the vulnerability arising from dependence on imported energy and other raw
materials.

THE AMBIGUOUS WEST GERMAN POSITION

The *Spiegel* texts, with the contrast in German strengths and weaknesses
which they clearly bring out, and with their stress on some points combined

with silence on others, indicate the very ambiguous international position of the Federal Republic today.

The paradoxical nature of this position — in which strength coexists with vulnerability, influence with interdependence, and active involvement in some international issues with reticence towards others — can only be explained by considering how the international system has changed at the same time as Germany's potential influence has risen. It can be said that the foreign policy of the Federal Republic has developed on the basis of steadily growing economic strength, combined with originally non-existent diplomatic and military resources, with the aim of inserting the embryonic West German state into a succession of international relationships, each of them designed to shape part of the external environment in accordance with Germany's as well as her partners' interests. The principal relationships which may be identified have been (not necessarily chronologically, as they have in fact coexisted over time): firstly, the integration of the Federal Republic into a West European entity expressed essentially by the Coal and Steel Community and by the Common Market (as well as the Council of Europe, etc.); secondly, the binding of Germany into the Atlantic alliance through NATO, WEU, and the most intimate relationship possible with the United States; thirdly — much delayed in time, and much more diluted in character — a relationship with the Soviet bloc which began with Adenauer's very limited agreement with Moscow, blossomed via the 'small steps' of the 1960s into the *Ostpolitik* of Brandt, and is maintained sceptically but determinedly by Schmidt; and fourthly, the even more diffuse set of relationships involving the Federal Republic in world economic management and specifically the 'North-South Dialogue', including the UN agencies, the Conference on International Economic Cooperation and its aftermath, and most especially the industrial world's relations with OPEC.[3]

Despite all their manifest differences, these four sets of relationships have in common, from the German point of view, that they were designed to provide a framework — a dependable and as far as possible predictable set of mutual obligations — within which certain of Germany's major needs, and those of her partners in each case, could be fulfilled. Such a structure, although obviously important for any state in the modern international system, was particularly desirable for a country in the position of the Federal Republic, which had to make its way in the post-war world from a position of economic near-bankruptcy and political isolation and which in any case purported to regard itself as no more than a provisional entity, destined to disappear when the goal of national reunification was achieved. Pending this obviously long-term prospect, the Federal Republic expected to find status, stability, and solutions to its economic and security needs in its membership of a succession of overlapping but widely different international structures: West European, Atlantic, East-West, and North-South.

An accumulation of unrelated developments has in the event made the Federal Republic a leading partner (though by no means the dominant one) in each of these relationships. Even without national reunification, which has receded to an infinitely remote horizon, the economic weight of the

Federal Republic has made it by far the most influential member of the European Community; a power in Atlantic relations which has been nominated by some of its American admirers as worthy to run the alliance in 'bigemony' with the United States; in the East-West context, a power which the Russians, and to some extent the Chinese, treat with great respect and attention; and in global terms a power with a substantial voice in North-South and other economic debates.

The stature of the Federal Republic in each of its international roles is due, of course, not only to its intrinsic strength, but also to the fact that each one of these international frameworks has failed, in different ways, to develop the cohesion which some of its architects anticipated: a cohesion in which the element of interdependence would be so strong that the power of individual states, even the largest ones, would be constrained and even progressively diminished. This proposition must be examined in relation to each of the four principal partnerships in which the Federal Republic has been engaged.

(i)   The European Community Connection. In the first of these, the West European one, both the preponderant weight of the German economy and the scope for German influence in an essentially inter-governmental rather than supranational negotiating framework have become very obvious during the 1970s. In terms of size, a West German economy which represents one-third of the resources of the entire Community puts Bonn in a strong bargaining position and the fact that this has not been used to press for specific lines of Community policy results mainly from the fact that the present balance of Community policies and spending programmes is broadly acceptable to the Federal Republic.[4]

German policy in the Community has concentrated in the main on promoting economic integration by the removal of obstacles to the free movement of goods, capital and labour, by the development of a strict competition policy and by related measures of 'negative' integration. The Common Agricultural Policy had also, by the 1970s, proved to be advantageous to the Federal Republic. On the other hand, any further measures of interventionist, or 'positive' integration, such as large-scale industrial, regional, or social policies, have proved less welcome to Germany on grounds either of economic doctrine or of financial cost, and Germany's influence, in the economic recession from 1973 onwards, has been used to check the development of policies of this kind.

In any case, the reluctance of Germany's Community partners to pursue integration beyond the scope of the area under Community control at the start of the 1970s — essentially agriculture and trade — ensured that steps towards supranational integration would be much less likely than the growth of inter-governmental cooperation. In this inter-governmental framework, the Federal Republic has made important contributions, for instance by actively promoting the system of European Political Cooperation between the foreign ministries of the Nine, by making effective use of the European Council meetings of the heads of government, and by pressing in 1980 for a strengthened role for the Secretary-General of the Council of Ministers. However, the net effect of all these developments, at the start of the 1980s has been that the Federal Republic stands in a class of its own as an economic power in a Community whose supranational authority is unlikely to grow, and which is likely to prove only a limited framework for containing German national power and a limited vehicle for the promotion of German national interests in the years ahead.

(ii)   The American Relationship. Some of this analysis also applies to the second of Germany's main international partnerships, the Atlantic Alliance and especially the relationship with the United States. It was never expected, of course, that this relationship would develop into an institutionalised community of the kind envisaged by the pioneers of the Common Market — except, perhaps, for specific occasions, as for instance when the Multilateral Force of the mid-1960s (MLF) was seen by its begetters as the nucleus of an Atlantic Defence Community. However, Bonn's relationship with Washington was and still is seen as the most important single element in the Federal Republic's foreign policy: a close understanding with Washington has been of vital importance in some of the most critical phases of Bonn's foreign policy, including the worst years of the cold war when Dulles (with reservations) supported Adenauer, and also the years of active *Ostpolitik* when Kissinger (again with reservations) supported Brandt.[5]

An indication of current German-US differences of opinion, and of a more independent German stance, has already been cited in Schmidt's remark to the *Spiegel* that the United States needed allies who were not afraid to speak their own minds, and to indicate divergences as well as points of agreement with American policies. Behind this formulation there lies a four-year-long history of bad communications and outright conflict between Schmidt and the Carter administration. Quite apart from the temperamental and other personal barriers between the two leaders, German-American relations have been marked in the late 1970s by a number of real conflicts of interest, including many which reflect Germany's growing status and the declining authority of the United States as the leader of the West. The conflicts have covered such diverse issues as German sales of nuclear technology to Brazil, disputes about how to handle the question of human rights in relations with the Soviet bloc, the appropriate Western response to the Iranian seizure of hostages and the Soviet invasion of Afghanistan, and finally, the whole future of East-West détente in the aftermath of this invasion.

Washington's concern that Bonn's wish to maintain détente might crucially weaken the Western alliance, expressed in a tactlessly-worded letter from Carter to Schmidt on the eve of the latter's Moscow visit in June 1980, is certain to recur with increasing force under the Reagan administration. Even though the new administration contains men who will be able to avoid some of the errors of the recent past, there are enough serious conflicts of perspective and of real interest between Bonn and Washington to ensure that the 1980s will not be an easy time for an increasingly fissiparous Atlantic alliance containing an increasingly powerful Germany.

(iii)   The Ostpolitik. The third of Germany's substantial relationships — that with the Soviet bloc which has developed essentially from Brandt's *Ostpolitik* of the early 1970s — has always had a much less intimate

character than either of the two Western partnerships: despite some Western fears that a 'new Rapallo' was in the making, or Strauss's allusions to the sinister machinations of the SPD's 'Moscow faction', the *Ostpolitik* has been firmly rooted in *Westpolitik*, and both Brandt and Schmidt have refused to allow the Federal Republic's involvement with the Soviet bloc to grow to a point where it threatened their country's fundamental commitment to NATO.

Despite this, the importance of continued détente to Germany has become very clear in the year since the Afghanistan crisis, which has seen the Federal Republic, despite its strongly pro-American stand on strategic issues and its solidarity with the Olympic buoycott, trying to insist that détente in Central Europe should not be jeopardised by a crisis in Central Asia. The importance of détente for Germany lies not only in the economic significance of Soviet orders from the German engineering industry, especially in a period of recession, or in the value to West Germany of Soviet natural gas supplies which will soon provide three or four per cent of Germany's energy requirements. There is also the vital human dimension represented by the fact that détente does something to soften the harsh division of the German nation: as a West German foreign policy expert recently argued to a congressional committee in Washington, the West should not forget 'those eight million West Germans that can now annually go to East Germany, those 1.5 million East Germans annually visiting the West, or the 60,000 German emigrants we extract every year out of East Europe'.[6]

Even though the GDR authorities, shortly after the West German election, imposed restrictions that may considerably cut down the number of West Germans visiting the East, and even though the Eastern position on détente in general remains tough and uncompromising, the Federal Republic is likely to persist in its efforts. The main point to note, in the context of the present argument, is that in East-West relations, as elsewhere, the Federal Republic is tending to emerge as an autonomous international actor, negotiating its way through a confused and partially disintegrating environment, rather than functioning as a wholly integral part of a cohesive East-West structure of the kind envisaged when President Nixon proclaimed the 'Era of Negotiations' at the start of the 1970s.

(iv)   North-South Relations. In the fourth and last of Germany's international partnerships, the North-South dimension, the underlying pattern is even harder to perceive, partly because the original design was a more multifarious and in some ways less ambitious one than in the other three contexts. However, the same basic theme of a comprehensive design becoming fragmented, and Germany emerging as a more autonomous and more influential actor, can be discerned in the process by which the original picture of Europe-Third World relations (German and other European aid being distributed partly bilaterally, and partly through the EEC's Yaoundé and Lomé Conventions, in return for the quid pro quo of raw materials and markets) has given way to a much more differentiated world: a world which involves Germany in relations with oil-rich and newly-industrialising, as well as with under-developed countries, and which has brought to light

increasing divergencies of views between the industrialised countries themselves on the proper approach to North-South relations.

These divergencies are partly a reflection of more general disagreements about the philosophy of political intervention in economic policy, whether international or domestic: for instance, disagreements between Germany and some of her partners in the Conference on International Economic Cooperation have their roots in the German principle of non-intervention in market forces.

Currently, German approaches to the problems of North-South relations, despite Schmidt's emphatic public endorsement of the Brandt Commission's report, appear to be marked by pessimism about the chances of any foreseeable economic aid from the industrial countries being adequate to cope with the problems. German thinking heavily stresses the degree to which existing Western aid programmes have been eroded in real terms by the population explosion and by the soaring cost of energy in the Third World, and the lesson appears to be drawn that future Western aid — to the extent that it can be afforded — should be concentrated on certain developing countries where some positive effects can be anticipated, and perhaps also on specific sectors of development, such as energy resources. Such an approach implies a more nationally-oriented German development policy than hitherto, and the same phenomenon, of a more independent German stance in relation to world economic issues, can also be detected in such different fields as economic cooperation agreements with oil-producing countries and others, or possible sales of German military equipment to countries as far apart (politically as well as geographically) as Chile and India.[7]

CONCLUSION

In all the main areas of Germany's international involvement — Western Europe, the Atlantic alliance, the East-West relationship, and the North-South complex — we can thus detect signs of the same underlying pattern: an increasingly authoritative Federal Republic emerging into a position of growing influence over an unstructured and less predictable environment. Many Germans regret that the structures within which the Federal Republic sought to integrate itself into the international system have failed to develop as they were expected to do. However, the fact that they have failed — at least relatively — by no means signifies a return to the worst features of the international anarchy of the 1930s. The Germans and their neighbours have learned to practise many of the habits of cooperation during the years when interdependence appeared to be the dominant rule of their lives, and there are few if any forces within the German political system which would dispute the need for foreign policy to be conducted as if structures of interdependence were still being strengthened instead of weakened.

NOTES

1. For a further discussion see the author's *West Germany's Foreign Policy Agenda*, Beverly Hills/London: Sage, 1978

2. These and other quotations from *Der Spiegel*, 29 Sept. 1980.
3. Cf Hans-Peter Schwarz, 'The Roles of the Federal Republic in the Community of States', in K. Kaiser & R. Morgan (eds.), *Britain and West Germany*, London: OUP for RIIA, 1971.
4. For a further discussion see the author's chapter on Germany in C. & K. Twitchett (eds.), *Building Europe*, London: Europa, 1981.
5. An analysis of post-war US-German relations is given in the author's *The United States and West Germany, 1945-73*, London: OUP for RIIA, 1974; current issues are covered in W. R. Smyser, *German-American Relations*, Beverly Hills/London: Sage, 1980.
6. Karl Kaiser in *United States-Western European Relations in 1980, Hearings before the . . . House of Representatives*, Washington: US Government Printing Office, 1980, p. 215. For a general survey see Michael Kreile, 'Ostpolitik Reconsidered', in E. Krippendorff and V. Rittberger (eds.), *The Foreign Policy of West Germany*, Beverly Hills/London: Sage, 1980.
7. Cf. *Die Zeit*, 26 Dec. 1980. On general economic aspects, see the chapters by Czempiel Zeitel, Dingwort-Nusseck and Schartzel in Wolfman F. Hanrieder (ed.), *West German Foreign Policy: 1949-1979*, Boulder, Colorado: Westview. 1980

Détente at Work — The Record of Inter-German Relations

Helga Michalsky

POLITICAL DETERMINANTS OF INTER-GERMAN RELATIONS

As the crisis in East-West relations deepens, there is growing concern in the Federal Republic that the freedom of manoeuvre for West German diplomacy is being reduced. This applies to East-West relations in general and to the relations between the two German states in particular. Since the state of inter-German relations is dependent on the relationship between the two alliance systems, the future development of East-West relations is of vital importance for the Federal Republic.

The Federal Government, however, does not view its role in the process of détente as merely passive, for it has always considered the *Ostpolitik* and *Deutschlandpolitik* conducted over the last decade as an active contribution to détente between East and West. For this very reason, the government believes that a continuation of détente between the two German states may contribute to keep the overall process of détente alive. This idea is based on the conviction that there is no acceptable alternative to détente. If the Western alliance should come to an assessment of the international situation that diverges from that made by the Federal Government, such a development would undoubtedly have critical repercussions on the *Deutschlandpolitik*. To a great extent the current concern expressed in government circles and by elite opinion reflects the fear that West German foreign policy may be at such a turning point, although a fundamental revision of policy is considered neither necessary nor inevitable.

The developments following the Soviet invasion of Afghanistan have brought changes in several respects. On the one hand, within the Western alliance, an increasing number of politicians consider détente as dead or — what almost amounts to the same thing — demand that it be put on a new footing. On the other hand, both German states initially made an effort to prevent the general deterioration in the international climate from spilling over into their bilateral relations. To give an example: the meeting between Chancellor Schmidt and Chairman Honecker, which had been scheduled to take place in the spring of 1980, was cancelled by mutual agreement and without any spectacular gesture. In their announcements, both sides explicitly referred to the international tension but did not engage in mutual recrimination. The development of the relationship under the impact of the Polish events during the last quarter of 1980 provides little ground for optimism. However, a pessimistic forecast would be premature, relations between the two Germanies in the past have always been characterised by ups and downs.

Yet, bearing in mind the international factors which conditioned the revision of the *Deutschlandpolitik* in the late 1960s, it seems practically impossible for the two Germanies to isolate themselves from a fundamental change in East-West relations. Just as the Federal Government in the 1960s was only temporarily able to resist the momentum of the détente process, so would a new consensus formed by the Atlantic Alliance force the Federal Republic to conform to the new line. The German Democratic Republic, for her part, is exclusively dependent on the basic foreign policy decisions of the Soviet Union. Early in 1980, this situation could be interpreted in a way suggesting that the continuation of détente policy by the GDR was also designed to demonstrate the unaltered Soviet commitment to détente.

Among the factors likely to determine the relationship between the two Germanies are the attitudes of the West German electorate towards the *Deutschlandpolitik*. In the pre-détente period, this policy had no operational criterion of success as it basically relied on the legal fiction of a united Germany. The current policy, in contrast, can be evaluated according to the volume and the quality of contacts that take place between the people in the two German states, since the growth of contacts has been one of the foremost objectives of the *Deutschlandpolitik* conducted during the period of the SPD-FDP coalition.

The current policy involves a considerable financial burden for the Federal Republic. Each measure of *Abgrenzung* (demarcation), for instance the restrictions on travel and communication, imposed by the GDR is therefore bound to raise the question of the distribution of costs and benefits in the bilateral relationship. If the GDR leadership were to push its policy of *Abgrenzung* to the point of cutting back on existing opportunities of contact and communication, the majority of the West German population might feel that the game was not worth the candle and withdraw its support for the Government's policy. If a temporary stagnation in inter-German relations were replaced by a determined reduction of contacts decreed by the GDR leadership (or the Soviet Union for that matter), in other words: if *Abgrenzung* received priority over détente, the Federal Government would have to conclude that this undermined the very foundations of the Basic Treaty.

The political controversy within the FRG surrounding inter-German relations and the *Ostpolitik*, ever since 1969, has always been — on the part of the critics — an ideological attack on political reality. But it has also been a debate over the success or failure of the policy put into practice. Eight years after the conclusion of the Basic Treaty, an assessment of the state of inter-German relations has still to take into account the effects of certain legal theories concerning Germany as a whole, but the following analysis will deal primarily with the results of the process of normalisation between the two German states which the Basic Treaty was intended to set in motion.

THE DIFFICULT GROUNDWORK: THE BASIC TREATY

When the Federal Government crowned the revision of the *Ostpolitik* with the conclusion of the Basic Treaty in 1972, the architects of this policy had set themselves more ambitious goals than bringing the Federal Republic into the mainstream of Western détente policy. They were convinced that the political and material disadvantages experienced by the Germans who lived under a socialist regime could only be tempered or mitigated through a policy of cooperation, for they realised that an end to the partition of Germany was not in sight. They did not adhere to theories of 'convergence' but their priorities were different from those of their predecessors. Bahr's formula of securing 'change through *rapprochement*' (*Wandel durch Annäherung*) did not refer to changing the political order but to making living conditions in different social systems more equal. In a 'Memorandum of the Federal Government regarding the "Treaty on the Basis of Relations between the Federal Republic of Germany and the German Democratic Republic" ', the Government pointed out its success in making such stipulations 'which confer to the treaty a tangible substance to the benefit of individuals and will thereby gradually render the actual conditions more tolerable'.[1] At the provisional signing of the Basic Treaty on 8 November, 1972, Bahr had emphasised that this was the beginning of a road, 'which would lead beyond organised coexistence (*Nebeneinander*) to good-neighbourly relations (*Miteinander*). This treaty is not only being concluded because the governments want it so, but because the people in the two states need it. Therefore we have set great value on the practical measures affecting all important aspects of everyday life.'[2] Article 7 of the Basic Treaty, which constitutional lawyers have criticised for its lack of specificity,[3] outlines the conception as well as the areas of cooperation:

The Federal Republic of Germany and the German Democratic Republic express their readiness to settle practical and humanitarian questions in the course of the normalisation of their relations. They will conclude agreements in order to develop and to promote — on the basis of this treaty and for mutual benefit — the cooperation with respect to economic relations, science and technology, traffic, legal cooperation, postal and telephone services, public health problems, culture, sport, environmental protection and other fields. Details are guided by the additional protocol.[4]

Behind this concept lay the expectation that continuous economic progress in the GDR would enable the SED leadership to grant their citizens freedoms which are considered self-evident in the Federal Republic without jeopardising its own power. In the long run, *rapprochement* would come about as the GDR would give up her 'demarcation' efforts. The political stability of the socialist system and the loyalty of its citizens would thus represent an intermediate stage on the way to a higher level of community. This developmental framework for the future of German unity does not imply the concept of a unitary nation-state, but it is based on an idea of national solidarity which transcends the territorial division. The specific character of inter-German relations which in terms of international and constitutional law represent a construction of remarkable complexity, appears in this respect as a natural complement both to normalisation and a lasting commitment to national unit. The connection between normalisation and the specificity of inter-German relations, however, was bound to raise questions from the outset. Yet, its realisation did not seem altogether impossible — at least at the beginning of the 1970s.

In the first half of the 1970s, the economic development of the GDR was promising. The political leadership displayed a new sense of self-confidence and demonstrated flexibility in some areas, such as in the treatment of writers and working conditions for West German journalists in the GDR. The high-flown hopes which, at the European level, manifested themselves in the Conference on Security and Cooperation (CSCE), were followed by the sobering experience of international tension before the practical and humanitarian potential of détente policy had been fully exploited. The erosion of the optimistic approach to the *Deutschlandpolitik* was also caused by the domestic debate over the constitutionality of the Basic Treaty and the ruling of the Constitutional Court of 1973. The Court recognised the constitutionality of the treaty but only within the limits of its own interpretation.[5] This was a high price for the Government to pay. Those stipulations of the treaty which according to the Government were designed to keep the German question open and conferred to the relationship between the two German states a status *sui generis*, were forced by the Court into the Procrustean bed of traditional legal theory concerning the unity of Germany as a whole.

The Court's ruling has given different emphases to certain provisions of the treaty:

(1)   The preamble of the treaty states that the Federal Republic and the GDR have different views 'on fundamental questions, including the national question'. The Court ruling held that the only solution to the national question compatible with the constitution is the restoration of the unity of the nation-state. This goal is a constitutional imperative for any Federal Government. Only the choice of appropriate instruments is left to the competent constitutional bodies. According to the Court, the German Reich still exists; it only lacks the capacity to act. However, the Federal Republic's claim to the sole representation of Germany as a whole (*Alleinvertretungsanspruch*) which previous governments had defended by means of the Hallstein doctrine was explicitly renounced by the Court. The Court's *Deutschlandtheorie* (theory concerning Germany) which constitutional lawyers[6] have termed a *'Teilidentitäts-theorie'* (a theory of partial identity with reference to the relationship between the Federal Republic and the German Reich) or criticised as a mixture of several theories, lends support to the proponents of the 'classical reunification theory' (*klassische Wiedervereinigungstheorie*) who generally opposed the Basic Treaty.[7]

(2)   Several articles of the treaty affirm the *independence and autonomy of both German states* in their internal and external relations. The Court's interpretation explicitly restricts this status to the relationship with third countries and, referring to the continuous existence of one German state (i.e. the Reich), characterises the

relations between the two German states as *'inter-se'* relations. The Federal Government has consciously avoided relying on such legal concepts, with the advantage that normalisation could be interpreted, though not explicitly, as normalisation of contracts and communication. The ruling by the Constitutional Court, however, subjects any definition of normalisation its compatibility with the *Deutschlandtheorie* formulated by the Court.

(3)   Regarding the question of *nationality*, the two contracting parties had stated their contrasting positions in an additional protocol. The GDR hopes that the Federal Republic will come to recognise a separate GDR nationality. This would mean that the Federal Republic would no longer automatically confer her own nationality upon GDR citizens who move to the Federal Republic. The recognition of a separate GDR nationality which would be equivalent to the *recognition of the GDR under international law* is, according to the Constitutional Court, incompatible with the Basic Law. As a consequence, the GDR is repeatedly able to drag up this bone of contention, not so much in order to achieve her objective but rather to deny concessions or to advance her other demands.

(4)   As the Federal Government was not prepared to recognise the GDR formally under international law, the GDR accepted the special status of the Permanent Missions in Bonn and East Berlin. For the time being, this formula was the only way in which the GDR could obtain treatment as a subject of international law on the part of the Federal Republic. By declaring the status of the Permanent Missions constitutional, the Court has precluded changes of their status (e.g. an upgrading to the level of embassies) for the future.

(5)   The Court has created an additional problem by using *inter-German trade* as an example of the implementation of the treaty in conformity with the constitution. This implies that the status of trade relations cannot be changed. Ironically enough, the Federal Republic may be confronted in the near future with the demand by her European Community partners to repeal the protocol on inter-German trade to the Rome treaty. The case of trade relations demonstrates that the court's tendency to prejudge future developments carries a high risk of immobilism.

The SPD-FDP coalition had never left any doubt that the formal recognition of the GDR under international law was out of the question. It had successfully referred to the principle of Four Power responsibility for Germany to justify its programme of normalisation. On the other hand, the Brandt-Scheel government had relied on a terminology which took into account the realities as well as the apprehensions of other European states about the problem of reunification. Whereas the Government interpreted the 'reunification imperative' as a mandate 'to keep the German question open' — reunification being nothing more than a long-term perspective — the more rigid formulations of the Constitutional Court limit considerably the freedom of action of future governments.

Moreover, the Court's ruling left a negative impression on many foreign

observers in both East and West, and the ruling was considered a provoca-
tion by the co-signatory of the treaty: it was the Federal Government which
had put at risk the spirit of reconciliation and détente [to which it had
attached so much importance when the treaty was concluded. In the
domestic battle over the *Deutschlandpolitik*, in which the CDU/CSU
opposition postured as the guardian of the constitution, the Government
was led more often than necessary (or tactically sensible) to base its own
position on the ruling of the Constitutional Court. When one recalls that the
GDR and the Federal Republic had written into the treaty their fundamental disagreement with respect to some key problems, it will come as no
surprise that the GDR considered the Court's ruling as an attack on the spirit
of the treaty. Both sides had agreed that the value of the treaty resided in the
fact that, in spite of different motives and interests, a constructive cooperation was possible.

The two states pursue different objectives. For the Federal Republic one
of the main goals of the treaty is 'to prevent a further drifting apart of the
Germans in East and West by increasing contacts and cooperation between
people, organisations and institutions'.[8] For the GDR, these contacts are
only tolerable as long as they do not threaten her social and political system
(hence *Abgrenzung*). The GDR was primarily interested in achieving international recognition. The de facto recognition by the Federal Republic
provided the key, and the admission of the two states to the United Nations
symbolised the achievement of a long-cherished goal. The GDR leadership
also interprets the Basic Treaty as recognition under international law. In an
amendment to the GDR constitution in 1974 and in the party platform of
1976, the SED rejected the concept of German national unity.

The Federal Republic has sought to avoid further concessions that would
enhance the 'state-ness' (*Staatlichkeit*) of the GDR. Instead, the
Federal Government has concentrated its efforts on safeguarding and
improving the existing opportunities for travel and communication as well as
the transit conditions between West Berlin and the Federal Republic. The
Government emphasises the disagreement on principles written into the
treaty and stresses the need to cooperate on practical matters. In the
preamble to the treaty, both states declared their readiness, 'to make a
contribution to détente and security in Europe'. The GDR relies on the
spirit of the preamable to justify her policy of *Abgrenzung*. Détente and
security, in her view, include the domestic security of states. The GDR
authorities also claim that 'factual situations', such as the special status of the
Permanent Representatives or the position taken by the Federal Republic
on the question of nationality constitute violations of international law.
Given the legal theories advanced by the Federal Republic, in the long run it
could very well be that the GDR will have more chance of having her
position accepted by countries other than the Federal Republic.

During the CSCE process, the socialist countries tended to give priority to
the goals of 'Basket 2' (economic cooperation) and to play down the
humanitarian obligations of 'Basket 3' (communication). The same holds
true for the GDR's approach to inter-German relations. Her main fields of
interest are trade relations and agreements that provide her with foreign

exchange. The economic interests of the GDR constitute the main lever for the Federal Republic in working out compromises. To put it simply: the Federal Republic *buys* humanitarian concessions from the GDR. Both sides find their benefits in this arrangement, but the GDR runs higher risks. As the raising of living standards represents an important instrument of political stabilisation for the present GDR leadership and requires cooperation with the West, the GDR had to make concessions on travel arrangements, working conditions for journalists, and 'Basket 3' of CSCE.

However, these measures so far have tended to thwart international stabilisation rather than to promote it. This has given a new impetus to the policy of demarcation. The effects of détente such as applications for the release from GDR citizenship or demands for freedom of expression, have led some observers to ask whether the GDR might not actually be interested in the demise of détente.[9]

THE FRUITS OF COMPROMISE: ACHIEVEMENTS IN INTER-GERMAN RELATIONS

In a report entitled '10 Jahre Deutschlandpolitik (1969-1979)', the Federal Government listed the most substantial achievements in inter-German relations as those agreements which concern *mutual information and contacts* between the people in the two German states (travel, tele-communications, media reporting) and the *conditions of existence of West Berlin*. *Inter-German trade* stands out as an area of comparable importance. During the initial phase of normalisation it had a particularly significant function, and the subsequent development of bilateral economic relations shows that the political importance of a particular area of cooperation may consist precisely in its isolation from day-to-day politics. Inter-German trade has been one element of continuity and stability. The semi-annual Leipzig Fair where the Federal Republic is traditionally the largest Western exhibitor, offers a useful opportunity for high-level economic contacts.

In the light of earlier crises, the agreements guaranteeing the status and the viability of West Berlin assume particular relevance. Berlin remains the most vulnerable point of the Federal Republic in the context of East-West relations. Yet, détente has worked in the case of Berlin; and for that very reason this achievement has almost vanished from the public mind. Before entering into negotiations with the GDR on the organisation of transit traffic to West Berlin, the Federal Government had ensured that the Four Power responsibility for securing access to Berlin was laid down in the Four Power Berlin Agreement of 1971. The co-responsibility of the Soviet Union for the Federal Republic's guaranteed access to Berlin and the recognition of the existing 'links' or 'ties' (the GDR, supported by the Soviet Union, insists on the weaker term) between the Federal Republic and West Berlin have created unprecedented legal guarantees for the access routes.

On this basis, a transit agreement was concluded between the two German states in the same year. The Berlin Senate reached an agreement with the GDR authorities concerning visits by West Berliners to East Berlin and the GDR. Over the following years, laborious negotiations on practical improvements of traffic movement from and to Berlin took place, and tensions that emerged in other fields did not affect this process. An exchange of letters between Chancellor Schmidt and Chairman Honecker and a first meeting between them in Helsinki during the Final Conference of CSCE opened the way to the comprehensive 'Traffic Agreement' of December 1975. The agreement provided for construction and improvement of access routes for commercial and passenger traffic by road, rail and water. These measures, which were primarily in the Federal Republic's interest but which also improved the GDR infrastructure, were financed to a substantial degree by West Germany. The co-financing of highway renewal in the GDR (259.6 million DM out of a total of 405 million DM) and the reimbursement of costs for the opening of a new border crossing for trains (51 million DM) represented a valuable source of foreign exchange for the GDR. This pattern of balancing interests was repeated later. The lump sum for transit fees was raised from 234.9 to 400 million DM per year for the period 1976-1979. For the GDR, these highly attractive arrangements did not create any domestic problems; only the commercially-organised smuggling of refugees from the GDR involves a problem of internal security for the SED leadership. The Federal Government, for its part, has condemned these activities as an abuse of the transit routes and has announced its intention to prevent them.[10]

A second package deal was concluded in November 1978. The Federal Republic agreed to take over a large share of the costs (1.2 billion DM) for the construction of a motorway between Hamburg and Berlin, for the improvement of transit waterways (120 million DM) and for the opening of the Teltow Canal (70 million DM). Additionally, 500 million DM were allowed for measures on which agreement would be reached in 1980. At the same time, the annual lump sum for transit fees was raised to 525 million DM for the following ten years. This increase was justified by the expansion of transit traffic, the smooth functioning of transit being of vital importance for the economic viability and competitiveness of West Berlin. The volume of transit trade from Berlin to the Federal Republic increased from 2,737,000 tons in 1969 (air freight excluded) to 3,793,000 tons in 1978. Tourist traffic by land has increased steadily since the coming into force of the Transit Agreement in June 1972 (from 10.5 to 18.1 million persons in 1977). The cost-benefit ratio of these agreements has been the subject of vehement public debate in the Federal Republic. The Government's position was expressed by Chancellor Schmidt in his 'State of the Nation' message before the Bundestag in January 1975 when he referred to the forthcoming agreements:

> We will . . . make sure that an adequate relation between costs and benefits is established. We will not be able to limit the cost-benefit analysis to economic categories; we will also have to weigh the humanitarian and political improvements.[11]

Commenting on the 1978 agreements, the Chancellor pointed out that they brought 'additional elements of stability into the still fragile relations between the two states'.[12]

The CDU/CSU parliamentary opposition and large sections of the conservative press believe that it is mostly the GDR which benefits from the agreements. The critics also charge that the government showed weakness in the negotiations, but sometimes they rely on flawed calculations. It is said, for instance, that the Government has transferred to the GDR the sum of 5.7 billion DM over the period 1970-1977, without even mentioning quid pro quos obtained from the GDR.[13] In spite of the efforts aimed at discrediting the *Deutschlandpolitik* of the SPD-FDP coalition, the majority of the West German population supports this policy. Those who remember the situation that existed before the new era of *Deutschlandpolitik* value its achievements highly and are prepared to pay the price. But they are also particularly sensitive to recurrent interference with transit traffic on the part of the GDR authorities (e.g. the barring of certain travellers, the threat of restrictions in cases where the Federal Republic is alleged not to respect the special status of West Berlin). In the final analysis — the transit agreement notwithstanding — the Federal Republic is dependent on the credibility of the Western allies' commitment not to tolerate violations of the Four Power Berlin Agreement.[14]

The room for compromise narrowed considerably when it came to improving the opportunities for contact between the citizens of the two German states. It was clear from the beginning, that the GDR would hardly go much beyond the concessions made in the Traffic Treaty (*Verkehrsvertrag*) of 1972, the first treaty to be concluded between the two states and a precondition for the conclusion of the Basic Treaty. The Traffic Treaty created the conditions for tourism and visits to relatives in the GDR. This kind of travel is subject to certain formalities and compulsory currency exchange, varying with purpose and duration of the trip and the age of the traveller, but otherwise — with only few exceptions concerning certain categories of former GDR citizens — free of restrictions. Considering the SED's fear of capitalist subversion, this degree of freedom of travel appeared as a fundamental change compared with the GDR's previous self-isolation. Immediately after the conclusion of the treaty, the flow of visitors to East Berlin and the GDR reached a level of about 8 million visits a year, a figure which has remained relatively stable.[15] For many West Berliners, who had only had a few specially-negotiated opportunities to visit East Berlin after the erection of the Wall in 1961, the treaty ended a period of callous separation of families.

The statistics show that the amount of currency that had to be exchanged significantly affected the number of visitors. At the end of 1973, when the GDR decreed an increase of the daily amounts to be exchanged and introduced compulsory exchange for pensioners, the visits from West Berlin (which has a high share of pensioners) as well from the Federal Republic declined.[16] At that time, the Federal Government successfully negotiated a reduction of the daily amounts which took effect exactly one year after the increase had been introduced. The number of visits then rose to the previous level. Already at that time, most observers agreed that the GDR leadership had intended to reduce the number of visitors from the West in order to contain the threats to internal stability. The partial repeal of the 1973 measures more-or-less coincided with a new round of negotiations on transit traffic to Berlin and a prolongation of the substantial 'overdraft facilities' granted to the GDR in inter-German trade (see below).

In a surprise move the GDR announced a drastic increase (from 13 to 25 DM) in the compulsory exchange on 9 October 1980 — four days after the elections to the Bundestag. As in 1973, the number of visitors declined sharply. It is doubtful, however, whether a repeal of the imposition can be negotiated this time round. The GDR seems to have embarked on a new phase of *Abgrenzung*, the motives and extent of which cannot yet be assessed with certainty. The Federal Government has stated that the GDR's action contradicts the spirit of the Basic Treaty (Article 7) and the Traffic Agreement. In his inaugural address Chancellor Schmidt deplored the 'serious set-back for all Germans'.[17] The GDR, for her part, has put forward a number of different reasons and countercharges. The Federal Republic is accused of having violated her commitment to peace and détente in Europe laid down in the Basic Treaty by playing an active role in the NATO decision on the modernisation of nuclear forces. The economic justification given is that the loss of value of the DM caused by inflation requires compensation.

This case illustrates the difficulties and frictions that plague inter-German relations, leaving behind a sense of perplexity and frustration. It also demonstrates that the treaty framework is only filled with real meaning when there is goodwill on both sides. The events in Poland may have strengthened the advocates of an uncompromising demarcation policy within the SED Politburo. Another indication in this sense are the renewed demands for the complete recognition of the GDR under international law by the Federal Government, the upgrading of the Permanent Missions to full-fledged embassies and the recognition of GDR nationality. These demands can hardly be interpreted as an overture to negotiations, because the GDR knows full well that with regard to these issues the hands of the Federal Government are tied by the Constitutional Court's ruling.

The GDR's decision to increase the amount of compulsory exchange came also as a surprise for the following reason: when the meeting between Schmidt and Honecker in the GDR was being prepared — the meeting was finally called off because of the Polish crisis — it was generally expected that the Chancellor would seek a reduction of the age requirement (65 years for men, 60 for women) applying to GDR citizens before they can receive permission to travel to the Federal Republic and West Berlin. It was felt that the travel opportunities for West Germans were satisfactory. Given the glaring disparity in travel opportunities between the two countries, the Federal Government has been urging for years that there should be a general reduction of the age requirement and an extension of the category of 'special cases'. Since 1974, the number of visits by GDR pensioners has averaged about 1.3 million a year. Visits to the FRG and West Berlin on 'urgent family affairs' (births, weddings, marriage jubilees, serious illnesses, deaths) amount to about 40,000 a year. These limitations on travel opportunities are among the main grievances people in the GDR harbour against their own government. It was hoped in vain that the SED leadership would become sufficiently self-confident to give up the idea that every person wishing to travel to the West was a potential 'refugee'. On the one hand, the emergence of dissidents who were encouraged by the Helsinki Charter to voice demands for freedom of expression and freedom of residence and the increasing number of applications for 'release' from GDR citizenship have made the SED more insecure. On the other hand, living standards have progressed more slowly than in the early 1970s. In spite of rises in productivity and incomes, consumers have experienced restrictions in certain areas (quality goods, imports from the West) over the past few years.

The difficulties just outlined should not obscure the fact that the opportunities for travel belong to the positive side of the balance sheet. Improvements have also taken place in frontier region traffic, non-commercial transactions (gift parcels), and telephone communications.[19] The working conditions for journalists have been subject to the requirements of demarcation policy. The activities of West German journalists were gradually restricted as the GDR leadership felt increasingly uncomfortable about the effects of media coverage, with the large majority of the population being able to receive West German television.

PROBLEMS OF INTER-GERMAN TRADE

The relationship between economic progress in the GDR and the self-assurance of the political leadership constitutes one of the main variables in inter-German relations. As economic progress is also in the interest of the GDR population, the Federal Government holds that trade relations should be developed on the basis of mutual economic interests to serve this goal. The continuity of trade relations is considered politically significant. As long as cooperation works in at least *one* field even during periods of crisis, inter-German relations are not reduced to an erratic pattern of stop-and-go policies. The Government's commitment to stable trade relations has grown out of experience. Previous governments had believed that economic pressure would force the GDR authorities to make political concessions. This assumption turned out to be mistaken. In 1960, the Federal Government had reacted to GDR interference with the traffic from and to Berlin by cancelling the Interzonal Trade Agreement of 1951. When it became clear that the GDR authorities were prepared to suspend deliveries of vital East German goods to West Berlin and to use the revocation of the Berlin Agreement on interzonal trade as an argument against the four-power responsibility for Berlin traffic,[20] the Adenauer Government was forced to retreat. It agreed to reinstate the trade agreement in its revised form of August 1960 without first having obtained the formal repeal of the traffic restrictions.[21]

The 1960 Berlin Agreement is still in force. Since then, technical procedures for the conduct of trade have been greatly facilitated. The licence requirement on a 'case-by-case' basis for deliveries to the GDR was lifted for 50 per cent of the goods traded (1969). The most important measure, however, was the introduction of the variable 'swing' in 1968, an overdraft facility whose ceiling was raised to 25 per cent of GDR deliveries of each previous year. This arrangement, which originally would have ended in 1975, was extended in 1974 up to 1981. At the same time an absolute ceiling of 850 million Units of Account (corresponding to DM) was introduced. Other instruments for the promotion of inter-German trade include a special VAT regime, tied financial loans for cooperation between Eastern and Western firms (since 1978), and a long-term agreement (1979) providing for deliveries of coal and crude oil to the GDR and for purchases of oil products by the Federal Republic. These measures were designed to stimulate GDR deliveries (the terms 'exports' and 'imports' are not used by West Germany for inter-German trade). The 'cooperation loans' represent an alternative to the compensation deals which the GDR prefers as a method of saving hard currency.

The development of inter-German trade reflects both the impact of the various agreements and the GDR's market chances as well as her capacity to pay. In 1969, trade figures started to rise steeply. Between 1969 and 1976, trade increased at an annual rate of 14 per cent. Over this period the volume of trade tripled, although subsequently, trade growth slowed down considerably. In his 'State of the Nation' Report of 1979, Chancellor Schmidt addressed this problem in the following terms:

> During the past year, economic relations between the two states have not developed to the extent which the Federal Government tries to realise in the common interest of both states. Of course, the total volume of exchange is still at a high level — almost 9 billion DM. But in comparison with the previous year, inter-German trade in 1978 has only increased by 1 per cent. The deliveries from the GDR even declined.
>
> I do not want to dramatise the situation, but we must recognise that it requires efforts from both sides to develop trade relations in line with overall economic growth. This implies the creation of favourable political conditions, but also the political will to promote trade. This political will is present on the part of the Federal Government. We assume that the GDR, too, is interested in a steady and balanced development of economic relations.[22]

In 1979, despite a nominal increase of 8.9 per cent, inter-German trade declined by 5 per cent in real terms.[23] It remains to be seen how significant the nominal increase of 34 per cent during the first half of 1980 will prove to be.[24]

During the first few years following the introduction of the 'swing', the facility was used by the GDR at a growing rate (1969: 270 million UA; 1976: 786 million UA = Units of Account). In 1978, the overdraft amounted only to 677 million UA and rose again in 1979 to 748 million UA. In 1980, the GDR, for the first time, actually achieved a surplus. This reflects a determined effort by the GDR planners to cover imports from the FRG through GDR exports (1978: 86 per cent; 1979: 96 per cent).[25] Nevertheless, the suggestion made by the industrialist Wolff von Amerongen, an authority on East-West Trade, that the 'swing' is a relic of the 1950s, was met with surprise in the government camp.[26] The experts of the *Deutsches Institut für Wirtschaftsforschung* believe, on the contrary, that a phasing out of the 'swing' would be a mistake, and they advocate further measures of trade promotion such as the lifting of quotas which restrict deliveries from the GDR.[27] The swing is, indeed, a controversial issue in West German politics. The Government is opposed to using the swing for imposing economic sanctions (by reducing or suspending it) whereas the opposition makes this proposal in reaction to almost every instance of GDR misconduct.

In order to evaluate the importance of inter-German trade as a factor in the economic development of the GDR, one has to look at the commodity structure of exports and imports. The increase (nominal and real) in GDR exports to the Federal Republic is accounted for by products of the basic and production goods industries, especially petroleum products. As for engineering products which, in general, represent the most important category of East German exports, the GDR has proved unable to penetrate the West German market. Their share in total exports to the FRG only increased from 2.8 per cent in 1978 to 3.1 per cent in 1979. On the other hand, engineering products accounted for 18.2 per cent of total imports from the FRG in 1979. Their absolute value of 858 million DM amounted to a decline of 10.9 per cent with respect to 1978 (964 million DM). The share of investment goods in total imports from the FRG declined from 31 per cent (1978) to 26.2 per cent (1979) — an ominous sign for the development of the GDR's productive capacities.[28] Although the volume of inter-German trade amounted to nearly 11 billion DM in 1980, the commodity structure is less than satisfactory for the GDR considering the pace of technological development.

The overall importance of these bilateral economic relations is very different for the two Germanies. Trade with the GDR amounts to 1.6 per cent of total foreign trade. The Federal Republic however, is the third largest trading partner of the GDR.[29] What the aggregate figures do not show is the fact that a number of West German medium-sized engineering firms are heavily dependent on intra-German trade and that food supplies for West Berlin are provided in large part by imports from the GDR.[30] The asymmetry in trade relations in favour of the Federal Republic does not mean that she is able to blackmail the GDR politically even though Erich Honecker deliberately tried to create this impression when he visited Vienna in autumn 1980. On the occasion of this visit, the order for the construction of a new steel works (worth 1.5 billion DM), which Krupp had hoped to win, was placed with an Austrian state company.

Even if there is no direct linkage between agreements in the areas of Berlin traffic, contracts and communication and trade, it can be safely assumed, however, that the governments in Bonn and in East Berlin do take into account their interdependence.

UNFINISHED BUSINESS AND AN UNCERTAIN FUTURE

Other areas where a cooperative working relationship has been established have received less public attention. They include postal and telephone communication, public health, and frontier problems. In areas such as environmental protection, legal cooperation and cultural relations, cooperative efforts have not yet produced significant results. Of course, there is a limited degree of legal cooperation, and cultural contacts do take place. But there is no contractual basis for these activities, as agreements that would be acceptable for both sides could not be reached. A cultural agreement foundered on the demand made by the GDR that the Federal Government turn over works of art in the possession of the *Stiftung Preussischer Kulturbesitz* (Foundation Cultural Possessions of Prussia) to which the GDR lays claim. The Federal Government, on the contrary, holds that they have to remain in the Federal Republic as the possessions of the *Stiftung* are governed by dispositions made by the allies and by Federal law in accordance with international law.[31]

As far as environmental protection is concerned, the main issue is river pollution. But the potassium wastes which in the GDR are introduced into the Werra and the Weser are not a burning political problem; similar problems arise with other neighbouring countries such as France and Switzerland. One of the most sensitive issues in inter-German relations is the legal emigration of GDR citizens. According to Honecker, between mid-1976 and mid-1977, 15,000 GDR citizens were allowed to leave the country, and between mid-1977 and mid-1978, 15,454.[32] Chancellor Schmidt gave the figures for 1978 as approximately 12,000, of whom more than 8,000 entered with the permission of the GDR authorities. Schmidt welcomed this development as a result of the humanitarian efforts undertaken by his government.[33]

At the beginning of 1981, however, it appeared that further progress on humanitarian questions would be very slow at best. The measures taken by the GDR to reduce the inflow of West German visitors clearly demonstrate that the SED Politburo is determined to give priority to domestic stability even at the risk of a loss of prestige and a deterioration of relations with the FRG. The Polish crisis has enhanced the importance of the GDR as a member of the Warsaw Pact, and this implies that the SED leadership is under a special obligation to preserve its ideological orthodoxy. Any concessions that might undermine the control exercised by the Party over all areas of public life are completely ruled out for the foreseeable future. Inter-German relations have reached a stage where the room for concessions has shrunk. This is due in part to the very achievements of the *Deutschlandpolitik*. The escalation of *Abgrenzung* reflects the fact that the SED perceives increasing risks associated with détente. At the same time, the Federal Republic's readiness to make concessions is likely to be affected negatively by the GDR's behaviour. The cancellation of the Schmidt-Honecker meeting because of Polish events became an open political embarrassment for Schmidt as it occurred shortly before the Bundestag elections. For the CDU/CSU opposition, each new demarcation measure applied by the GDR gives further proof of the failure of the *Deutschlandpolitik* as conducted by the government. On the other hand, it is difficult for the Federal Government to test the bona fide character of the demands that Honecker has recently re-stated: recognition of GDR nationality, exchange of ambassadors, recognition of the frontier between the GDR and the Federal Republic (Gera speech, 13 October 1980). All of this has been precluded by the 1973 ruling of the Constitutional Court, and the Government therefore has little room for flexibility in negotiation. Inter-German relations may thus be entering a period of stagnation, even if a new Cold War between the super-powers can be avoided.

NOTES

1. 'Denkschrift zum Vertrag über die Grundlagen der Beziehungen zwischen der Budesrepublik Deutschland und der Deutschen Demokratischen Republik, 22 Dec. 1972,' in: *Zehn Jahre Deutschlandpolitik. Die Entwicklung der Beziehungen zwischen der Bundesrepublik Deutschland und der Deutschen Demokratischen Republik 1969-1979*, Bonn: Bericht und Dokumentation, (Bundesministerium für innerdeutsche Beziehungen) 1980, pp. 213-16, 215.
2. Op. cit., p. 21.
3. Kay-Michael Wilke, *Bundesrepublik Deutschland und Deutsche Demokratische Republik*, Berlin: Duncker and Humblot, 1976, p. 125 f.
4. *Zehn Jahre Deutschlandpolitik.*, p. 206.
5. Cf. the text of the court ruling, op. cit., pp. 232-43, 233.
6. Cf. Wilke, op. cit.
7. Cf. Dieter Blumenwitz, 'Fünf Jahre Grundvertragsurteil des Bundesverfassungsgerichts', in: Gottfried Zieger (ed.), *Fünf Jahre Grundvertragsurteil des Bundesverfassungsgerichts*, Köln: Carl Heymanns Verlag, 1979, pp. 7-22.
8. *Zehn Jahre Deutschlandpolitik.*, p. 11.
9. E.g., Wilhelm Bruns in an unpublished conference paper, Berlin, 1980.
10. Declaration by Minister Franke, in: *Zehn Jahre Deutschlandpolitik*, p. 374.
11. *Zehn Jahre Deutschlandpolitik.*, p. 416.
12. Ibid., p. 434.
13. Cf. *Frankfurter Allgemeine Zeitung*, 12 Dec. 1978, p. 5; 12 Dec. 1978, p. 10.
14. Cf. Chancellor Schmidt's inaugural address of 24 Nov. 1980, in: *Bulletin* Nr. 124 (25 Nov. 1980), p. 1053.
15. Cf. *Zahlenspiegel Bundesrepublik Deutschland / Deutsche Demokratische Republik-Ein Vergleich*, Bonn: Bundesministerium für innerdeutsche Beziehungen, 1978, p. 97.
16. Ibid.
17. *Bulletin*, loc. cit., p. 1052.
18. *Zehn Jahre Deutschlandpolitik.*, p. 44.
19. Cf. ibid., p. 44.
20. Cf. Robert W. Dean, *West German Trade with the East: The Political Dimension*, New York: Praeger, 1974, p. 61.
21. Cf. Siegfried Kupper, *Der Innerdeutsche Handel. Rechtliche Grundlagen, politische und wirtschaftliche Bedeutung*, Köln: Markus Verlag, 1972, pp. 28-30.
22. In: *Zehn Jahre Deutschlandpolitik.*, p. 434.
23. *DIW-Wochenbericht* 9-10/1980 (7 March 1980), p. 105.
24. Cf. *Der Spiegel* 43/1980, p. 22.
25. *DIW-Wochenbericht* 9-10/1980, p. 105.
26. Cf. *Frankfurter Allgemeine Zeitung*, 26 Aug. 1980.
27. Cf. *DIW-Wochenbericht* 9-10/1980, p. 108 f.
28. Figures from ibid., p. 106 f.
29. Cf. *Der Spiegel* 43/1980, p. 24; *Die Zeit* Nr. 44/1980 (24 Oct. 1980), p. 29.
30. Cf. *Handelsblatt*, 16 April, 1980.
31. Cf. *Zehn Jahre Deutschlandpolitik*, p. 50.
32. *Frankfurter Allgemeine Zeitung*, 8 July 1978, p. 2.
33. Cf. *Zehn Jahre Deutschlandpolitik.*, p. 434.

The 1980 Bundestag Election: A Case of 'Normality'

Geoffrey Pridham*

The significance of parliamentary elections may not always be what appears on the surface or even become clearly evident at the time they are being conducted. Some are indeed perceived by contemporaries as possessing 'historical' importance, such as the Bundestag election of 1972 which, following the political crisis over the *Ostpolitik* and the government's fragile majority, decisively confirmed the Left-liberal coalition under Brandt in power. In general terms, elections usually decide various obvious questions, as in West Germany: firstly, which of the two chancellor contestants will hold national office in the ensuing legislative period, and related to this the respective roles in government and opposition of the three main parties; secondly, the state of the parties' popular strength, even though short-term factors may in part influence the outcome; and thirdly the salience or priority accorded different issues, depending on the divergent commitments of the rival parties to their programmes, although this aspect is by no means always so clear-cut as was the 1972 result with respect to the *Ostpolitik*. The election of 5 October 1980 certainly settled the first two questions, but its outcome for the third was not so definite as might have been suggested by the high degree of personal-political polarisation between Schmidt and Strauss and apparent differences of policy, at least in style and approach, if not in content.

These factors do not, however, provide the full significance of a given election, if only because this ultimately depends on its longer-term repercussions on party development (such as the 1957 Adenauer election triumph as a further compelling argument for the SPD's Godesberg revisionism; or the 1972 election result in persuading the CDU finally to embark on party organisational reform), not to mention that sometimes election victories may contain paradoxical or ambivalent seeds — deriving more immediately from the failure of leaders or parties in government to capitalise on their popular mandate, or more probably from expectations aroused by the election outcome concerning government performance. Furthermore, some election successes may be founded on distinct but unstable or temporary moods of public opinion. This short account of the 1980 Bundestag election cannot predict such eventualities, except tentatively, but it is worthwhile assessing this, the ninth national election since the establishment of the Federal Republic, in the light of underlying trends.

*The author wishes to acknowledge the financial assistance received from the German Academic Exchange Service (DAAD) for his visit to the Federal Republic during September-October 1980.

The 1980 election, in terms of the campaign and apparently in the outcome, could best be described as 'normal' — in the sense that for once it was not perceived as a crucial test of German democracy. The fact that this election was more of a 'normal' event than in previous cases should not itself be underrated or perhaps even be welcomed, given the background of modern German history. We can trace the conditions of normality in reviewing the results of the election and related aspects of political behaviour.

THE RESULTS: CONFIRMATION OF STABILITY OR NEW POINTERS TO THE FUTURE?

The interpretation of election results is subject to the necessary distinction between the 'subjective' and 'objective'. That is, the 'subjective' importance of an election outcome is intrinsically linked to media and individual party expectations and of course to the aims which leading politicians set themselves. With the strong executive orientation of party electoral competition, this perspective focuses first and foremost on winning power in Bonn. Thus, in 1976 the CDU/CSU performed remarkably well in terms of electoral trends (its best result since Adenauer's unique victory in 1957), and that from the position of opposition to a visibly competent chancellor but, in fact, its close failure to win a hoped-for absolute majority was profoundly disappointing for the CDU/CSU and provoked the worst crisis of internal dissension between its two component parties. Nevertheless, expectations are not exclusively determined by this factor, as illustrated by the 1980 elections.

TABLE 1
RESULTS OF BUNDESTAG ELECTIONS 1972-80

PARTIES	1980		1976		1972	
	%	Seats	%	Seats	%	Seats
CDU/CSU	44.5	226	48.6	243	44.8	225
SPD	42.9	218	42.6	214	45.9	230
FDP	10.6	53	7.9	39	8.4	41
GREENS	1.5	—	—	—	—	—
EXTREME RIGHT	0.2	—	0.3	—	0.6	—
EXTREME LEFT	0.2	—	0.3	—	0.3	—

On election night, it was the SPD rather than the CDU which revealed the greater disappointment with the result; for the former had clearly failed to benefit from the customary 'chancellor effect' and, while achieving its first aim of maintaining the coalition in power, had not succeeded in its second aim of becoming the largest *Fraktion* in the Bundestag. Somewhat in contrast, the CDU (though less so the CSU, which had remained more intimately bound to the hope of its chairman becoming Chancellor) had already lowered its expectations to the stated aim of continuing as largest *Fraktion* and retaining the Bundestag presidency. It hardly needs mentioning that the surprise success of the FDP, itself taken unawares by the degree of its electoral increase which surpassed all poll predictions, was the event which made the greatest impression.

The most obvious political result of the October election was the confirmation of the Left-liberal coalition under Schmidt in power by a comfortable majority. This outcome compared well with the majorities held by the same coalition in the preceding three legislative periods:

TABLE 2
MAJORITIES OF LEFT-LIBERAL COALITIONS

	Lead in seats	Lead in popular vote (%)
1969	12	2.4
1972	46	9.5
1976	10	1.9
1980	45	9.0

The coalition success therefore compared numerically most with that of 1972, except that the balance of strength between the two parties in government was in 1980 tilted more favourably towards the FDP. What, however, lay behind this political result with respect to electoral trends, viewed in the 'objective' sense of reflecting on the popular strengths of the various parties?

There are two bases of comparison in the Federal Republic for general electoral trends: with the results of the previous Bundestag election, if not also with earlier ones; and with the collection of results in the series of *Land* elections in the intervening years. Both comparisons provide useful reference points for measuring the general degree of party voting support, even though differential political factors also help to determine such results, e.g. the impact of campaign events, international or domestic, in different national elections, or variations in governmental performance between them; the tendency in *Land* elections for a 'swing' against the governing parties, modified where applicable by the salience of regional issues or by the circumstances of the time at which a particular *Land* election takes place.

Comparing the 1980 results with those of the 1976 Bundestag election, the most striking differences are in the degree of support for the CDU/CSU and FDP as against the stability suggested by the SPD vote. Since 1953, when the CDU/CSU had stabilised as a party of mass appeal, its range of support in national elections had been 44.8 — 50.2 per cent, but it now sank slightly below that with 44.5 per cent. The heaviest losses were incurred by the CDU (whose national vote outside Bavaria fell by 3.8 per cent from 38 per cent in 1976 to 34.2 per cent), especially in north Germany, rather than by the CSU (whose national share of the vote fell by 0.3 per cent from 10.6 per cent in 1976 to 10.3 per cent. This regional variation in Opposition losses was as follows:

TABLE 3

REGIONAL DIFFERENTIATION IN CDU/CSU LOSSES, 1980 CF. 1976 (%)

Lower Saxony	— 5.9	Hesse	— 4.2
Schleswig-Holstein	— 5.2	North-Rhine Westphalia	— 3.9
Baden-Württemberg	— 4.8	Saar	— 3.9
Hamburg	— 4.7	Bremen	— 3.7
Rhineland-Palatinate	— 4.3	Bavaria	— 2.4

Regional differentiation has in West German voting behaviour been essentially a consequence of variation in socio-economic structure between the *Länder* and not of any regionalisation of political consciousness.[1] For instance, the presence of Catholic sub-cultural ties buttressing the CSU vote in Bavaria, but their absence in notably Schleswig-Holstein making the CDU electorate there relatively less stable, accounts basically for this North/South divide. The greater 'vulnerability' of the CDU electorate in the northern Protestant *Länder* makes it more subject to the impact of political determinants related to a particular election. In the case of 1980, two such political influences were evident: the unpopularity of the Strauss candidacy above all in the North, where his negative image was long-standing,[2] even occasioning some disaffection among CDU activists as in Lower Saxony; and the issue of the Catholic bishops' letter which caused some consternation among Catholic voters (especially those with a looser church connection)[3] and was anything but encouraging to Protestant voters of the CDU.

The one unexpected regional result for the CDU was its above average loss in Baden-Württemberg, where there had in the past been much sympathy for Strauss's political positions among party activists. This result suggested a certain divergence between CDU voters and activists, for evidence pointed to a desertion of 'old liberals' among the former from the CDU to the FDP in this once traditional liberal stronghold.[4] Altogether, the CDU/CSU result was far from encouraging for Strauss's 'fourth party' solution for a national CSU. Despite his polemical use as in 1972 and 1976 of the greater stability of the CSU vote *vis-à-vis* that of the CDU, paradoxically it was his candidacy rather than any campaign deficiencies of the CDU which accounted for the relapse of party support outside Bavaria.

The FDP result also evidenced distinct regional variation with its strongest increases in the northern *Länder*: compared with the national increase of 2.7 per cent, these ranged from 3.1 in NRW, 3.4 in Lower Saxony to 3.9 per cent in both Hamburg and Schleswig-Holstein. Once again, this variation must be explained first and foremost with reference to socio-economic structure and the potential this offered for influence by political determinants. The FDP performed best in areas of relatively high mobility, that is where there was strong representation of the 'new middle class' (white-collar workers, civil servants) in a Protestant-dominated milieu.[5]

TABLE 4

SOCIAL-STRUCTURAL ASPECTS OF THE BUNDESTAG ELECTION RESULT, 1980

Selected Constituencies		Share of Votes Bundestag Election 1980			Change compared with 1976 (in brackets compared with 1972)		
		CDU	SPD	FDP	CDU	SPD	FDP
Share of Protestant population	low	56.8	33.9	8.3	-3.7 (0.1)	1.3 (-2.8)	2.1 (2.4)
	high	37.3	48.6	12.0	-5.1 (-2.1)	0.4 (-2.0)	3.4 (2.8)
Share of Catholic population	low	36.6	49.4	11.9	-5.0 (-2.1)	0.4 (-2.1)	3.4 (2.8)
	high	57.4	33.5	8.1	-3.7 (-0.2)	1.3 (-2.4)	2.1 (2.4)
Share of those with secondary education	low	49.3	39.8	9.6	-4.1 (-1.0)	1.3 (-1.5)	2.5 (2.2)
	high	40.9	44.3	12.6	-4.8 (-1.0)	0.4 (-2.8)	3.2 (2.4)
Share of those employed in agriculture	low	37.7	48.3	11.8	-3.3 (0.6)	-0.6 (-3.9)	2.8 (2.1)
	high	49.0	39.8	10.1	-5.7 (-2.7)	2.3 (-0.5)	3.0 (2.9)
Share of those employed in service trades	low	48.8	40.4	9.5	-3.4 (-0.2)	0.9 (-2.5)	2.5 (2.3)
	high	54.4	44.8	12.5	-5.6 (-0.9)	0.3 (-2.7)	3.1 (2.1)
Share of workers in employment	low	45.7	40.0	12.6	-4.8 (-1.2)	1.2 (-1.9)	3.0 (2.4)
	high	41.5	47.7	9.1	-3.7 (0.1)	0.0 (-3.1)	2.5 (2.3)
Share of those employed in trade + business	low	34.6	51.9	11.4	-4.0 (-0.8)	-0.4 (-3.3)	3.3 (2.8)
	high	54.4	35.9	8.5	-4.1 (-0.4)	1.8 (-1.5)	2.0 (1.7)
Degree of electoral participation	low	46.3	40.6	10.8	-4.0 (-0.2)	0.4 (-2.9)	2.5 (1.9)
	high	44.8	43.9	10.0	-4.5 (-1.1)	0.7 (-2.1)	2.7 (2.3)

Source: Die Zeit 10.10.80

This mobility derived from the growth of this sector as the most important social change in the post-war period (20.6 per cent of the occupational structure in 1950; 45 per cent in 1977) and its weaker traditional party ties in relation to those present among the working-class and the 'old middle class' (the self-employed and farmers).[6] The 'new middle class', therefore, comprised the main reservoir of voting support open to the influence of party competition. It was precisely in this area where the CDU/CSU, with its more sophisticated campaign there, had made significant gains in 1976, and where in 1980 it suffered losses most to the FDP. The Strauss factor undoubtedly played an influential part in this transfer of votes as indicated by the report of the Mannheim research group that a quarter of the FDP votes in 1980 came from the CDU/CSU because of Strauss's candidacy, especially from the 'new middle class',[7] thus confirming poll evidence over the previous year about reservations over the choice of chancellor candidate among Opposition supporters. This trend is further underlined by looking at regional voting behaviour with the direct correlation between CDU losses and FDP gains in the North. It was most noticeable among urban voters in the *Länder* of Hamburg and Schleswig-Holstein, but also in large cities elsewhere like Bonn, Wuppertal and Bremen.[8]

This trend represented the main location of voter movement between the parties, together with SPD supporters also voting FDP, for there was little direct transfer between the two main parties (according to one analysis about 5 per cent) which retained 90 per cent of their electorates of 1976.[9] In this connection, one distinguishing feature of electoral behaviour in 1980 was the degree of split voting, a practice allowed for by the two-vote system (first vote for constituency candidates; second vote for the party lists) in West Germany. This had become a more common feature in the 1970s, induced by the possibility in both national and *Land* elections that the FDP might sink below the 5 per cent minimum requirement for parliamentary representation, and was very noticeable in the 1972 Bundestag election between SPD and FDP supporters.[10] The difference in the 1980 election was that this practice favoured the FDP among supporters of *both* main parties to the extent that there was a difference of 3.4 per cent or 577,402 votes between the first and second votes for the FDP, comparable with that which occurred in 1972:

TABLE 5
FDP: DIFFERENCE BETWEEN 1ST AND 2ND VOTE SUPPORT (%)

	1st vote	2nd vote
1972	4.8	8.4
1976	6.4	7.9
1980	7.2	10.6

While it was the second vote that counted for entry to the Bundestag, the first vote strength was more indicative of the stable element in FDP support, which could come uncomfortably close to the 5 per cent hurdle. FDP leaders on election night openly expressed their concern about securing their new electorate in coming years, but the portents were not encouraging: the political influences promoting FDP success this time (the anti-Strauss factor, and the shock effect of the NRW *Land* result in May) were unlikely to repeat themselves on a future occasion; while the loose party allegiances among the 'new middle-class' did not suggest a solid basis beneath this party's breakthrough.

The outstanding characteristic of the SPD vote was the stability emphasised by its result of 42.9 per cent being a virtual repetition of those it achieved in 1976 (42.6 per cent) and 1969 (42.7 per cent). After the 'comrade trend' of the 1950s and 1960s, when the SPD had regularly gained in each successive Bundestag election of between 3-4.4 per cent up to and including the 1972 result, this party's support now had levelled out several (crucial) percentage points below the range enjoyed by the CDU/CSU. This picture of stability was reinforced by the regional patterns of voting where, except for the small Saar (+2.2 per cent), the SPD's gains or losses compared with 1976 were all 1.5 per cent or less. Broadly speaking, the SPD compensated for its losses to the FDP and the Greens by limited gains from the CDU/CSU and strong support from first-time voters; and so far as any trend was visible the SPD lost more in its strongholds (e.g. Bremen and Hamburg) and made slight gains in rural and Catholic areas.

As in 1969 and 1972, the significance of the latter feature should not be overrated, for despite a gradual decline in confessional ties the SPD has really failed to make substantial inroads among the Catholic and rural electorate, or at best any such gains have been localised. What above all distinguishes the SPD electorate, as indeed that of the CDU/CSU, is the maintenance of traditional social-structural ties in party support: the working-class and to a lesser extent white-collar employees in the former case; both middle-class sectors with the latter. Since the SPD electorate was the less homogeneous of the two, the development to watch in future voting behaviour is whether the party will maintain its integrative capacity across the cleavage between its middle-class and working-class supporters,[12] especially should adverse economic circumstances in the 1980s create new social pressures. In general, it may be said that the SPD has for a variety of reasons, both political and social-structural, failed to capitalise significantly on its role as governing party to make quantitative gains in voting support equivalent to those reaped by the CDU/CSU in the 1950s. The advance of the SPD to 45.9 per cent in 1972 was in the light of subsequent electoral trends a temporary development, for by the 1970s the social structural bases of the party system had stabilised compared with two decades previously.

As in the two elections of the 1970s, the vote for the minor parties on the extreme Left and Right in 1980 was minimal — totalling less than 1 per cent — but the new development in this election was the appearance of the Greens, the party-political channel for the ecologist movement. Polarisation between the main parties in the final stage of the campaign evidently squeezed the Greens' chances, so that their final share was only 1.5 per cent compared with poll indications in the summer of 2.5 per cent or more. They tended to perform better where there was a high proportion of young voters, the 'new middle class' and an above-average educational level,[13] but nowhere did they approach 5 per cent. There was slight regional variation with the highest scores in the *Länder* of Bremen (2.7 per cent) and Hamburg (2.3 per cent), but elsewhere their range was restricted to 1.1-1.8 per cent, with their highest constituency vote at 3.3 per cent. However, as the political force most closely associated with the post-industrial issues of the 'New Politics', the Greens' prospects could not be dismissed simply on the basis of the 1980 result. Moreover, their popular vote of 568,265 meant that state finance would allot them the sum of nearly DM 2 million as a useful contribution to their future activity.

The question of the Greens leads directly to the other basis of comparison for general electoral trends, namely the results of the series of *Land* elections from 1978 to 1980. There are various interesting conclusions to be drawn here which may be noted with reference to the different parties. Firstly, the CDU/CSU performance during the 1978/80 *Land* elections was distinctly less impressive than that in two preceding series in its Opposition period of 1970-1972 and 1974-1976. This was a serious portent for 1980, since an Opposition party has invariably tended to make gains in state elections, benefiting from stronger mobilisation and a 'swing' against the Government, and it needs to provide itself with a favourable background of electoral support to balance the 'governmental bonus' normally enjoyed by Government parties in the national election (commonly estimated at around 3 to 4 per cent). Whereas in the 1974-1976 *Land* elections the CDU/CSU scored an average vote of 51.4 per cent (compared with the national result of 48.6 per cent in 1976), giving itself a reasonable chance of an absolute majority in the Bundestag, in the 1978-1980 series the CDU/CSU average was only 48.8 per cent (with a subsequent national result of 44.5 per cent). Favourable circumstances certainly assisted the CDU/CSU in 1974-1976 — adverse economic trends following the energy crisis, the beneficial effects of CDU organisational reform — while in the 1978-1980 series the demoralising impact of the 1976 Kreuth crisis internally between the CSU and CDU apparently undercut the Opposition's appeal. The last elections in this later series even registered losses by the CDU (1.9 per cent in Bremen, 3.3 per cent in Baden Württemberg, 5.1 per cent in the Saar and 3.8 per cent in NRW), all of which occurred after Strauss's nomination as candidate.

Secondly, the SPD vote during 1978-1980 with an average of 42.9 per cent proved remarkably stable compared with its normal level in national elections during the 1970s. It made slight gains in several cases compared with preceding *Land* elections of 1974-1976, with its most impressive result in North Rhine-Westphalia in May 1980, gaining an absolute majority of seats. This *Land* election was, however, an important example of a different time-setting influencing the outcome compared with the national result, even though a period here of less than half a year. The *Land* campaign in North Rhine-Westphalia took place under the shadow of the Afghanistan crisis, so that the SPD successfully mobilised support on the 'peace' theme; while during the Bundestag campaign, as shown above, a combination of unfavourable election 'events' and organisational mistakes by the SPD reduced its effective appeal. Furthermore, the very impact of the North Rhine-Westphalia result in this most populous *Land*, on the very eve of the

Bundestag election, had a strong effect on the campaign conduct of all the parties, above all on the FDP, as already noted.

The FDP performance in *Land* elections was uneven and more than hinted at the relative instability of its electorate. Its average result for all eleven elections was 6.6 per cent, ranging from 4.2 per cent in Lower Saxony to 10.7 per cent in Bremen, including its expulsion from three state parliaments because its vote in Hamburg, Lower Saxony and North Rhine-Westphalia fell below the 5 per cent level. Because of its electoral instability — that is, the FDP's *Stammwählerschaft* was around 5 per cent, but it depended heavily on floating voters (above all from the 'new middle class') to assure its parliamentary representation — the FDP was particularly vulnerable to political circumstances in a given election. This was especially evident in the impact of preceding *Land* elections, for expulsion from one state parliament activated an 'FDP survival' syndrome among floating or coalition voters subsequently. Such behaviour had happened on various occasions during the *Land* elections of 1970-1972, when the FDP lost conservative liberal support following its national coalition with the SPD, and it occurred again in 1978 in Hesse and Bavaria after the shock of the FDP result in Hamburg and Lower Saxony a few months beforehand. This syndrome was, however, most visible in the 1980 Bundestag election after the impact of the North Rhine-Westphalia result. Compared with the *Land* vote less than five months before, the FDP result in North Rhine-Westphalia in the national election more than doubled its absolute total and its percentage strength. The same pattern in 1980 was clear from results in other *Länder*, where the FDP had performed weakly in state elections, e.g. compared with *Land* elections (in brackets) the FDP results in Hamburg and Lower Saxony were respectively 14.1 per cent (4.8) and 11.3 per cent (4.2).

TABLE 6
FDP VOTE IN NORTH RHINE-WESTPHALIA, LAND AND BUNDESTAG
ELECTIONS, 1980

Land Election, 11 May 1980	4.98%	488,946
Bundestag Election, 5 October 1980	10.9%	1,191,612

The strongest disparity between the Bundestag election result of 1980 and the trends in *Land* elections of 1978-1980 was in the vote for the ecologist Greens. Unlike their national vote of 1.5 per cent, their average in the ten *Land* elections in which they presented candidates (the one exception being the Rhineland-Palatinate) was 3.46 per cent, with a range from 1.8 per cent in Bavaria to 5.3 per cent in Baden Württemberg:

TABLE 7
VOTE FOR THE GREENS IN LAND ELECTIONS, 1978-1980

Baden-Württemberg	5.3	North-Rhine Westphalia	3.0
Bremen	5.1	Saar	2.9
Hamburg	4.5	Schleswig-Holstein	2.4
Lower Saxony	3.9	Hesse	2.0
West Berlin	3.7	Bavaria	1.8

In fact, the vote for the Greens (in many cases they campaigned under similar though different labels) was in each case of a *Land* election higher than the national result of 1980, while in two cases they passed the 5 per cent hurdle and entered state parliaments, not to mention their increasing representation in local councils. There are several reasons for suggesting that the Greens' greater strength in *Land* elections is more indicative than their disappointing result in 1980, at least with reference to the next series of *Land* elections in 1982-1984. Unlike, for instance, the NPD in 1969, the Greens' legitimacy as a political force was not so linked to their entry to the Bundestag; but, more importantly, the likely salience in the future of the energy question (on which the SPD was divided and the FDP vulnerable) and the continuing groundswell of public concern over environmental issues assured the Greens of a receptive audience. In short, they were well placed to act as a protest force and benefit from a 'swing' against the Government parties, although their actual performance could also be negatively affected by an improvement in the CDU/CSU's appeal after Strauss and any repercussions from their own internal divisions.

CONCLUSIONS

The significance of any election has to be assessed by considering both the political trends as revealed by the campaign (in West Germany a relatively long process, compared for instance with the UK) and the electoral trends indicated by the results. Taken together, these provide evidence about underlying tendencies in party development, in particular how much these are confirmed or otherwise modified by temporary factors surrounding the election in question. In assessing this evidence, consideration must be given to both 'subjective' and 'objective' perspectives, for the former is not without some reflection on the state of the individual parties and the party system as a whole.

Subjectively, it is clear that the criticism of the 1980 Bundestag election concerning its lack of substantial issue debate was justified, but it is important to look behind this complaint for its motivation and precise meaning. Its value was to pinpoint a certain weakness in the response of the parties to public concerns as well as changes in the quality of political attitudes and involvement among the electorate. Nevertheless, the active interest in discussing politics at the level of personal relationships was in 1980 very comparable to that in the election years of 1969 and 1976, though less so than in the exciting campaign of 1972. This did perhaps further suggest a 'normality' about the 1980 election; whereas the interpretation of the media, apart from their natural professional desire for drama, remained geared more to expectations arising from the political past. Some of the campaign rhetoric of West German politicians, questioning polemically the democratic credentials of their rivals or with references back to the Nazi period, obviously encouraged this interpretation by the media. 'Normality' in the 1980 election was above all underlined by the fact that the system of parliamentary democracy in the Federal Republic was not itself in question, despite the heat aroused by the Strauss candidacy, but rather some of its qualities — if anything, criticism of the behaviour of the parties arose from a wish among the electorate for more political information and certainly more accountability by the parties.

Objectively, the campaign and results tended to present a picture of stability in reference to foregoing or underlying trends. 'Stability' is of course a relative term, for as indicated above the votes of the smaller parties (the FDP and the Greens) did reveal elements of electoral instability, which politically could be significant, although in the FDP's case this was no new feature. With regard to the main parties, it is more difficult to estimate future trends and longer-term repercussions of the 1980 elections. The CDU/CSU, now in its fourth successive period of opposition, could re-establish its broader appeal especially to middle-of-the-road voters since it is freed of the Strauss candidacy, although this will depend on the performance of the Government parties and the popularity of its next chancellor candidate (Kohl, Albrecht and Stoltenberg being the three possibilities mentioned in the aftermath of the 1980 election). One positive sign for the CSU/CSU was that it managed to activate its campaign organisation effectively to mobilise the vast majority of its supporters notwithstanding popular reservations about Strauss. More worrying in this respect was the state of the SPD as a party, for not only were some of its organisational deficiencies highlighted in the campaign but it had still not resolved its prospective and complicated leadership succession. While its organisational condition has weakened during the SPD's 14 years of governmental respon-sibility in Bonn, it had not compensated for this by becoming in any essential way a 'Chancellor party'. The mistaken assumption by Schmidt and his official aides that the latter was so in their electoral strategy underlined this problem.

In short, there were no serious or fundamental signs that the West German party system might be moving towards the kind of structural changes experienced by so many other West European party systems during the past decade. However, future interpretations of its functioning as being 'normal' could well depend notably on whether a second 'change of power', with the CDU/CSU replacing the SPD as main governing party, were to be regarded as less of a fundamentalist and more of a routine event compared with 1969.

NOTES

1. See P. Hoschka/H. Schunck, 'Regional stability of voting behaviour in Federal elections: a longitudinal aggregate data analysis' in Max Kaase/Klaus von Beyme (ed.), *Elections and Parties: socio-political change and participation in the West German Federal Election of 1976*, 1978, chapter 2. Their conclusion is that 'one cannot speak of an increasing importance of regionalisation as an independent factor, as was surmised in the debate about a north-south gradient and the like' (p. 49).
2. See poll on Strauss after his nomination as chancellor candidate, *Der Spiegel*, 9 July 1979, pp. 25-8.
3. See poll on reaction among Catholics to the bishops' letter, *Der Spiegel*, 22 Sep. 1980, pp. 24-5.
4. Report on the result in Baden-Württemberg, *Süddeutsche Zeitung*, 7 Oct. 1980.

5. Analysis by D. Oberndörfer and G. Mielke in *Die Zeit*, 10 Oct. 1980.
6. D. Oberndörfer and G. Mielke, 'Der neue Mittelstand entscheidet die Wahl' in *Die Zeit*, 26 Sep. 1980.
7. Quoted in *Die Welt*, 7 Oct., 1980.
8. Election analyses in *Frankfurter Rundschau*, 7 Oct. 1980 and *Süddeutsche Zeitung*, 7 Oct. 1980.
9. W. Kaltefleiter in *Die Welt*, 7 Oct. 1980.
10. See Conradt in K. H. Cerny (ed), *Germany at the Polls*, 1978, pp. 33-4.
11. Infas analysis in *Frankfurter Rundschau*, 7 Oct. 1980.
12. See chapter by U. Feist, M. Güllner, K. Liepelt in Kaase, von Beyme, op. cit., esp pp. 185-7, on the difficulties faced by the SPD with its 'new middle-class' voters.
13. *Die Zeit*, 10 Oct. 1980.

What the 1980 Election did not Solve

Peter Pulzer*

One man's stability is another man's stagnation. Comparing West Germany's current political habits favourably with those of Britain, a recent letter-writer to the press asserted:

> There is a basic thing which is wrong with our so-called democracy. [A previous correspondent] mentioned various countries, but avoided the example of West Germany, where proportional representation has resulted in a succession of coalition governments, all of them roughly in the centre of the political spectrum, and all of them tending not to reverse the policies of their predecessors, as opposed to having two parties which change from government to opposition, or vice versa, every four years, and leave their country in a tangle, never knowing which policy is 'in' at any one moment.[1]

The sentiment is not new. 'It is admitted as a general principle', the founder of political science wrote, 'that moderation and the mean are always best'.[2] Hans-Dietrich Genscher could not have put it better.

Yet we must distinguish between elections that change nothing and those that decide nothing. The 1980 federal election decided a number of matters of considerable importance, at both the purely political and the institutional level. It decided, of course, that Helmut Schmidt rather than Franz-Josef Strauss should be Federal Chancellor, in itself of no mean significance. In doing so, it confirmed something about the German electoral process that was far from self-evident to the founding fathers of the Basic Law, namely the executive-selecting function of legislative elections. Although the elections of 1953 to 1961, in the formative years of West German 'chancellor democracy', were proclaimed as *Kanzlerwahlen*, they left a number of issues unresolved. Chief of these was the question of who the coalition partners of the chancellor's party were to be, if it failed to gain an absolute majority. In 1961, for instance, the FDP gave the impression during the campaign that it would make the resignation of Adenauer a condition of joining a CDU-led government. It nevertheless agreed to serve under Adenauer after the election and was widely criticised for doing so.

The anti-Adenauer posture of the FDP in the 1961 campaign is a striking contrast to its attitude towards its coalition partner in 1972, 1976 and 1980. The prior commitment to a particular party combination for the whole of the subsequent legislative period, at the federal level and the great majority of *Land* elections in the past decade, is a major evolution in German political practice and the 1980 election helped to reinforce it. It may not last, but as

*The author would like to express his appreciation to the German Academic Exchange Service, which enabled him to visit the Federal Republic in September and October 1980.

long as it does it represents a major departure from German party tradition as it evolved under the Empire and the Weimar Republic, but also as reconstituted at the end of the Second World War. One has only to consider the prevalence of grand coalitions in the *Länder* from 1945 onwards, designed to counter the divisions and polarisations of electoral conflict, the tone of the debates in the Parliamentary Council and indeed the intellectual effort invested in the formulation of Articles 63, 67 and 68 of the Basic Law which presupposes a predominance of legislative-executive conflict and therefore ministerial instability. They were debated as some of the most important components of the Basic Law and are now largely redundant.

THE UNCHANGING POLITICAL AGENDA

Why then did so many observers claim the election was boring and the campaign without substance — a verdict endorsed by the voters whose interest in the election declined, quite unprecedentedly, as the campaign progressed?[3] The answer must be that little has changed in the agenda of the political debate since 1972. The issues that surfaced were, with one exception, eight years old or more. The problems that have emerged since then failed, in the main, to become issues.

The first familiar theme to dominate the election was *Ostpolitik*. This is not surprising. Nowhere in Europe are domestic and foreign policy more intertwined than in the two German states. Relations with the neighbour in the other bloc are for many otherwise apolitical citizens a matter of personal emotional commitment and West Germany's relations with Poland, Czechoslovakia and the Soviet Union continue to be burdened by both guilt and resentment, the legacies of aggression and expulsion. On the other hand more than six years had elapsed since the Bundestag voted on the last of the five 'Eastern' treaties, that with Czechoslovakia. This lapse of time made it even less likely that the Federal Republic's belated recognition of the post-1945 *status quo* in Central Europe could in any way be reversed.

That some of the optimism originally invested in *Ostpolitik* had proved illusory is undeniable. The illusions in any case dated more from the Brandt-Scheel than the Schmidt-Genscher era and it is difficult to dissent from one sympathetic critic of the opposition's stance who argued five years ago that:

> Even after the change of government the majority of the CDU/CSU criticises the *Ostpolitik* of the SPD/FDP government with arguments almost identical to those it used in the era of Willy Brandt. At the same time it appears anachronistic if the CDU/CSU today criticises the SPD-FDP government with the same slogans that it had to endure twenty years ago from the SPD: betrayal of German interests, haste in negotiation, ambiguities or contradictions in the interpretation of treaties.[4]

That even some of the reduced expectations of the government were to be disappointed is equally undeniable. The events in Poland during the summer of 1980 further narrowed the scope of the government's Eastern policies and led to the cancellation of summit meetings with Edward Gierek and Erich

Honecker. In spite of these disappointments, foreign policy remained the topic on which coalition spokesmen displayed the greatest unity and the greatest confidence; it was also the issue on which the coalition had the greatest lead in popular confidence at the beginning of the campaign.[5] One of the functions of an Opposition is to use its enforced leisure to produce new ideas and stimulate policy innovations; on this criterion the Opposition failed to perform its allotted task.

A faded 'golden oldie' that revived, somewhat unexpectedly, was that of church-state relations. The post-1945 foundation of the CDU and the ecumenical movement of the 1960s had gone a long way towards healing the Protestant-Catholic split. The disengagement of the SPD from its traditional anti-clericalism helped it to build bridges to the Catholic Church and gain increasing support from Catholic voters. At least some of the wounds healing over the past two decades were re-opened by the Catholic hierarchy's Pastoral Letter,[6] the most explicit since 1969, which was widely interpreted as implicit support for Franz-Josef Strauss.

This derived less from the letter's first two paragraphs, which attacked the liberalisation of abortion and supported the integrity of the family, topics on which the Church's views are well-known and on which Strauss is not entirely orthodox, than from the last two paragraphs, which warned against an escalation of the public debt and urged that no candidate should be denounced as a threat to peace. This apparently partisan engagement evoked sorrow from Catholic members of the cabinet, such as Hans-Jochen Vogel, the Minister of Justice, and Hans Matthöfer, the Minister of Finance,[7] and anger from Helmut Schmidt, who unwisely suggested that the Churches should stick to saving souls. Strauss countered the clerical bogey with an anti-clerical one, hinting that the coalition parties were plotting to 'turn off the churches' revenue tap' by amending the tax-collecting facilities at present provided by the state. One of the principal developments of post-1945 German politics, the emergence of both catholics and socialists from their historically-determined corners, seemed for the moment arrested, if not reversed.

A third recurrent issue was that of internal security. Extremism and terrorism are serious problems; it is easy enough for the outsider to assume that the solutions propounded by German governments in the last ten years are clumsy and counter-productive. But these policies have led to a definition of extremism that is extensive on the Left and rather selective on the Right, and require an apparatus of surveillance and investigation that probably alienates more people from the prevailing values of society than is good for that society. The bomb blast at the Munich *Oktoberfest* reminded everyone that the risk of violent subversion remains. Rather more salutorily, it was also a reminder that subversion exists on the Right as well as the Left. But on this topic, too, the Opposition, by reacting instinctively, produced old answers, not new ones. Principally it blamed the FDP Minister of the Interior, Gerhart Baum, for trivialising terrorism, for instance by engaging in public debate with the ex-terrorist lawyer Horst Mahler.

There were well worn themes of the Left, too, for the splintered and debilitated Left opposition was no more capable of mounting an innovative challenge than the alternative government. What unity the Left was able to show grew entirely out of reaction to the adoption of Strauss as chancellor candidate. The cynic might say that the one needed the other: each behaved as the antagonist expected him to. In comparison with its often naïve anxiety to subvert in the 1960s, the Left's slogans in 1980 were totally traditionalist. It saw the opposition to Strauss as a further round in the great anti-fascist crusade, as if it were the Spanish Civil War all over again, or the Bundestag were about to go up in flames.

There are no doubt reasons internal to the CDU/CSU that explain the persistence of slogans and policy attitudes that have changed little since their loss of federal power in 1969. An outstanding example of this obstinacy was the CDU's choice of the slogan *Den Sozialismus stoppen*, although survey evidence had shown that the equivalent 1976 slogan *Freiheit statt Sozialismus* had been unfavourably received by voters, including a majority of unattached voters.[8] But beyond that the content of the campaign gave the impression that it is difficult to give superannuated hatchets a decent burial in Germany, that distant, often venial, sins remain unforgiven and that old scores can rankle for a long time. That in turn raises the question whether the inability of the political debate to move on to new ground is a cause or a symptom of a deep need for consolidation in the German policy. Much has changed in world affairs since 1972, but the internal political agenda of the Federal Republic has remained much the same.

THE PROCESS OF STABILISATION

The reason for this must be the profound change that the politics and society of West Germany underwent in the years immediately before 1972, and the need to digest that upheaval. This change was symbolised by the *Machtwechsel* of 1969, a 'critical election' in V.O. Key's sense,[9] but can be traced over the whole of the period from the retirement of Adenauer in 1963 to the re-election of Brandt in 1972. Those years marked the end of the post-war period in which recovery and security were the primary, at times the only, public concerns. They constituted, in many ways, a 'second founding' of the Federal Republic. A new political generation took over, not only at the parliamentary level but among those formulating new demands. Most of the enactments that were the fruit of this new mood date from the Brandt-Scheel period,[10] but their gestation can be dated from the Great Coalition (1966-1969) and, in foreign policy at least, from some of Gerhard Schroeder's initiatives under Erhard (1963-1966). The readjustments that the changed relationships with East and West demanded were evidently greater than many of their advocates anticipated; it should not therefore surprise us if the echoes of the polemics they released still dominate the debate.

Even greater, and evidently demanding even longer convalescence, was the impact of the protest movement of the 1960s. Like all such upheavals, it raised expectations that could not be satisfied and it induced in others, including some radicals of the first hour, a *grande peur*. The ferment was not all in vain. Few observers of the West German scene would deny that its society is today less narrow-minded, more pluralistic and more diverse in aims and values than 15 years ago. Nevertheless, those who constituted the infantry of change — never a very homogeneous cohort — have dispersed in ever more divergent directions.

Some have done well for themselves. The long march through the institutions has in many instances led to the triumph of the institution over the marcher. Ex-rebels now in middle management in education, the media, public administration or private corporations may retain some of their post-materialist ideals but also have material gains — in power as well as possessions — to defend. They constitute that section of the 'new *Mittelstand*' among whom liberal values are widespread[11] but who no longer constitute a driving force for change.

Others have entered politics and constitute either the cadres of citizens' initiatives and 'green' parties or the left factions in the SPD and FDP. In either case they are restricted to exerting pressure and are liable to suffer the frustrations of operating in a largely hostile or sceptical environment. Yet others perpetuate their youthful radicalism into nostalgic middle age by membership of the alternative culture in its multiple manifestations. This, too, has become institutionalised through its publications and internal communications network; its members are 'negatively integrated'[12] into the *status quo*: they do not belong to it but are dependent on it; they oppose it but have no hope of overthrowing it. Lastly, there are those for whom frustration has led to conspirational violence and whose numbers, as far as one can tell, are steadily reducing.

It is these last who most account for the nature and strength of antithesis to the party of movement, as it existed in the late 1960s. This, too, consists of a number of groups: those who were opposed to reform all along and only saw their worst suspicions confirmed; those who were initially welcoming, but ceased to sympathise once some initial modest gains had been achieved; and those whose lasting impressions of the era of reform are of some trauma of violence, intolerance and aggression, of seeing seminar rooms turned into battlefields and campuses into guerilla terrains. These, the casualties of protest, are as much a segment of the Federal Republic's spectrum of opinion as the perpetuators of protest.[13] Together with the 'first-hour' opponents of the reform wave, they explain why inner security enjoys such continuing prominence.

THE NEGLECT OF NEW ISSUES

Nothing illustrated the way the political agenda remained as it had been in 1972 more than the failure of newer problems to make an impact on the campaign. There is no shortage of these, and any list is bound to be arbitrary and incomplete.

Little was said about energy policy, beyond sloganising for and against nuclear power stations. Yet, given Germany's heavy dependence on imported fuel, the federal government's inability to evolve a long-term strategy is one of its more notable failures. Little was said about the future of the EEC and in particular the reform of the Common Agricultural Policy, although politicians of all parties were aware that they would have to make up their minds on this some time in 1981. Little was said about educational policy, although the multitude of reforms at both school and university levels has left few educators satisfied and many students and parents bewildered. Little was said about the prospects for industrial relations, although at least one aspect of this, the future of co-determination, has aroused strong feelings among unions, management and politicians.

Very little indeed was said about what is probably the biggest time-bomb ticking away in German society — the status of foreign workers, the social integration of their families and their claims for citizenship. Surprisingly little was said (in comparison with the prominence that the topic enjoys in other Western countries) on the social and economic impact of the new technology.

Now there is not much mystery about this public silence. These are complex topics, not well suited to the crude formulations of the hustings. Moreover, aggregative or majoritarian parties cannot afford too many hostages in the shape of specific policy commitments: they campaign on their general competence and not on a package of promise that few electors would accept without qualification.

There are other reasons why the parties preferred vagueness or silence. On some of these issues they are themselves divided: this is true of the FDP and SPD on nuclear energy. On others, a public front of unanimous enlightenment hides distrust of the instincts of the rank-and-file: that is true of the SPD on the subject of foreign workers. On others still, the coalition partners disagree: that applies pre-eminently to industrial co-determination, probably to education and, in a rather more complex way, to the CAP, given the peculiar status of Josef Ertl, the Minister of Agriculture, in the FDP. Some topics are avoided because there is more overlap of views between the SPD and the CDU than within the coalition: of those listed above, co-determination is one, but there are others, including the indexation of pensions. And there remain topics such as the new technology, on which no-one appears to have done much public thinking.

Nevertheless, elections are times when there is an optimum audience for political argument. The case against discussing these topics outside election campaigns is that then nobody listens. Therefore, unless one believes that parties are not issue-defining bodies and elections issue-defining occasions — and these functions are surely not incompatible with that of selecting executives — there was a loss to the West German political system in the way the agenda for the 1980 election developed.

THE PLACE OF THE MINOR PARTIES

The main agents for raising awkward questions were the minor parties and in this respect at least role expectations were fulfilled. Environmental and energy questions were emphasised by the alliance of 'Green' parties. Their poor poll (1.5 per cent) was well below their own expectations. It reflected their well-publicised internal divisions, which had not added to their credibility, and the squeeze that single-issue parties suffer in national elections when these are primarily executive-selecting. It also reflected the specifically polarising effect that the Strauss candidature had on the dissident groups of the Left. Having become obsessed with 'stopping Strauss', their members logically had to do so in the only effective way. While 38 per cent of Green supporters were undecided in mid-August whom they preferred as chancellor — a higher proportion than for any other party and a symptom of the Greens' general alienation from 'official' politics — of the remainder 60 per cent preferred Schmidt and only 2 per cent Strauss.[14]

The squeeze on the Greens is all the more significant since on a whole cluster of issues they give the appearance of being a libertarian version of the SPD and FDP rather than a monomaniac crusade. On the one hand, by no means all Greens oppose nuclear power (10 per cent are in favour); on the other, they give low priority to law and order (26 per cent think it the most important problem, compared with a national average of 45 per cent) and high priority to the protection of free speech (36 per cent; national average 14 per cent) and greater opportunities for citizen participation (35 per cent; national average 10 per cent).[15] Thus, even if one bears in mind the con-genital incoherence of the Greens as an organisation, one has to assume that in one form or another they will continue to contribute to the formulation of the Federal Republic's political agenda.

At the other end of the spectrum the only party to campaign for sending foreign workers home was the NPD. Its negligible poll (0.2 per cent) suggests that the party is virtually dead as a political force and the main plank in its platform has no drawing power. These were probably further reasons why the other parties chose to avoid raising this issue. But there could be long-term disadvantages in this. Liberal-minded Germans tend to be shocked at the suggestion that the question of foreign workers should be debated more openly and to congratulate themselves on not having produced an Enoch Powell or George Wallace. Yet one of the effects of the agitation of Powell and the National Front in Britain has been to mobilise a counter-force, to give anti-racialism a popular base and to make the problems of race relations a part of the political agenda. If and when communal conflict or violence were to flare up in the Federal Republic, the consensus of silence so far practised could leave the public and the parties unprepared and disoriented and, in this respect, at a disadvantage compared with France, Britain or the United States.

What success these or any other minor parties can have — leaving out of account any discussion of the merits of their programme — depends on the capacity of the West German political system to absorb change. And on this question one is bound to be sceptical, for what the 1980 election did not reveal was how to bring about that change. The inertia of party structures, of interest group cartels and the editorial choices by the media seems in 1980 to be overwhelming and immovable.

BARRIERS TO INNOVATION

Some of the obstacles to change in the Federal Republic are institutional and deliberate. The Basic Law was designed to prevent the abuse of power and it therefore must impede the exercise of power in general. The Bundestag is not a sovereign legislature. It is subject to the veto of the Constitutional Court (Article 93) and the qualified veto of the Bundesrat (Article 77). The Bundesrat may represent the claims of the *Länder*, as originally intended, and therefore of local as against central interests; or the mid-term fluctuations of electoral favours; or the pulling power of territorial potentates who do not compete directly against the chancellor but are nevertheless his rivals. Thus even a direct change of power in Bonn would not entail the kind of policy changes possible in a unicameral, centralised political system such as that of Britain.

There are, however, further obstacles to innovation in the Federal Republic and these are at the level of ideas. This is best illustrated by speculating on the possible outcome of the 1984 federal election. These are:

1. No change. This rests on two assumptions. Firstly, that the FDP is too firmly wedded to alliance with the SPD, both through shared interests and in response to the preferences of the majority of its own followers, to be able to play the pivotal role that might otherwise be expected of it. Secondly, that the continued alliance of the FDP with the SPD virtually ensures the re-election of the coalition, since the FDP is unlikely to drop below 5 per cent and the CDU/CSU unlikely to exceed 50 per cent.

2. An absolute majority for the CDU/CSU. This shares one of the above assumptions, that the division of German politics into 'blocs' remains. On the other hand it assumes that by 1984 Chancellor Schmidt will either have left office or lost his appeal to the electorate and that after 15 years the slogan 'time for a change' will be attractive enough to bring about the 6 per cent swing that the CDU/CSU need for a working majority.

3. A CDU-FDP coalition. This assumes that by 1984 the SPD will have become less attractive for the FDP, if only be becoming less popular, and the CDU more attractive by acquiring a more liberal leadership and policies.[16] It also assumes that a pre-election commitment to a coalition switch or to awaiting the outcome of the election will be acceptable to enough FDP back-benchers, regional leaders, rank-and-file members and voters. It will depend to some extent on the coalitions that emerge from the next round of *Landtag* elections, especially in Rhineland-Palatinate and Lower Saxony.

4. A great coalition. There is support for this among some elements in both major parties, especially the trade union wings. But in the main this is a solution for emergencies and unlikely unless an as yet unforeseen crisis supervenes.

From the perspective of 1980, therefore, (1) and (3) are the most likely outcomes. They have a common feature: in a CDU-FDP coalition Genscher or his successor would presumably be Foreign Minister, Count Lamsdorff or someone similar at the Ministry of Economics and — if only for reasons of party cohesion — someone from the left-wing of the FDP at either the Interior or Justice. Which would in turn raise the question: just how much of a change would that be? In two important senses, such an apparent *Machtwechsel* would be consistent with the traditions of the Federal Republic. Nine federal elections and over one hundred *Landtag* elections have resulted in very few complete changes of power: the most that has been achieved is shifts in coalitions, some admittedly more substantial than others. In the great majority of these coalitions the FDP has participated. SPD and CDU have held office in about half the post-war federal and *Land* cabinets, the FDP in 85 per cent.

Nor is this FDP dominance contrary to the wishes of the population. Opinion polls have repeatedly shown that about 70 per cent favour three parties in the Bundestag,[17] which means that only a minority of West German electors want absolute majorities and decisive shifts of power. This public reluctance to see alternation of power institutionalised and the public attachment to parties with a specifically 'corrective' or 'braking' role bestows on the FDP a position of enormous privilege. When one considers further that the FDP represents a fairly homogeneous stratum of urban, professional people with above average education and income, the policy veto that the present party system gives to this group emerges very powerfully. Indeed, deliberately or not, West Germany at the moment seems to follow closely the precepts of the founder of political science:

> We may therefore conclude that in the ownership of all gifts of fortune a middle condition will be the best. Men who are of this condition are the most ready to listen to reason . . .
>
> It is clear from our argument, first, that the best form of political society is one where power is vested in the middle class and, secondly, that good government is attainable in those states where there is a large middle class — large enough, if possible, to be stronger than both of the other classes, but at any rate large enough to be stronger than either of them singly; for in that case its addition to either will suffice to turn the scale, and will prevent either of the opposing extremes from becoming dominant.[18]

One can see the attractions of this stability; to many British observers it appears enviable. The adoption of its mechanisms in Britain, its supporters argue:

> . . . would reduce polarisation, because parliament would be more representative of the electorate and government would have to rest upon a majority of the nation and therefore not be tied to, nor identified with, one side of industry.
>
> I firmly believe that electoral reform will benefit industry in three ways. First: it will strengthen the moderate view in government and the influence of those who prefer consensus and consistency of government policy. Secondly: it will give to genuinely majority governments the legitimacy and support for necessary and difficult decisions. Thirdly it will produce fewer but more carefully considered laws, making it easier for industry to get on with our real task of wealth and job creation.[19]

Yet the dividing line between stability and stagnation is not easy to draw. What the 1980 federal election failed to establish, for the long as well as the short-term, is how to bring about change. Where will the impetuses for this come from? And who will be able to accommodate them? A partial *Machtwechsel* can usher in a change of policies, as in 1969. In 1980 the mood was different, for reasons we have speculated on. No one talked, as Willy Brandt did in 1969, of 'daring more democracy' or 'building a modern Germany'; no one offered, as did the FDP in 1969, to snip off the old pigtails. But this mood, too, can pass. If so, 1984 might decide what 1980 did not.

NOTES

1. 'Fair Voting Leads to Balance', *Sunday Times* (London), 2 Nov. 1980.
2. Aristotle, *Politics* 1295 b (trans. Ernest Barker), Oxford: Clarendon Press, 1947.
3. Data by Forschungsgruppe Wahlen, Mannheim, supplied by Professor Max Kaase.
4. Christian Hacke, *Die Ost- under Deutschlandpolitik der CDU/CSU. Wege und Irrwege der Opposition seit 1969*. Cologne: Verlag Wissenschaft und Politik, 1975, p. 116.
5. 'Aufgaben in Bonn: Wer löst sie besser?' *Der Spiegel* 12 May, 1980, p. 96.
6. *Wort der deutschen Bischöfe zur Bundestagwahl 1980*. Deutsche Bischofskonferenz, 25 Aug., 1980.
7. For Vogel's reaction, see interview in *Westfälische Rundschau*, 25 Sept., 1980; for Matthöfer's, see 'So wahr mir Gott helfe, was soll ich tun?' *Der Spiegel*, 22 Sep., 1980, p. 21.
8. Werner Kaltefleiter, *Vorspiel zum Wechsel. Eine Analyse der Bundestagwahl 1976. Verfassung und Verfassungswirklichkeit*, Jahrbuch 1977, p. 182.
9. V.O. Key, jr. 'A Theory of Critical Elections', *Journal of Politics*, Feb., 1955.
10. According to a calculation by the Federal Chancellor's office, 455 reform projects were considered during 1970 alone. 'Vom Ende der Reformen', *Die Zeit*, 26 Sept., 1980, p. 34.
11. For the social basis of value changes see Kai Hildebrandt and Russell J. Dalton, 'The New Politics: Political Change or Sunshine Politics?', Max Kaase and Klaus von Beyme (eds.) *Elections and Parties*, German Political Studies, Vol. 3, London & Beverly Hills: Sage, 1978.
12. Dieter Groh's phrase about the pre-1914 SPD in, *Negative Integration und Revolutionärer Attentismus: Die Deutsche Sozialdemokratie am Vorabend des ersten Weltkrieges*, Frankfurt: 1973.
13. 'Neben den Protest-Geprägten bilden die Protest-Geschädigten eine der unsichtbaren Parteien im politischen Leben der Bundesrepublik.' Hermann Rudolph, 'Eine neue unbewältigte Vergangenheit?' *Merkur*, Sept. 1980, p. 878.
14. Allensbach survey, *Stern*, 28 Aug., 1980, p. 51.
15. Nuclear power: 'Hat Strauss eine Chance?' *Der Spiegel*, 5 May, 1980, p. 44; other issues: Forschungsgruppe Wahlen, Mannheim, supplied by Professor Max Kaase.
16. It is worth noting that after the election Strauss himself spoke more favourably of 'uniting the bourgeois camp'. Speech at secret CSU meeting, Kreuth, reported in *Die Welt*, 3 Nov., 1980.
17. For instance, Infas survey, *Die Welt*, 28 May, 1980.
18. Aristotle, *Politics*, loc. cit.
19. Lord Caldecote, 'Time to stop the policy pendulum', *The Times*, 11 Nov., 1980.

Rethinking the German Past

Richard J. Evans*

Thirty-five years after the fall of the Third Reich, and almost half a century after the Nazi seizure of power, the shadow of the past still darkens the surface of German politics. It is not simply that the antics and outrages of neo-Nazis keep the memory of the Third Reich in the public eye; nor that there are still many former Nazis in high places, and that some of these, such as the former Minister-President of Baden-Württemberg, Hans Filbinger, have been at the centre of major controversies when unpleasant facts about their political past have been revealed: cases such as Filbinger's are likely to occur with increasing rarity as those who were adult before 1945 die out, while the neo-Nazi extremists seem to have even less support than the Baader-Meinhof group. History plays a less direct but more central role than this in West German politics.[1] It has been particularly in evidence during the most recent federal election campaign. Voters were allegedly repelled by the unsuccessful opposition candidate Franz-Josef Strauss because, among other things, the violence of his invective and the alarmism of his foreign policies reminded them all too much of Adolf Hitler. And if this is going too far, then Strauss had certainly identified himself on a number of occasions with the long tradition of German nationalism, while his emphasis on discipline and order, his *penchant* for authoritarian state action, and his unbridled attacks on Socialism, all called to mind, paradoxically in view of his Bavarian origins, the historical memory of the old Prussian State. More generally, West German politicians have frequently addressed historical problems in a way that is unfamiliar in other countries. In 1971, for instance, President Heinemann urged West Germans, on the centenary of the founding of the Bismarckian Reich, to see themselves as the successors not of the Empire which the 'Iron Chancellor' created, and those who ruled it, but of Social Democrats such as Bebel and Liebknecht, who sat in gaol as it was being proclaimed, and of other opponents of Bismarckian authoritarianism such as Eugen Richter, the left-wing liberal, or Ludwig Windthorst, the Catholic Centre party leader during the struggles of the *Kulturkampf*.

The connections between politics and historical (and other) scholarship in the Federal Republic are close. The political parties have their own educational committees which go as far as discussing school *curricula* in quite detailed terms; the State governments have to approve university appointments and frequently refuse to do so on political grounds; examinations are also vetted by the State, which is also represented on the examining bodies. A major political party such as the SPD has its own research institute as part

*This paper originated as a contribution to a conference on 'History and Politics in West Germany' held at the German Historical Institute in London by the Association for the Study of German Politics in December 1979.

of the Friedrich Ebert Stiftung, which publishes a large quantity of historical literature, from general party histories to highly specialised monographs, and sponsors a large quantity of research. All these connections, while producing nothing like the rigid 'party line' familiar in East German historiography, do constitute a consistent set of pressures operating in the direction of the politicisation of historical research, above all as it applies to the history of the last 150 years.

Since the end of the Second World War, German historians themselves have also been acutely conscious of the political relevance and importance of their discipline. In his opening address to the first post-war Congress of German Historians (*Deutscher Historikertag*) in 1949, entitled 'Present Situation and Future Tasks of German Historical Scholarship', Gerhard Ritter, the President of the Congress, laid particular stress on the sins of the past in this respect.[2] In his view, the historians of previous generations had been all-too-characteristic examples of the 'unpolitical German':

> Since Ranke, German historical scholarship has always been especially proud of its objectivity. And certainly one may say in retrospective praise that its development was less closely connected with party-political tendencies than, for instance, English or even French historical scholarship was . . . But frequently this objectivity was the result not of a real sense of truth and justice but rather of cautious or unworldly neutrality . . . [This] also robbed it in many cases of political nerve and did not protect it from . . . the intrusion of political prejudices in favour of Prussia and Germany, from the spirit of nationalistic arrogance. (p. 6)

He called therefore for a stronger political engagement on the part of historians; for a sober and self-critical reappraisal of the German past and of the methods by which German historians had hitherto approached it. Similarly, many younger German historians in the early 1970s argued that history had an important role to play in the creation of a new, more securely rooted democratic consciousness among the citizens of the Federal Republic. History, as one of the most prominent of these historians remarked, should aim to contribute consciously to the development of 'a freer, more critical social consciousness', it should 'work out the consequences of decisions taken, or the social costs of decisions not taken, in the past, and thus increase the chances of a rational orientation of our behaviour and our lives, and to embed them within the horizons of carefully-considered historical experiences.'[3]

German historians since the end of the Second World War, therefore, have addressed the recent past with very specific political questions in mind. Chief among these has been the obvious one of how Germans can learn from their past in order to avoid repeating its mistakes. The questions which everyone wants to answer to are: How can the Bonn Republic survive where the Weimar Republic failed? What do Germans have to do to prevent the advent of another Hitler? Not surprisingly, the answers which historians have provided have differed widely according to their political position. A historian whose sympathies lie with the CDU/CSU, for instance, is likely to have a very different view of the past from one sympathetic to the SPD or the FDP. Correspondingly, any interpretation which an historian advances of the historical origins of the Nazi seizure of power is bound to have direct political implications for the present. Of course, the view that was put forward by Allied propaganda during the war, of the immutable wickedness of the 'German character', could only have the implication that never again could Germans be allowed to take charge of their own destinies. Not surprisingly, therefore, for this if for no other reason, it has always been rejected by the Germans themselves. This posed the problem, however, of what should replace it.

The purpose of this essay is to discuss two sharply contrasting interpretations of German history, advanced respectively in the early years of Konrad Adenauer's chancellorship and the early years of the SPD/FDP coalition. They are, despite the inevitable personal idiosyncracies of their authors' views, representative interpretations: the first, by the late Gerhard Ritter, doyen of German historians in the 1950s and early 1960s, if only by virtue of his position as President of the German Historians' Association on its foundation in 1949; the second, by the still very much alive Hans-Ulrich Wehler, because the views which he has put forward are probably shared by a majority of the younger German historians working on the history of the Empire and the Weimar Republic, at least if their appearance in published articles, dissertations and books since the second half of the 1960s is anything to go by.[4] The concern in the following analysis is not to discuss the changes in historical methodology which have taken place over the intervening period, great though these have been; nor is it to offer an assessment of the validity or otherwise of the views that are analysed, a subject which would extend far beyond the bounds of this brief discussion and which in any case remains unaffected by their political origins and implications. What is envisaged rather, is to explore some of the ways in which historians have been rethinking the German past since 1949, and to show how a great deal of this rethinking has been strongly political in character.

GERHARD RITTER AND GERMAN HISTORY

The interpretation of German history put forward by Gerhard Ritter in the early years of the Adenauer era provides our starting-point. Ritter's main concern was to dissociate what he regarded as the central traditions of German history from what he argued were the novel and alien ideas and practices introduced by Hitler. In his essay on 'The Historical Foundations of the Rise of National-Socialism', written in the early 1950s,[5] he therefore launched a strong attack on the 'continuity thesis' advanced, above all, in Allied propaganda during the war:

> Up till the present there has been a strong tendency to seek the sources of National-Socialism in the dim past of German history. Attempts to do this were started in the Vansittart group's propaganda in the Second World War, when they tried to show that National-Socialist methods of violence existed among the Cimbri and the Teutons. More serious are the efforts of various foreign and German experts to explain the

distinctly militarist nature of German nationalism by its origins at the time of the wars of liberation, and the glorification of war throughout the nineteenth century, which is shown by quotations from all kinds of authors. Others trace the prehistory of National-Socialism back to Frederick the Great, or even to the Reformation. (pp. 385-6).

Ritter objected strongly to such views, which he said were 'sterile if they are used to explain the rapid decline of the Weimar Republic and the triumphal ascent of the Hitlerian Party from 1930 to 1933' (p. 386). Indeed, at some considerable risk to himself, he had already objected publicly during the 1930s to the Nazis' own attempt to portray Luther, in what appeared to them to be positive terms, as a predecessor of Hitler.[6]

Ritter countered these arguments by suggesting that the methods used by these historians were faulty. 'History', he wrote, 'can never be written by means of quotations from literature, since it is almost always possible to find such quotations contradicted elsewhere.' (p. 386) Quotations illustrating nationalism, racism, militarism and anti-democratic criticism could be found in the literature of any European country. In Germany, moreover, literature was more than usually abstruse, personal, and 'not representative of real tendencies alive in the people.' More specifically, Ritter argued that historical experience showed that, 'In general German people did not like political adventures.' (p. 387) He also attacked the idea that Germans had no natural sense of liberty. 'Only a completely superficial study of German history can ignore the thousands of examples of a true sense of freedom, examples which are numerous since the early Middle Ages, and which frequently made the rulers of the German people think them unruly and difficult to govern'. (p. 388) Enlightened despotism, liberalism, local autonomy and the Weimar Republic had all contributed to the political education of the Germans. The Weimar Republic failed not because it was a democracy, but 'because it did not succeed in winning general confidence, in becoming genuinely popular through successes which could be appreciated from a distance' (p. 389).

For Ritter, the historical origins of National Socialism lay not in old-established traditions of German life and thought, but in the destruction of these traditions after the First World War. That is not to say, of course, that he was entirely uncritical in his attitude towards them; but he undoubtedly saw them, for all their faults, as an influence that might, under other circumstances, have prevented the rise of the Third Reich. The origins of the Hitler regime lay first of all, he argued, in the destruction during the First World War and the following inflation of private incomes, of the financial independence of the educated middle classes:

Modern industrial society, a mass society of innumerable individuals united by common needs, has taken the place of the former *bourgeois* society, consisting of a layer of economically independent notables who were the great landowners and *bourgeois*. The First World War accelerated and intensified the process of economic and social levelling, by removing differences during wartime, especially in Germany. The whole of society was ground down to a uniform mass, grey as the soldiers; it was subjected to overall state control, to a totalitarian power which deeply affected even private life. (p. 390)

Universal suffrage meant the end of political parties composed of notables, of 'men who were socially and financially independent, who knew something about politics and were interested in them' (p. 391). Parties became bureaucratic machines; they abandoned 'political education, real discussion, individual thought' in the search for mass appeal. 'In order to interest the masses, they must be attracted by sensationalism. He who is best is also the most popular. The most effective method is always the sermon of hatred, the least effective the voice of peacable reason . . .' Secondly, the struggle for liberty and national unity characteristic of the nineteenth century were replaced in the era of mass politics by 'the struggle for a higher standard of living'. 'Liberalism was attacked and discarded in favour of Socialism. Political thought became more and more materialistic'. (p. 391) The material interests which replaced ideals in politics were irreconcilable, so parliaments became discredited and people became more and more discontented, using extra-parliamentary action (strikes, marches, pressure-groups, mass meetings) and seeking for a 'strong man.' Thirdly, religious values declined. 'Christian teaching scarcely reached the populations of industrial towns.' Materialism, Social Darwinism, the glorification of power, and the Marxist idea that, 'The only political reality was the conflict of material interests, and political ideals were only ideological camouflage' replaced it. (pp. 392-3) Finally, new technical facilities for political propaganda made it far easier than before to mobilise the masses behind the new ideas.

For Ritter, then, the Third Reich represented the triumph of democratic radicalism over the principle of representative parliamentary liberalism: the triumph of direct popular sovereignty expressed through the rule of one man over 'political compromise reached by discussion, the just balancing of the opposing desires and interests of different classes, groups, and individuals'. Nazism was a revolutionary force directed against all the central traditions of German history:

Hitler himself never sought a restoration; he sought its opposite . . . Hitler's propaganda was based not on the memory of 'our forefathers' deeds', but on an indomitable will for the future. His state was to be completely new, something that had never before been seen, contemporary and modern, a state that could be created only once. He poured criticism and scorn on the institutions which existed under a hereditary monarch under which the ultimate orders were made not by the most able, but by those in power on account of an accident of birth and of heredity, as he said in private . . . It is a very great mistake to believe that the modern function of leader of the people is in any way the heritage and continuation of the old, monarchic power of the princes. Neither Frederick the Great, Bismarck, nor Wilhelm II were the historian precursors of Adolf Hitler. His precursors were the demagogues and Caesars of modern history, from Danton to Lenin and Mussolini. (pp. 298-9)

Thus Hitler's party was composed of 'uprooted individuals whose mentality was revolutionary', and its strongest attraction to the masses lay in 'the fact that it was contemporary' and in the fact that it was led, not by one of the traditional notables, but by a man of 'obscure, popular origins'. (p. 400)

It is easy to see the apolgetic aspects of Ritter's arguments. He was, to begin with, concerned to spread the guilt well beyond the frontiers of Germany. 'It is difficult', he wrote, 'to understand how the Hohenzollern dynasty would have collapsed so quickly without foreign intervention (Wilson!), in spite of the serious moral uncertainty caused by the Wilhelmian regime and the disastrous result of the war.' (p. 397) Similarly, the Treaty of Versailles united 'all German parties and groups' in violent opposition to it, then aggravated the conflicts between parties, 'since right and left each placed the responsibility for the disaster at the door of the other'. (p. 406) Humiliation caused by foreign influence continued through the French occupation of the Ruhr in 1923 and the running sore of reparations. By the time things began to improve, with the Young Plan and after, it was too late: 'No government could survive without injury such serious and humiliating failures in foreign policy as did that of the Weimar Republic.' (p. 407) Finally, Hitler himself was an outsider:

> The history of Hitler's intellectual background certainly bears little relation to the general intellectual history of Germany. It is more related to the history of his own country, Austria, [where] . . . the 'cultural superiority' of Germanism in the face of the Slavonic races was a battle-cry which was continually raised . . . There were, no doubt, similar conflicts in the German states which bordered on Poland; but a nationalist born in the Reich would never turn his energies to these, instead of to the traditional rivalry with the West, with the hereditary enemy, France . . . In this respect, therefore, the historical origins of Hitlerism are to be found outside the Reich. (pp. 413-5)

Moreover, Ritter argued, 'when the causes of Hitler's great electoral successes are examined, his racial doctrines cannot be regarded as very important', for the masses never understood them. Hitler's anti-Semitism was more influential, especially among the lower middle class, but when, under the Third Reich, he passed from words to action on a huge scale, 'it is true to say that his popularity diminished rather than increased'. (p. 415) Most important was the doctrine of *Lebensraum*, which was 'not invented by Hitler, but came from Darwinian theories which had been influencing the political literature of Europe for many years, and which caused disturbing symptoms in the writings of other countries too'. Nonetheless, this too had little influence in winning over the masses. 'It is certain', wrote Ritter, 'that Hitler would never have dared to make his warlike plans for conquest known to the public earlier than 1933, for fear of destroying all the electoral success of his party. A war of conquest was certainly not a slogan for elections.' In fact, he concluded, Nazi ideology 'never became really popular'. It was not Hitler's ideas and programmes that won him support, but 'his gift of radiating confidence in the future', his personal appeal, and the sophisticated propaganda techniques used to project it. (p. 416)

Ritter's apologetic and exculpatory intentions also had a more precise and specific thrust. He was concerned above all to provide a justification for the behaviour of his own class, the educated bourgeoisie, during and prior to the Nazi seizure of power. While politics remained the province of the financially independent and educated middle classes, he argued, Nazism was impossible. Representative liberal parliamentarianism, in which the masses took no direct part, was clearly Ritter's ideal. Even more striking than the explicit elitism of Ritter's arguments were the implicit assumptions which informed them. There was, for example, an implicit equation of the 'educated bourgeoisie' with 'the Germans':

> The Germans themselves were more surprised than anyone else by the rapid rise of the National-Socialist Party to a position in which overall power in the state was at its disposal. Up to 1930 the vast majority of educated Germans thought Hitler's disciples to be a group of loud-mouthed extremists and super-patriots without any practical importance. The theatricality of their processions and meetings, the strangeness of their uniforms and of their bright red banners might awaken the curiosity of a tasteless crowd or seduce the more vulgar lower-middle-class members of the large towns; but it all seemed absurd to educated people . . .' (p. 381)

Ritter's account continued then to equate 'the Germans' with his own class by writing in the passive voice: the November 1923 *putsch 'was* generally *considered* to be' a piece of Bavarian comic opera; Hitler '*was regarded* as a man who had had his day'; after 1930, however, 'Hitler's movement *was taken* seriously.' (emphasis added) Ritter did not say by whom it was taken seriously after 1930. Implicitly, however, he disqualified the 'masses' who supported it from being able to take anything seriously, and he went on to describe how, 'the majority of educated Germans — that part of the nation which was consciously aware of its historical traditions — was very distrustful of the Hitler propaganda'. (p. 384) In other words, Ritter assumed an equation between being educated (i.e., with a university degree), being aware of Germany's historical traditions, and being German.

In advancing these views, Ritter believed that he was taking his stand on old, sound German traditions which had been perverted or overthrown by the Nazis. He was not entirely uncritical of these traditions. He pointed out, for example, that the men from the liberal professions who ran the civil service and ministries of the Empire were uninspiring people who made no attempt to win general popularity, administrators rather than politicians; that Wilhelm II was equally incapable of gaining the heart of the nation; and that while Bismarck's rule gave German people the feeling that their nation had in the world the status it deserved, this was no longer true under Wilhelm II, when

> . . . the rivalry with England, the ambition to become a people of the world (*Weltvolk*) and a sea-power began. In this forced atmosphere,

composed of the national consciousness of strength, of inferiority complex, and the fear of being cut off from other countries, was born the radical nationalism of the Pan-Germanists, whose writings contained many characteristics of National-Socialist propaganda. (p. 406)

Finally, Ritter thought that the conflict between bourgeoisie and proletariat which gave Hitler his chance to project himself as a unifying force was 'the old, fatal relic of Bismarck's Reich'; both sides were to blame, but Ritter was critical of 'Bismarck's efforts to suppress, by police methods, the Social Democratic Party'. (p. 403) Despite these reservations, however, Ritter still believed that it was the destruction of the German Empire in 1918 and the overturning of its traditions which was the decisive influence in opening the door to the alien demagoguery of Hitler. Ritter regarded the German Empire as a 'constitutional monarchy' whose stability offered the best guarantee of order and civilisation. (p. 388) Under this system, the rule of the notables, of educated, propertied and responsible men, had secured the best interests of all. Ritter did not say explicitly in this particular essay in what he thought German traditions consisted, but he was clear that, 'Hitler's victory . . . did not represent the culmination, but rather a contradiction, of tradition, particularly of the German Prussian and Bismarckian tradition.' (p. 384)

WEHLER'S OPPOSING INTERPRETATION

Two decades later, in the very different political circumstances of the aftermath of the student revolt and the early years of the Social Democratic-liberal coalition government in Bonn, a very different, indeed in many ways diametrically opposed interpretation of the historical origins of Nazism was gaining wide currency. Its most characteristic expression was in Hans-Ulrich Wehler's popular and widely-read account of the history of the German Empire, *Das deutsche Kaiserreich*, first published in 1973 reprinted many times, and most recently in its fourth edition. In total contrast to Ritter, Wehler was concerned above all to establish the links between the 'Prusso-German tradition' and the rise of Nazism. Wehler accepted the main thesis of the Allied propaganda which Ritter had so strongly objected to: the uniqueness of Germany's history, and its disastrous divergence from the path followed by the Anglo-Saxon nations. Hitler's seizure of power took place little more than 12 years after the end of the Empire; 'How could one manage to explain this without the historical dimension, which means the history of the Empire?' (pp. 12-15) Conservative historians such as Ritter, he charged, had stifled any self-critical discussion of the problem of continuity in German history, in order to defend their notion that all was well with the world before 1914. This, he said, was mere 'escapism', which sought to overcome the problem of National Socialism by presenting it as an illegitimate perversion of German history, 'instead of recognising it as a result of deep-rooted continuities'. (p. 16) The majority of the preconditions for radical fascism were present in German society under the Empire, or were the result of the Empire's policies.

Nonetheless, Wehler realised that it was impossible to go back to the rather arbitrary procedures of intellectual history by which older writers on the Allied side had attempted to support the theory of continuity in German history, and which Ritter himself had so trenchantly criticised. Instead, Wehler argued, it was necessary .o look more deeply into the socio-economic and political structures of German society in the late nineteenth and early twentieth centuries. In Wehler's analysis of these structures, almost all of Ritter's major arguments were sharply contradicted. To begin with, the elite groups which Ritter regarded as the major guarantors of political rationality before 1914 were presented by Wehler as the groups with whom the primary responsibility for the catastrophe of 1933 lay. The feudal aristocracy, the Prussian *Junkers*, who controlled the Empire through their predominance at Court, in the Army, in the Civil Service and in the Prussian Parliament, used their power to preserve their social primacy, exclude the mass of the people from participation in political decision-making, and bolster up their faltering economic viability as agrarian landlord-farmers. Much of Wehler's book, indeed, was devoted to an exposition of the methods by which, he argued, the aristocracy had managed to retain its dominance — 'the unholy trinity of social imperialism, social protectionism and social militarism', (p. 237), the authoritarian employment of police and justice as instruments of repression, the use of the educational system as a means of conservative political indoctrination, and so on. While Ritter saw the old ruling class as preserving solid virtues and values against the vulgarity and materialism of the masses, Wehler alleged that the old ruling class, using modern propaganda methods, was stirring up nationalistic ambition, anti-Semitic hatreds and anti-democratic passions among the masses as a means of preserving its own traditional, privileged position. The vulgar 'democratic radicalism' of the masses and the suscepti-bility to demagoguery and political sensationalism which Ritter had so reviled as the negation of the rational politics of the elites, Wehler saw as the very creation of these same elites through a strategy of political manipula-tion in which bread and circuses were offered instead of equality and justice, nationalism instead of participation, prosperity instead of emancipation. Ritter's own class was not immune from such criticism either, for Wehler argued that it had been co-opted into the ruling class by a process of 'feudalisation' in which it had largely come to share the socio-political attitudes of the aristocracy, and hence to share its burden of historical responsibility for the rise of the Third Reich as well. Thus the exclusion of the masses from political equality was in this view a fundamental reason for the rise of Nazism, rather than the major factor preventing it.

Wehler's account directly contradicted Ritter's in other ways too. While Ritter saw the Empire as a constitutional, parliamentary system, Wehler saw it as a *pseudo*-constitutional semi-absolutism in which Parliament had little real power. Ministers and governments were appointed by the Kaiser and were not responsible to the Reichstag, and a similar lack of ministerial responsibility obtained at the level of the individual federated States. Decisions on central matters were taken by the Kaiser and his entourage, the chancellor and the generals, and the Reichstag could do little but attempt to obstruct them, and even then not very effectively. Whole areas of major importance in the State, such as the army and the police, were more or less outside the control of elected assemblies. Not only were the majority of people denied effective participation by property-qualified franchises in Prussia and other states, therefore, but even those who did have the vote (all adult males could vote for the Reichstag), and who sat in Parliament, had little effective power. Moreover, where Ritter saw religion and Christian values as an essential moral defence against the 'materialism' which he believed had so encouraged people to listen to Hitler's message, Wehler regarded religion as an 'ideology of legitimation' through which pre-industrial and anti-democratic, authoritarian values were purveyed: 'Precisely in order not to be outbid in his claim to be a loyal citizen, the Catholic became equally as subservient and circumspect a subject of the monarchical State power as did his Lutheran neighbour.' (p. 122) Both churches offered effective opposition to the forces striving for freedom, emancipation and equality. In dealing with 'materialism' and 'idealism' on a more general level, the two historians were similarly at opposite ends of the interpretative spectrum. While Ritter implicitly suggested a contrast between the 'idealistic' elites and the 'materialistic' masses, Wehler explicitly argued that the elites' main concern was the preservation of their own economic position, and suggested that it was the masses who in their struggle for political equality, above all in Prussia, were idealistic.

Of course, Wehler's account in fact went beyond this to give a more complex and differentiated view of the relationship between ideology and material interest than I have space to discuss here; feudal values, he argued for example, had their own influence among the elite, while the search for an escape from poverty was certainly a major concern among the masses. In this respect, indeed, we come up against the fact that the two historians differ not only in their interpretation of the past, but also in the way they approach it and the concepts of human nature and human society which they employ. On the narrower question of their interpretation of the *Kaiserreich*, however, it is clear that while both regarded the reduction of political parties to economic interests, and the intrusion of economic pressure groups into central areas of the political system, as unfortunate developments, the real objects of the criticism were once more quite different. Ritter directed his fire in particular against Socialism and Marxism. In his view, they undermined political morality by portraying political ideals as mere camouflage for economic interests. Moreover in 1914-1918: 'It was undeniable that the radical propaganda of Socialists and Communists had weakened or destroyed the will to fight of many sections of the army' and so had assisted foreign powers in their destruction of the Empire. Wehler, by contrast, aimed his criticism at the employers' associations and industrialists' pressure-groups, which, he argued, financed and promoted radical nationalism as a means of winning new markets and new sources of raw materials abroad, and deliberately stymied the growth of democratic institutions which would have allowed more power to their employees.

It follows from all this that Wehler, in contradistinction to Ritter, saw Bismarck and Wilhelm II as precursors of Hitler, not as statesmen who bore little or no resemblance to the later dictator. Bismarck, in Wehler's view was himself a dictator, and he quotes a number of authorities, from the historian Friedrich Meinecke to the contemporary English ambassador Lord Ampthill, all of whom echo this view with phrases such as 'the German dictator', 'the all-powerful dictator' and so on, in their descriptions of the 'Iron Chancellor'. Bismarck is compared by Wehler to Napoleon III of France; his regime was a 'Bonapartist dictatorship' cemented by plebiscites or plebiscitary elections, and characterised by a mixture of concessions to progressive demands with sharp repressive measures; conservatism pursued by radical, even revolutionary means, such as the granting of universal manhood suffrage within Germany, or the disturbance of the European international order outside. After Bismarck's departure, there was no serious successor, despite Wilhelm II's attempt to fill the gap with a 'personal rule', for the Kaiser lacked the ability to impose himself on the country in any consistent way:

> Not Wilhelm II but the traditional oligarchies, in conjunction with the anonymous forces of the authoritarian polycracy, put their stamp on the Imperial policies of his time. Their power sufficed even without a half-dictator, though with help of a Bonapartist strategy of defending their ruling position — to be sure, with fatal consequences. (p. 72)

There were, then, in this view, elements of the modern dictatorships already in the Germany of Bismarck and Wilhelm II.

So too was the racism which Ritter presented as an alien importation into German culture. Wehler saw the isolation and stereotyping of 'enemies of the Reich', such as Catholics and Socialists, as one of the central manipulative techniques of Bismarckian rule. There was systematic discrimination against minorities such as the Poles, and above all there was a pervasive anti-Semitism on a 'massive' scale (p. 113). Jews, Socialists and other minorities were excluded from the most important posts in the State, and from full recognition as equals, with equal opportunities to others in society. Bismarck and his aides such as Minister of the Interior von Puttkamer, encouraged the radical and 'vulgar' anti-Semitism which was ultimately to triumph in the person of Adolf Hitler. In 1885, for instance, Bismarck inaugurated mass expulsions of some 32,000 Poles from the Eastern Prussian provinces; a third of these unfortunates were Jews. Nationalism, racism and anti-Semitism, then, were in this view important elements of the Bismarckian Reich and the rule of the old elites. In foreign policy, as well as in domestic affairs, Social Darwinism militarism and a radically racist and expansionist pan-Germanism gained increasing acceptance among the 'opinion-forming upper and middle strata' of society and, even if only indirectly, had a powerful influence on the government (p. 181). In all these ways, therefore, contrary to what Ritter maintained, many of the central elements of Nazism were already present in the Bismarckian Empire; and Prussian traditions such as militarism, deference to authority, absolutism and autocracy, hostility to parliamentarism and democracy, joined with more novel techniques of rule such as Bonapartism, Social Imperialism and the conscious manipulation of mass opinion, to lay the foundations of the Third Reich well before 1914.

Indeed, it was not the destruction of the old elites and the traditions they represented in 1918, but their persistence into the Weimar Republic, that paved the way for the triumph of Hitler; for in 1933 these same old elites, aided by the petty-bourgeois pre-industrial strata, the *Mittelstand*, which they had so successfully manipulated into supporting them, were the people who put Hitler into office. Correspondingly, in this view, Hitler was not a revolutionary but a reactionary; he offered not modernity, but a return to an (admittedly fictitous) remote past, where the pre-industrial values so prized by Junkerdom, the 'feudalised bourgeoisie' and the peasants and shopkeepers of the *Mittelstand*, would once again rule supreme.

Viewed from a political angle, these more recent arguments have a double-edged character. On the one side, they are a sharp attack on the conservative traditions of Prussia, a fierce critique of the old ruling classes whom Ritter was trying to defend, and a plea for a complete reassessment of the German past. The 'conquest of the past' by the Germans demanded the self-conscious rejection of a large part of their heritage, and the recognition that those aspects of German history formerly most admired above all the nineteenth century unification, should now be seen as ominous developments leading directly to the barbarism of the Third Reich. On the other hand, there is a positive side to these arguments which verges on the apologetic or exculpatory; for if pre-capitalist classes such as the Junkers and the *Mittelstand* were primarily responsible for the rise of the Third Reich, then present-day West Germans have little to feel guilty about, for in the meantime those classes have long since declined drastically in number and lost virtually all the power they once had.

Similarly, if the industrialists helped Hitler to power not because they were industrialists but because they were 'feudalised', then there is no necessary connection between capitalism and fascism; indeed, quite the reverse, since, as Wehler argues, what was wrong with the German Empire was that economic 'modernisation', the triumph of capitalism, failed to bring with it is 'natural' consequence, the triumph of liberal democracy. Correspondingly, it was with the foundation of the Federal Republic that the process of 'modernisation' was finally completed. Once again, it is easy to see how these arguments serve to legitimise the Federal Republic by dissociating it from the evils of the German past. Here, 1945 rather than 1918 marks the decisive discontinuity in the development of modern Germany; and everything that happened before 1945 is consigned to pre-history, having an increasingly tenuous connection with life in present-day West Germany.

HISTORY AND CONTEMPORARY POLITICS

It would be wrong to suppose that any simple or straightforward equation could be made between the first interpretation which I have discussed and the CDU/CSU conservative opposition, and the second interpretation and the SPD/FDP government in West Germany, between Gerhard Ritter and Konrad Adenauer and between Hans-Ulrich Wehler and Helmut Schmidt. Both these historians' writings are naturally stamped by their individual personalities, their intellectual idiosyncracies and their personal views. Their interpretations in no sense have any official public endorsement from any of the political parties, nor were they written at any party's behest. Nonetheless, no historian can remain immune from the surrounding political atmosphere, and no historian's writing is uninformed by political beliefs of some kind. In the Federal Republic, as suggested in the first part of this essay, the surrounding political atmosphere is particularly 'thick', and historians tend to be a good deal more concerned about the political implications of their work than elsewhere. It is therefore justifiable to view the two representative historical interpretations as representative not merely of the very different eras in which they were developed, but also of the two major political tendencies in the Federal Republic, CDU/CSU and SPD/FDP.

Such a political background can be glimpsed in many of the elements in these two views of German history. For example, Ritter's essay made little distinction between Hitler and Stalin (or Lenin), and drew explicit comparisons between the Third Reich and post-Revolutionary Russia. Indeed, it ended on a pessimistic note, criticising the 'Western leaders' of the day for weakness and lack of resolution in confronting the Communist menace. For Ritter, therefore, the danger of a renewed collapse into barbarism and dictatorship was only too close; in his view, it came once more from outside Germany, from the East. Writing as the Cold War was at freezing-point, Ritter was clearly an adherent of the doctrine of totalitarianism, in which the 'rise of mass society' was made responsible not only for the rise of Hitler but also for the rise of Stalin. Wehler, by contrast, writing at a time when, with Brandt's *Ostpolitik* in full swing, détente was at its warmest, presented Nazism as a variety of fascism, and located its predecessor, the 'Bonapartist dictatorship' of Bismarck, specifically within the context of capitalist society, albeit with feudal admixtures. Totalitarian theory was much less in evidence in this account. Again, while Ritter stressed the importance of Christian values in resisting the totalitarian urge, an emphasis reflected in the presence of the word 'Christian' in the names of the two major conservative parties, Wehler echoed long-standing liberal and Social Democratic tradition in voicing his suspicion of the role of organised religion in the *Kaiserreich*. Similar parallels and connections can be drawn from most of the rest of the two historians' arguments.

Despite these close connections between history and politics, however, both major parties have been attempting to cut themselves off from their historical roots, as Wehler's advocacy of a sharp discontinuity in 1945 suggests may well be the case. The Marxist ideology of the pre-1933 Social Democrats has become increasingly embarrassing to their presentday successors. Among historians close to the SPD, there has been a marked tendency to portray Marxism as an alien ideology imposed on the pre-1914 Social Democrats by intellectual outsiders unaware of the real aspirations of the German working class, and accepted by the party activists as a means of protesting against the discriminatory practices of the Imperial authorities. The CDU/CSU, on the other hand, after the failure of Strauss, must surely be reconsidering once again the problem of its identification with the nationalist legacy of the past. Here again, as soon as a politician such as

Franz-Josef Strauss begins to utter phrases reminiscent of the nationalists and reactionaries of previous eras, voters are apparently repelled. By the end of the campaign, when giving considered answers to the interviewers' questions, both candidates were all too conscious of these difficulties, and it is significant that when asked what historical figures they sought to emulate, Strauss and Schmidt carefully avoided any reference to the recent past: Strauss took refuge in a series of generalisations before naming a number of safely remote and obscure figures such as Maximilian II of Bavaria and the Emperor Charles V, while Schmidt, apart from commenting that Bismarck's cautious foreign policy of the 1870s and 1880s was (unlike the Iron Chancellor's domestic policies) relatively acceptable, steered clear of German history altogether and opted for President Lincoln and the Founding Fathers of the United States of America. And in their policy discussions on the place of history in the school curriculum in the early 1970s, the SPD even went so far as to propose that it be removed altogether as a separate discipline, to reappear in another guise as the provider of 'historical examples' for political science and sociology.[10]

West Germany's Federal Republic increasingly appears, despite the occasional panic about urban terrorism or the activities of equally tiny groups of neo-Nazi extremists, to be a stable and well-established parliamentary democracy. Those who played a prominent part in Hitler's regime are now mostly dead or in retirement. Prosecutions of major Nazi criminals are increasingly prosecutions of old men and women. West Germany seems in many ways to have overcome the problems of the past: the *Ostpolitik* settled remaining accounts with Poland, Czechoslovakia and Eastern Europe; people speak increasingly seldom of *Vergangenheitsbewältigung* (coming to terms with the past) as if it were a problem; West Germany has taken her place, along with East Germany, in the councils of nations and is playing an increasingly assertive role in the Western Alliance. To the current generation of university students, mostly born after 1960, even Konrad Adenauer is a historical figure, and the generational conflicts so characteristic of the 1960s, as angry children confronted their parents with the question: 'Daddy, what did *you* do in the Third Reich?', have largely subsided. Interviews with school-children have established that few of them know much about Hitler, who must appear to them by now to be as remote a figure as Bismarck or Napoleon. All industrial societies are losing their historical consciousness, and in the long run Germany will be no exception to this general rule.

NOTES

1. See Karl Dietrich Bracher, *The German Dilemma*, New York: Praeger, 1975.
2. Gerhard Ritter, 'Gegenwärtige Lage und Zukunftsaufgaben deutscher Geschichtswissenschaft', *Historische Zeitschrift* No. 170, 1950, pp. 1-22.
3. Hans-Ulrich Wehler, *Das deutsche Kaiserreich 1870-1918*, Göttingen, 1973, p. 12.
4. This is not to say that the views represented by Ritter have entirely disappeared. There has recently been a resurgence of conservative historiography in West Germany: see, for

example, Manfred Rauh, *Die Parlamentarisieuring des Deutschen Reiches,* Düsseldorf: Droste, 1977, or Volker Hentschel, *Wirtschaft und Wirtschaftspolitik im Wilhelminischen Deutschland,* Stuttgart; 1978. These authors' consciousness of being in a minority is perhaps the origin of the shrill and hysterical attacks on the work of Wehler and others that disfigure the footnotes to their books.

5. In: International Council for Philosophy and Humanistic Studies, *The Third Reich,* London: 1955.
6. See Helmut Heiber, *Walter Frank und sein Reichsinstitut für Geschichte des neuen Deutschlands,* Stuttgart, 1966, for an account of Ritter's activities in this period.
7. Ritter, 'Historical Foundations', p. 404.
8. See the introduction, 'The Sociological Interpretation of German Labour History', to Richard J. Evans (ed.) *The German Working Class 1888-1933: The Politics of Everyday Life,* London: Croom Helm, 1981, for an elaboration of this argument.
9. *Der Spiegel,* vol. 34, No. 40, 29 Sept. 1980, p. 25.
10. Klaus Bergmann, Hans-Jürgen Pandel (eds.), *Geschichte und Zukunft,* Frankfurt: 1975.

The State, University Reform and the 'Berufsverbot'

Roger Tilford*

If men and women do not learn at university to fulfil their duty within the social body it will be impossible to avoid a new political catastrophe. Universities which do not teach their pupils in this way must expect to be faced one day, not with constructive proposals for their reform, but with indiscriminate revolution.[1]

West German universities are widely considered to have undergone a profound intellectual and organisational upheaval in the late 1960s and early 1970s. If this were true, it would follow that the political culture of the university has changed as well, with significant consequences for the quality of politics in West Germany. But is it true? The political culture of an institution/social sub-system is shaped crucially by its *basic* organisational structures and relationships, as is the content and the style of intellectual discourse cultivated in it. The question pursued in this essay is: How profound were the organisational changes? Were not underlying structures and relationships and consequently the core of the traditional university political culture, in fact, left unquestioned and even reinforced, amid the apparent upheaval? Do not the *Radikalenerlass* and its effects amount to a powerful restatement of the traditional political culture of the German university? It will follow from these questions that the concern here is not with an analysis of intellectual fashion — for instance, that of the Frankfurt School — and its impact on university disciplines of study and on university politics, but rather of the institutional determinants of political culture, and hence of intellectual fashion at the university. A reductionist advocacy of institutional structure as the sole determinant is not intended but it is perhaps more illuminating than an emphasis on the movements of ideas themselves.

GERMAN INTELLECTUAL TRADITIONS

One important basis of the modern German university derives from German Idealism and in particular from one of its finest representatives, Wilhelm von Humboldt. The *freedom* and *unity* of teaching and research and the *community* of teachers and taught — subsumed under the notion of academic freedom, have helped shape the ethos of German universities

*Parts of this article originally appeared in the author's contribution to the Special Number for L. W. Forster of *German Life and Letters*, October, 1980 as 'The Political Responsibility of the West German University' (pp. 126-39).

since the early nineteenth century. An equally significant root — one which pre-dates Humboldt and the new university foundations of the early nineteenth century but which was taken over at the time — was the explicit subordination of the university to the purposes of the state.[2] German academic freedom and subordination to the purposes of the state, as well as detailed regulation by the state, have historically gone hand in hand. This dualism is intimately related to, and possibly developed prior to, several other historically dynamic German dualisms, including those of *Geist* and *Macht* and *Staatsverdrossenheit* and *Staatsfrömmigkeit*. It is this contrast of freedom and detailed state regulation, too, which is still central to the political culture of the German university.

The notion of freedom posited here is not one tempered by the constraints deriving from the university being politically and (within limits) financially autonomous; for the university did not have that responsibility — its regulation by the state is too detailed and too intimate. 'Freedom without responsibility' is perhaps putting it rather polemically, but the freedom of the university, as with the notion of freedom in general in German political development, tended to be a notably abstract one, not to be bound in with substantive political freedoms — such as freedom from state interference — nor with the notion of political responsibility. Spiritual and intellectual freedom was viewed as something divorced from concrete political freedoms and consequently had anarchic and irresponsible inclinations. The question of the extent to which the upheaval of West German universities ten years ago took place *within* the accepted framework of this dualism and the extent to which it challenged the framework itself is a crucial one for us.

Dahrendorf, writing in *Die Zeit*,[3] has maintained that while the Federal Republic may, particularly in its early years, have approximated to a market economy (*Marktwirtschaft*) (and for this reason may be thought to have made good, at least in economic terms, part of Germany's historical liberal deficit), it is not a 'market society' (*Marktgesellschaft*). In other words, liberal economic forms have not been accompanied by a liberalisation of social forms. He mentions in particular the manifold and intimate involvement of the state in many social institutions, including those of education, where a framework, ground rules and overall supervision may properly be established by the state but where, for the rest, a liberal abstinence on the part of the state and responsible autonomy on the part of the social institutions themselves are necessary if a liberal-democratic frame of mind or political culture is to thrive. The distinctive and perhaps rather incongruous 'mix' of economic liberalism and administrative regulation of society by the state may be an important key to the quality of contemporary West German society and to its political culture — not least its industrial relations and economic efficiency. The West German university's intimate links with the state — university budgets which have to be approved in detail by *Land* legislatures, university teachers who are *Beamte*, students of whom 51 per cent go into the public service, the state's control of academic appointments, these are only some of the most obvious examples — appear to lend support to Dahrendorf's thesis. The indirect administrative regulation of political behaviour at the universities represents a powerful anticompetitive strand in German society. The intellectual climate which it engenders is likely to be one of indifference or slavish obedience to established scholarly or philosophical authorities punctuated by a shrill and occasionally violent rejection of all established authorities. Neither condition is conducive to the fruitful competition of ideas and philosophies. The German university, in this interpretation, is not well equipped to be a support of a competitive or 'market' society.

Is there evidence here, not only of a survival of the historical dualism of the German university, but also of the importance of the survival of this dualism to the characteristic West German mix of economic liberalism and social regulation? A fundamental organisational and intellectual change in West German universities would, it may well be thought, have threatened this efficacious, if incongruous, societal mix. However, let us not advance too rapidly.

A major aspect of the crisis which universities in many countries found themselves in in the late 1960s was that their central organisational principles of hierarchy and collegiality which survived in their conventional form, were no longer adequate to the changing governmental needs of universities. Chief among these changes were the need to formulate coherent policy for the university as a whole in response to growing demands made on it by government and society, and the emergence within universities of groups with a perception of sharply differing interests, requiring the articulation, management and reconciliation of these interests within an agreed set of rules, as well as their accommodation to the requirements of university-wide policy. In other words, the university was becoming much more overtly a *political* system; it was not primarily this, of course, but its basic function could only be well served if it also operated efficiently as a political system.[4] The German university, by virtue of its own tradition, especially its dualistic origins, was especially ill-equipped to meet this challenge.

At the broadest level, there has long been considered to be an important link between the Idealist intellectual tradition and the phenomenon of the 'unpolitical' German, the excessively privatistic figure with an inadequately-formed sense of political and social responsibility and realities, whose political naïvety may result in a predilection for unpolitical utopias. In this interpretation, the tradition of Idealism, whatever its merits, has rendered difficult an adequate understanding of the subtle and complicated relationship between the individual and society (*pace* Hegel), of the university as a *social* as well as a scholarly institution, of the complexity and the importance of the border between the public and the private spheres, all essential requirements of a liberal understanding of politics. This, in turn, partly accounts for a dualism characteristic of German thought and political behaviour: the tendency to veer sharply between an ahistorical, asocial individualism on the one hand and historical or social determinism on the other, in scholarship between the headiest speculation and the most rigid positivism.

More specifically, the *community* of teachers and taught and the *unity* of teaching and research, central tenets of German university tradition and rhetorically invoked still by a surprising coalition of interests, are — in their anachronistic and unrealistic assumption of the self-sufficiency of the world of knowledge and of a community or identity of interest where in practice divergent interests prevail — not readily compatible with the notion of the university as a political system, posited as this notion is on the recognition, articulation, reconciliation and management of divergent interests within the university and between it and the outside world.

DEFECTS OF THE UNIVERSITY STRUCTURE

The traditional structure of authority[5] in the German university reflected and reinforced these weaknesses. The full professor, the *Ordinarius*, was confronted within his domain only by untenured assistants without public-service status or any other form of job security, who were excluded from conventional collegiality and participation in decision-making. Authority at the faculty, and particularly at the university level, was weak. Rectors were elected by full professors for a short-term (usually one year) and rarely had the time or the inclination to develop political skills commensurate with the task of managing a university. Decisions were particularistic and discrete, geared to the needs of professor-dominated units and long-established disciplines. Decision-making therefore tended to lack cohesion at university level. The dominance of the *Ordinarien* was reinforced by the state, which maintained direct financial links with chair-holding institute directors, frequently by-passing both the central and faculty levels of the university. Collegiality, then, was very selective, and central executive authority weak. This situation, taken in conjunction with the extent and manner of the state's control of the university, militated against the efficient independent operation of the university as a political system and against the emergence of a mature notion of political responsibility.

Further light is thrown on the institutional arrangements of the German university and on its political culture, by an examination of the distinction drawn between academic and financial matters. University autonomy in Germany has traditionally been restricted to the 'academic' sphere: 'financial' autonomy did not exist. No German university received an independent budget to distribute within the university as it saw fit and according to academic priorities which it determined. The budget of each university constituted part of the annual budget of the *Land* and was therefore subject to approval annually by the *Land* government. Forward planning and policy-making of the kind facilitated by the British quinquennial plan for individual universities was therefore difficult and inertia was encouraged. The *Land* had, and despite important recent changes in university government and financing still has, the power (in law at any rate) to moderate the development of universities through its annual budget; some areas of· research might be promoted at the expense of others; the university's accounts could be open to the examination of civil servants, M.P.s might criticise the estimates and block them without reference to the university. Theoretically every expenditure in the university required direct negotiation with and authorisation by the relevant department in the Education or Finance Ministry. Clearly, university autonomy under these circumstances is not what is understood by the term in Britain, nor is it that on which British liberal doctrine with respect to universities is premissed.

The problematic nature of the distinction between 'academic' and 'financial' or administrative autonomy was demonstrated when the regional governments authorised a rapid expansion in numbers of university teachers and appointed them. The universities failed to reform the system of study, with the result that the problems of overcrowding and staff-student ratio were actually exacerbated. The 'financial' measures — the government releasing money for new staff — were not accompanied by the appropriate 'academic' action on the part of the university: introducing courses divided into years, syllabuses to match, and so on. Such reforms were anathema to the professoriate — and to organised student opinion — as being an unacceptable curtailment of 'academic freedom'. Effective university autonomy, it may be concluded, implies a strong executive in the university with increased budgetary powers and the power to make policy for the university.

In an ideal society the inevitable tension that exists between an autonomous university and the society of which it is part would be alleviated by mutual trust and confidence built up over years of cooperation. If a healthy relationship is to be maintained, any attempt to define too closely the university's autonomy would probably be mistaken. Similarly, out of a sense of responsibility to the society which provides its means of existence in the form of finance and students, the university would be prepared to sacrifice some part of its autonomy and accept some kind of supervision and control by the State. In Britain this tension has been alleviated and is stable: so far the universities and the state have found a mutually acceptable *modus vivendi*. In Germany the tension has been inadequately understood or recognised, possibly because of the dichotomous origins of the modern German university, and therefore not accepted as positive and fruitful. After 1945 the British and American authorities in Germany attempted unsuccessfully to introduce lay participation into German university government as a way of relating the university to society. The German universities were prepared to accept only *Universitätsvereine* or *Beiräte*, which acted rather as patrons. Completely lacking in Germany has been a body such as the University Grants Committee which mediates between the universities and the state and preserves an independence from both.

THE POLITICAL CULTURE OF THE GERMAN UNIVERSITY

A notion of 'academic freedom' in which, on the one hand, academic decisions need not be tempered by the political constraints of financial self-management, while, on the other, financial management is a matter of detailed regulation by the State, may contribute, albeit indirectly, to a political culture whose characteristic intellectual expressions are: extremes of revolutionary and utopian politics and of subaltern thinking, of activism or 'decisionism' and of passivity, of complete rejection or unquestioning acceptance of the institutional framework of the university or of the wider political framework, punctuated by periods of mute alienation. The chronological relationship of such polarities varies. The poles may coexist in time; they may follow each other. At the root of them all is the historical lack of institutional pressure to develop the habits of compromise and accommodation — in other words to develop necessary political skills. In this sense, the German university can be seen as a microcosmic and antiquated survival of the situation of the educated classes in Germany in the early nineteenth century: excluded from political responsibility they were free to indulge in the headiest speculation. Philosophy flourished; the art of government did not. And the philosophy, if viewed as a plan for political action, as opposed to a theoretical construct of ideas, was deficient, as became obvious when the politically unprepared intelligentsia attempted to impose inappropriate ideas on an intractable reality. All of this was echoed in 1968 at German universities.

Central to the tradition of the German university and to its dualism was the concept of Bildung. The educational philosophy associated with Bildung was marked by an emphasis on ideas as things unconditioned by social circumstance (Marx of cou.se went to the other extreme), on man as an autonomous being. Man as an intellectual and aesthetic being was the prime concern. The concept of freedom to which this tradition contributed was one in which freedom of the spirit was the highest form of freedom and which was compatible with a lack of concrete political freedoms which were accorded lower priority.

An important part of the origin of the 'unpolitical German' evoked so vividly by Thomas Mann at the end of the First World War lies here. The world of practical concerns and politics was contrasted with and despised when set against the heady world of the spirit and the intellect. Here, too, is one of the roots of that dichotomy of Geist and politics, that divorce of public and private morality which was to have such profound consequences in subsequent German political development. It is the divorce of the world of mind from the world of practical concerns which tended to result in Geist, and with it the Geisteswissenschaftliche Fakultät, being regarded as something immutable and immune to the influence of social forces and change. This, too, is an essential attribute of the ahistorical, asocial quality of the notion of Bildung. As Thomas Mann said, 'The educated German is indifferent to politics because he is so much more interested in things of the mind'. Mann recruits Schopenhauer, Wagner and Nietzsche in support of his view that the political element is rightly missing from Bildung.

Clearly the Idealist tradition of scholarship and that of close state control have not excluded each other. Indeed, one is the corollary of the other. A tradition of exaggerated scholarly self-sufficiency is, in the German context, the other side of the coin of state supervision. Resentment of the state and suspicion of its motives — more marked at universities in Germany in the nineteenth and twentieth centuries and more justified than in Britain or the United States — have contributed to the tendency for the academic autonomy of the university to be interpreted as something directly opposed to, even as an escape from, a concern with political and social reality. This characteristic is reflected both in the traditions of knowledge and scholarship pursued and in many aspects of the academic organisation of the university. Resentment in the universities at the intervention in their affairs represented by the *Hochschulrahmengesetz* (1976) and the *Land* university laws which preceded it led to renewed recourse to the rhetoric of Humboldtian academic freedom.

The universities, after 1945, remained inward-looking, though here the difficulty of establishing in Germany a healthy, educationally-fruitful tension between the university and the world of political and social concerns should not be under estimated. In Britain and the United States the critical propensity of the university has traditionally been considered an *educational* asset. Through the young being confronted with new and unorthodox political and social ideas, inherited beliefs are challenged and they are forced to adopt and defend positions based on rational consideration, rather than prejudice. This was only possible in societies marked by an absence of ideological or profound political cleavages (or both) in their recent past, by breadth of consensus and homogeneity of political culture. In Germany, the depth of political and ideological cleavages in recent times precludes the sort of political confidence required to view social criticism at the university as an educational function, just as it renders difficult a stable tension between state and university. Social criticism has, perhaps inevitably, been seen as primarily political in intent rather than educational, with the resultant risk of the university being riven by partisan politics and exposed to outside criticism and interference.

What is argued here is that the institutional ambivalence of the German university, because it retards the development of political skills and responsibility at the level both of the institution and of the individuals in it, contributes to this incapacity to view political and social debate and criticism as an *educational* function of the university. Dogmatic intellectual polarisation stems partly from the fact that habits of responsible political debate are not anchored institutionally in the university. Institutional ambivalence contributes ultimately, then, to the extreme radicality, irrationality and incontinence — *another* version of the *furor teutonicus* of the occasional intellectual/ideological upheaval at German universities.

The extreme politicisation occurring in West German universities in the years following 1967/68 (not in all of them, nor in all departments) may be seen as an example of the institutionally-determined dualism of political over-engagement and under-engagement. The political content of this bout of extreme politicisation was clearly different from that of the late 1920s and 1930s ('democratisation' was the label, though that ship was flying many flags), but in its radicality of content and style it is perhaps an indication that the vulnerability to messianic and utopian politics engendered by the 'unpolitical' tradition is still a force in German society.

The opposite, and corollary, of the exaggerated individualism and privatism of German Romanticism — of the lack of appreciation of the complex relationship between the individual and society — was the development of a predisposition to collectivist models of society, to organic forms of social organisation: a form of society with no conflict, in which the individual counts only in so far as he is a member of the group and where freedom is defined as the honour of belonging to the group, where individuals are seen as little more than the product of their social environment. Such an approach is as unpolitical, in its denial of choice and conflict, as its opposite and concomitant: privatistic individualism.

Part of the 'student revolt' was representative of such collectivist reaction. The quiescent, soporific, unpolitical university of the 1950s was rapidly converted into a highly politicised institution in which the intensity and dogmatism of conviction excluded the liberal politics of accommodation and compromise.

THE CONTENT OF UNIVERSITY REFORM

It is against this background that demands for reform, their discussion, and the partial implementation of changes in the organisational structures of the universities took place. These changes, affecting the internal governance of the university and, much less, its relationship with the state have since the late 1960s been imposed on sometimes reluctant universities through laws passed by most of the respective *Land* legislatures, and subsequently by the *Bund*, in framework federal legislation, the *Hochschulrahmengesetz* (1976), with which *Land* legislation was to have been brought in line by 1979. The salient features of these laws, in as far as they directly affect the governance of the universities are: the replacement of the one or two-year Rector with a President with from four to nine years' tenure; the fusing of academic and financial administration in a single bureaucracy within the university under the president; the reduction in the powers of the *Ordinarius* through the replacement of the *Fakultät* and *Institut* by the *Fachbereich*, (which is somewhere between the faculty and a department in size), and by the allocation of resources to the *Fachbereich* and not to individual chairholders, who no longer negotiate the size of their budget and support staff directly with the *Kultusminister*; and the widening of participation in decision-making, resulting in what is widely referred to as the *Gruppenuniversität*. The logic of these provisions is that the university should receive a global budget to spend according to priorities which it determined and indeed many of the *Land* laws were linked to an economic measure to this effect; this change is a sharp break with traditional German arrangements and it remains to be seen how it works in practice. The signs are at the present that whereas universities may now draw up a global budget, every expenditure in it still has to be approved annually by the *Land* parliament.

Participation in decision-making, including that in the highest collegial body, the Council (variously termed the *Konzil, Grosser Senat, Universitätsversammlung*), is determined through an apportionment formula which gives different groups within the university a certain proportion of the available seats in the decision-making bodies. The number of these groups, their definition and the proportion of the seats to which they are entitled has been the subject of sharp controversy which has tended to dominate the debate about reform of the university's organisational structure; it is almost certainly, however, not the most important of the changes that have taken place.

The Council may consider all aspects of university policy but its chief power is the election of the President. The President may come from outside the institution but so far the majority have been senior professors from within the university. The Council's control over policy lies mainly in its power to elect the President. It may influence and change the policy of the executive (the President); however, once elected he has tenure for between four and nine years. In this way group participation in the Council is carefully balanced by the increased executive power of the President.

It is too early to say how the reforms are working in practice. At some universities, Bonn and Cologne among them, there has in fact been little change and considerable and rapid adaptation will be necessary if the *Hochschulrahmengesetz* is to be complied with. However, from the point of view of the type of analysis attempted in this essay — the efficient functioning of the political process, including managerial and participatory arrangements, in the university — these far-reaching organisational changes at least create the opportunity for the German university to function more successfully as a political entity than in the past. This possibility is in itself perhaps surprising in view of the unpropitious intellectual and political climate at the universities when reform discussions were initiated. Groups previously excluded from influence on decisions are now included; divergent interests and expectations regarding policy are recognised and structures created for the articulation of those interests (group representation in the Council and in the *Fachbereichsrat* are the most important examples); a measure of control is exercised by those interests over the executive; the executive itself has been greatly strengthened *vis-à-vis* the state by the length of tenure granted to the President, by the administrative resources now put at his disposal and by his formal and informal policy and decision-making powers. Together with a further requirement of the *Hochschulrahmengesetz* that universities draw up a development plan several years ahead and bring it up to date each year, these new provisions facilitate coherent and efficient policy-making at the level of the university. In the new President the university has for the first time, in theory at any rate, an adequate negotiating partner for government, who is also powerful enough and legitimated in such a way as to preserve and increase the university's independence of government.

Increased budgetary powers for the university, while leaving ultimate financial control over academic policy with *Land* parliaments, deprive the professoriate of its financial independence of the central university executive and create a situation in which the university, through its elected Council and chief executive, will, particularly in any era of financial stringency, itself have to decide on the priorities — as between disciplines, teaching and research, vocational and non-vocational emphasis and many other matters besides — for which state approval is sought. The broadening of representation in university government affords the chance of universities to be less inward-looking. Drawing up a proposed budget for the university as a whole, with the consequent pressure to formulate priorities of policy at the level of the university, will require the development of those political skills of accommodation and compromise which are necessary if the political process within the university is to be adequate. Political manners of this kind, if widely enough diffused in the university, might act as a barrier to further outbursts of utopian and dogmatic irrationality. Institutional engineering may not, of course, result in such a change of attitude and behaviour in the short term; change may take a long time or, in the event of underlying relationships and institutional traditions proving too strong, may not occur at all. The present signs are that many West German universities are uneasy with the new structures; in the light of their own tradition it would be surprising if they were not.

'DEMOCRATISATION' OF THE UNIVERSITIES

That little had changed from the state's point of view, despite the *Hochschulrahmengesetz*, emerges from a statement issued in 1979 by the (admittedly conservative) *Land* of Baden-Württemberg:

> In the fields of teaching and research the universities are public-law corporations which enjoy the right to regulate their own affairs through their collegial organs; for the rest they are, as state institutions, subject to the state's directives in such matters as personnel, finance and state examinations. Whereas, in the field of teaching and research, the state merely scrutinises the legality of university decisions, it is in the fields mentioned above, as well as in the areas of student numbers and admissions, the administrative staff of the university, the competent supervising body. This means that in these areas it scrutinises and controls not only the legality of university decisions but also their appropriateness (*Zweckmässigkeit*) and their funding (*Wirtschaftlichkeit*) . . .[6]

This is in fact a restatement of the traditional legal relationship between state and university.

In important respects, however, there must be doubts whether the new institutional arrangements, even were they to become firmly established, would work a significant change in the political culture of the German university and hence in the determinants of intellectual and ideological debate and fashion. These doubts concern the basically unchanged nature of the relationship between state and university, the manner of the introduction of those reforms that have been implemented, as well as the substance of one of the reforms.

To take the last reservation first. Whereas, for instance, there is little doubt that there are legitimately differing interests within the university and that both 'democracy' and efficiency will be served by making institutional allowance for them, there is also little doubt that this process must remain subordinate to the primary purpose of the university, namely teaching and research. However, such was the priority given to 'democratisation' and participation, both in university and in public discussion, and such was the political climate in the country at large at the time, that there was a tendency for the representation of group interests — a political process — to be seen as the central concern of the university. The Federal Constitutional Court ruled in 1973 that the *Gruppenuniversität* was compatible with the constitutional guarantee of academic freedom, thus giving the notion a constitutional blessing and making it a figure of law. The undue prominence given to this notion contributed to the politicisation of an institution whose *primary* task is not political. That appointments in a few disciplines and universities were politicised needs no comment here. Inadequately developed political skills and a malformed political culture made the university vulnerable to such politicisation. As a result of the nearly universal acceptance of the *Gruppenuniversität*, intellectual furore and ideological polarisation, when they came, were 'institutionalised' in the university in quasi-parliamentary groupings.

The emphasis on participation and the surprisingly uncritical acceptance of the notion of the *Gruppenuniversität* has also to be seen against the background of the *Demokratisierungswelle* in West German society at large in the late 1960s and early 1970s, a movement which was possibly necessary and one which had authoritative support from the highest political level. However, this movement tended to confuse participation with democracy, to think participation a sufficient condition of democracy, it gave inadequate thought to how to apply a political principle, even that of democracy, to institutions whose primary purpose was not political. Legislation by the *Länder* in the late 1960s and early 1970s was deeply affected by this climate of opinion and marked by the naïve or possibly opportunistic belief that if university decision-making structures were 'democratised' — which at that time tended to mean *Drittelparität* — the problems of the university, including those of its governance, would simply go away.

The *Gruppenuniversität* can be seen as analogous to a development which is characteristic of West German politics and society at large since 1945: the invasion by political groupings, the political parties in particular, and domination by them, through their proportional representation in governing bodies, of institutions and areas of life in which such immediate party-political involvement would in the pre-Nazi past, or in Britain today, have been resisted; broadcasting is the obvious example. *Proporz* is a fact of life in the government of many institutions which are not primarily political in function. The void in political authority left by the political collapse of 1945; the lack of an appreciable national tradition in politics which was congruent with the values of the new liberal-democratic regime and which might have prevented the major contemporary political parties from being identified so completely with foundations of the new regime; the weakening — though not disappearance — of Hegelian notions of an (often spurious) 'above-party' state: all of this contributed to a political vacuum which was filled by the political parties. Germany, which historically had been slow to recognise the necessity of 'party' and to accord parties a major function in government (as opposed to representation), has in West Germany, swung a considerable way toward the other extreme.

In this sense West Germany is now much more completely a *Parteienstaat* than Britain. The pervasiveness of party-political *Proporz* as a principle of political organisation is, it may be argued, a major reason for the receptiveness of legislators to the notion of the *Gruppenuniversität*. However, the West German *Parteienstaat* may be benevolently interpreted as a fusion of, on the one hand, Western political pluralism and party government and, on the other, more traditional German thinking about the state, with the latter providing the source for a public-service ethic and notion of the common good among the parties which acts as a counterweight to party egoism. The threat of group egoism in the *Gruppenuniversität* is perhaps greater in the absence of such a unifying bond. This bond would have to consist in a common understanding of the purpose of the university; it is precisely a redefinition of purpose, however, which has for so long eluded the German university and prevented a change of its political culture. However, the analogy of the *Parteienstaat* has other facets. Just as too close a fusion of university and state may promote a dichotomy of utopian and conformist politics so may the parties' tendency to give priority to governmental, legal and administrative values contribute to a confrontation between the *staatstragende Partei* and the imperative mandate.

What is perhaps at work here with the *Gruppenuniversität* is another form of state intervention. Not this time intervention in substantive issues of university life but the imposition, admittedly with the assistance of large groups within the university, of a whole principle of the state (a dominant principle of political organisation) namely *Proporz*, on the universities. This principle in itself, it may be argued, results in part from the inability, stemming from historical cleavages in society and deficient political maturity and trust, to discuss and decide issues in accordance with criteria largely intrinsic to a particular institution or sphere of activity (in this case teaching and research) while taking into account (but not being dominated by) extrinsic political and ideological criteria. *Proporz* is posited on the culturally-conditioned notion that extrinsic (political) criteria of judgement will inevitably dominate and that the important thing is to prevent a monopoly by any one political/ideological viewpoint. The 'institutionalisation' of radical ideological dissensus by way of the *Gruppenuniversität* may be the result.

Perhaps a more fundamental reservation about the reforms is that the *manner* of their introduction will inhibit their chance of increasing the political efficacy of the university. The reforms have been imposed on largely reluctant universities by state legislators and officials at *Bund* and *Land* level after years of abortive attempts on the part of the universities to reach agreement themselves. The difficulties facing the universities should not be underestimated; the severity of these difficulties can be gauged from the fact that the *Land* governments, too, despite legislation by some of them, were unable to solve the problems of the universities satisfactorily and that, as a result of this frustration, increased powers, necessitating constitutional amendment, have accrued to central government, the *Bund*. The *Hochschulrahmengesetz*, a federal law, is a result of these increased powers. However, the failure of the universities was ultimately a measure of their political inefficacy. Their failure invited the intervention of the state. Inevitably perhaps, but not without irony, it is the quality of that legislation which is now seen by many critics within the university as a major source of its problems.[7]

From the point of view, however, of the future political efficacy of the West German university it is not the quality of the legislation which is the major handicap, but that responses to the university's problems were left to or allowed to originate with the *Bund* and *Land* legislator at all. The tendency to seek legal solutions to problems which are not a fitting subject of legal adjudication and are sometimes not justiciable at all, is an important strand of the 'unpolitical' tradition which is part of the German university's heritage and problem. Hence, no matter how much the content of the organisational reforms may, if accepted by the universities, in time enhance the political efficacy of the university, the manner of their introduction may help to perpetuate more traditional ways of responding to problems.

AN UNRESOLVED STRUCTURAL AMBIVALENCE

But the chief doubt about the reforms concerns their failure to tackle the traditional relationship between university and state. This is the 'embedded structure' of the problems of West German universities, their institutional ambivalence and resulting under-developed political responsibility. Ultimately it is this deficiency, particularly if it is shared in other educational institutions, for instance, the *Gymnasium*, which helps shape the content and style of intellectual movements.

Rather than restrict the state's rights with respect to the universities, the reforms have on balance reaffirmed them. A reminder is the provision of the *Hochschulrahmengesetz* that at least 50 per cent of the members of the *Studienkommission* (committees to investigate course design and syllabus) for courses of study leading to the *Staatsexamen* should be representatives of the state. This provision and the restatement of the state's traditional role in examinations have surprisingly not been resented or resisted in the universities. Ultimately, if the redoubled activity of the State in and with respect to the universities prevents the reforms of the university's organisational structure bearing fruit — and therefore denies a new sense of political independence and responsibility — it is the intermeshing of university education with entry qualifications for employment in the public service (particularly the Higher Civil Service), including school and university teaching, which must perhaps be attacked.[8] To make this aspect of the state-university relationship solely responsible for the ills of the German university or to claim that breaking this link (giving the university sole control over all its examinations and taking entry qualification for the Civil Service outside the university) is a necessary condition for any significant reform of the university is perhaps to act as an apologist for the university's own lack of initiative in the past.

Nevertheless this link, considered together with the wider definition of the public service in West Germany than in, for example, Britain; the status of the university teacher as a *Beamter*; the special relationship to the state that status has traditionally signified; the fact that over 50 per cent of West German university graduates currently enter the public service, not to mention the oath of loyalty to the Constitution required under the *Beamtengesetz*. These considerations not only illustrate that characteristic West German societal mix of a degree of economic liberalism on the one hand and fairly tight administrative regulation of society and of the life chances of individuals on the other hand; they also illustrate that the resulting discipline or stability may be more apparent and real. A large part of the future political elite in the universities are constrained in their intellectual and political development by the knowledge that they will be going into the public service of a *streitbare* (vigilant) *Demokratie*. This is a burden on the development of balanced political criticism and opposition and contributes to the preservation of that oscillation between *Staatsfrömmigkeit* and *Staatsverdrossenheit* which has been characteristic of German political culture. A dichotomy of *Laufbahndenken* (careerism or opportunism) and utopian politics is another way it may be expressed. The majority conform; the minority rebel with a radicality and ferocity which is perhaps some measure of the strength of the pressure to conform in the first place.

Students of German politics often have difficulty reconciling two apparently conflicting generalisations often made about German political culture on the one hand the 'subject mentality', on the other the tendency to break all bounds. The political socialisation of future political elites at West German universities provides an interesting case-study in the coexistence and mutual conditioning of these apparently dichotomous tendencies. The distinctive characteristic of the West German 'student revolt' and subsequent politically motivated terrorism, compared with contemporaneous varieties elsewhere, is perhaps its implacably dogmatic ideological rejection of *Das System*. The semantics of that word and its derivatives and compounds in the years following 1968 is itself an illuminating study. Overtly the 'system' objected to is that of capitalism. But it is not the intellectual content of the opposition to 'the system' which is, in the longer term, significant. It was not the political complexion of the critics from the Left that was a major source of the damage done to — and changes wrought at — West German universities. The change brought about by the intellectual predilections of the neo-Marxist Left — dramatic though its impact on appointments, teaching, text-books and university decision-making structures appeared to be for a time — appears in hindsight to have been transient and negligible.

What was significant was the utopianism, the radicalism of the views, the dogmatism of content and style and the ferocity of advocacy, which on that occasion emanated from the Left but could on a future occasion come from the Right. This characteristic, it has been argued here, is bound up with the structural characteristics of the university, in particular the dualism of 'academic freedom' and subordination to the state, which are at its root, and the resulting lack of political independence and responsibility in the university's political culture. What the 'covert' system reacted against was the indirect pressure to conform politically exercised through the state's links with the university.

After the intellectual ferment of 1968 and after, the passive conformism of

the 1950s and early 1960s has reasserted itself. West German universities in
the early 1980s are beginning to resemble those of the 1950s in the political
abstinence or passive accommodation of their students. The reforms of
university governance and organisation left untouched the structural
ambivalance which partly determines the quality of intellectual debate. To
change this would require a dissociation of state and university; it would
have meant challenging the framework of the institutional dualism. Such a
challenge to the framework was not mounted.

A POSITIVE INTERPRETATION

It is improbable that the dissociation of state and university will take place in
West Germany — particularly at the present time when the egoism of
powerful autonomous social groupings and institutions is under attack and
when the 'ungovernability' of Western democracies is causing such concern.
Such a separation is also unlikely when it attacks such a central strand in
German social tradition — what might be called the *durchorganisierte
Gesellschaft*.

Indeed, it may be tempting for some to argue that, in a time of uncertainty
and failing nerve in liberal democracies, the wide West German definition of
public/civil service and the resulting dependence of larger groups than
elsewhere on the state; the survival of a notion of the state that transcends
politics but has fused with Western party government; the practice of filling
a great many politically sensitive civil-service posts with known supporters
of one or other of the political parties, it may be tempting to argue that all
these features contribute to a sense of responsibility for the whole, counter-
acting the group and individual egoism that appears to plague other liberal
democracies, and at the same time ensuring that the self-interest of large
numbers of people is identified with that of the state, rather than political
stability being dependent on the enlightened self-interest of liberal doctrine.

This is a seductive line of thought. If it were true, it would mean that the
Germans in a sense by marking time had become 'supermodern', that
paradoxically the survival of just those traditions — including older notions
of the state and its role in politics — which had been thought to have
obstructed the development of a liberal-democratic form, is, far from being
an anachronism, precisely the reason why West Germany has accommo-
dated so well to 'big' government, the welfare state and other exigencies of
political organisation in industrial states. And, indeed, the apparently
felicitous blending of this older tradition with the forms of Western political
pluralism appears to have led to a widespread admiration of the West
German political model in other countries. The West German political mix
may also be seen as another, up-to-date, version of Germany's historical
pivotal position between West and East, for the purpose of this argument,
between political pluralism and state paternalism.

A NEGATIVE VIEW: THE RADIKALENERLASS

However, the other side of this coin is that the political 'learning process',
which historically accompanied the formative age of unfettered and less

inhibited economic and political competition in other countries, was not
experienced deeply enough in Germany to result in a secure, durable
libertarian tradition. The inequity of the *Radikalenerlass* and the lack of
effective resistance to the erosion of civil rights in the train of government
measures against terrorism are vivid, and for the purposes of this essay, are
relevant instances of this nether side of the West German political blend.
They also illustrate the relative lack of impact that 'academic freedom'
appears to have had on libertarian sentiment. The *Radikalenerlass*,
taken in conjunction with the oath of loyalty to the constitution required
under the Civil Service Law, risks putting a gag on that responsible independence of spirit and expression at the universities which is essential to the
nurture of a libertarian tradition. Ultimately the West German political mix
may be lopsided; the roots of its pluralistic component may be shallower
than those of its monistic component.

The *Radikalenerlass* itself is perhaps the best example of how
improbable a disentanglement of state and university is. Although it did not
emanate from the universities and is not aimed specifically at them, the fact
that over half of German students go into the public service makes them a
prime target. We have seen that the state anyway has powerful mechanisms
at its disposal for regulating political behaviour at the universities. Almost as
if these mechanisms were considered to be too weak rather than too strong,
the ban on the employment of radicals (a term interpreted differently and
dubiously by the authorities) was introduced in the public service, not
merely in 'security-sensitive' posts.

At a time when, despite all the subversive complications arising from the
existence of the arch (but German) enemy across the border, the conditions
in West Germany seemed propitious for an increase in generosity and
tolerance to the politically uncomfortable and a relaxation of the administrative regulation of society, the state's control of the university students
was boosted gratuitously by the imtimidatory *Berufsverbot*. The unchal-
lenged survival of the university's institutional tendency to promote a
dichotomy of *Staatsfrömmigkeit* and *Staatsverdrossenheit* was reinforced from the outside by this measure, whose major impact would be to
further inhibit the intellectual and political expression of the university
youth and in all probability help to produce precisely the kind of political
behaviour it is intended to deter: the alienation of an important part of one
of the major pools from which future political elites are drawn.

In the light of this interpretation the *Berufsverbot*, and the inhibition of
open debate to which it leads, is not an exceptional measure taken to deal
with a uniquely difficult situation. It is merely a graphic and topical
expression of a long-standing structural tendency in the political socialisation process of the university in West Germany. It reflects and reinforces a
tendency inherent in the structural ambivalence of the German university, a
tendency which both helped produce, and ultimately has been strengthened
by, the intellectual upheaval affecting the universities in the years after 1967.

NOTES

1. Foreign Office, *University Reform in Germany*, Report by a German Commission, London: His Majesty's Stationery Office, 1949, p. 6.
2. See, for instance, R. von Westphalen, *Akademisches Privileg und demokratischer Staat*. Stuttgart: Klett/Cotta, 1979, p. 77f.
3. *Die Zeit*. 17. Oct. 1980., p.16.
4. For another statement of this view see J. van de Graaf, 'Evolution in Higher and Professional Education: Questions of Authority', *1977 Annual Review of Social and Educational Change*, ed. Edmund J. King, London: 1977.
5. This account of the structure of authority at the German university owes much to van de Graaf's analysis.
6. *Pressemitteilung*. Ministerium für Wissenschaft und Kunst. Baden-Württemberg. 28 May, 1979.
7. An example of this is W. Hennis, 'The Legislator and the West German University'. *Minerva* 15, 1977.
8. This step, radical in the German context, is advocated in Westphalen, p. 165.

Does West German Democracy
Have An 'Efficient Secret'?

Gordon Smith

Discussions of modern Germany attract almost obligatory questionmarks. Well back in the nineteenth century, the 'German Question' originally set the style, and furrows have since been traced across German history in attempts to pose the correct questions as much as in finding the right answers. The 'Question' turned out to be an all-embracing quest: the barriers in the way of securing unity for the German nation, the problem of Germany's place in Europe, faults in the structure of German society, the difficulties of overcoming resistance to democratic government, the idiosyncrasies of German intellectual thought, especially in its implications for the relationship between state and society. Rather like Jeremy Bentham's view of the British Constitution, the German Question came to resemble 'a nose of wax' that anyone could twist to his purpose.

A similar quality attaches to the interpretation of post-war Germany. That was to be expected: the old questions were up-dated through the failure to find solutions at an earlier stage, and the Federal Republic was a direct product of previous failure. In the immediate post-war period, and even well into the 1960s, the issue of German reunification was an insistent preoccupation. But — with the emergence of two separate and stable German state systems 'reunification' has become an unpromising line of debate. The idea of a German nationhood and even Germany's 'place in Europe' are topics attracting a balanced interest rather than anxious speculation.

EVALUATIONS OF WEST GERMAN DEMOCRACY

The focus of attention has instead turned steadily inwards. Perhaps the problem of establishing democracy in Germany had been the basic one all along. Thus Ralf Dahrendorf regarded it as the key question underlying all the others when he asked: 'Why is it that so few in Germany embraced the principle of liberal democracy?'[1] His formulation underlines the difficulties of explaining how a stable — and in some respects even a model — parliamentary system managed to take such firm root in a country not noted for the strength of its democratic traditions.

We have at least passed the stage of questioning the stability of the West German system, and a curtain can finally be drawn on the legend of the frailty of the democratic institutions. That doubting attitude persisted in Germany long after others began treating the Federal Republic as among the most stable in Western Europe. Still, it was reasonable to wonder whether basic political values had sufficiently altered to be supportive of liberal democracy. Would not the well-known German leaning for a more authoritarian style of political rule win through once more? Questions in this vein have constantly been rekindled by Germans themselves, and it is a paradox that in spite of all the manifest signs of stability, the storm-warnings of 'crisis', imminent or impending, have been a recurrent — almost obsessive — theme throughout the life of the republic. Expressions of uncertainty about the viability of liberal democracy in Germany were dressed up in academic garb in the 1960s and early 1970s to appear as an overtowering 'crisis of legitimacy', even though most Germans were quite unaware of what the scholarly turmoil was all about.

From the perspective of the 1980s those concerns have abated; and there is a general acknowledgement that the quality of political culture is entirely different from what it was at the beginning of the republic and even further removed from that of Germany in the Weimar period — as David Conradt has concluded: 'The Bonn Republic, unlike its predecessor, has built up a reserve of cultural support which should enable it to deal with . . . future issues of the quality and extent of democracy at least as effectively as other "late capitalist", Western democracies.'[2] Remaining reservations about the essential strength — and moderation — of the liberal democratic system should surely have been dispelled by the outcome of the 1980 election, notable for the failure of Strauss's attempt to win power — and to radicalise German politics.

Yet the Federal Republic is still the target of strong criticism from within Germany. It comes in particular from German Marxists, and they — although electorally emasculated — maintain an important intellectual presence. For them, any 'secret' of West German democracy is fairly straightforward: post-war German capitalism has been extraordinarily successful in imposing favourable terms for its own development, and at the same time it has 'allowed' the political system to operate on a liberal-democratic basis, as the means of promoting a necessary level of mass integration. According to the German Marxist view, there is an ever-increasing contradiction apparent between the bourgeois parliamentary system and the 'fascist' potential of the West German state, as shown by such measures as the '*Berufsverbot*' and the passing of the anti-terrorist laws. On a strict Marxist analysis, strenuous efforts have to be made to demonstrate that there is an underlying economic malaise and that German capitalism is near the limit of its potential.[3] Such argumentation easily slides into a wish-fantasy that gives German Marxists such a bad name.

In a more moderate tone, others invoke Marcuse and find Western Germany to be the model of a 'repressive tolerance'. Hans-Magnus Enzensberger is representative of the moderate critics.[4] He sets out specifically to reveal the 'secret' of German democracy, and he finds that it consists of a 'progressive form of social control' and that the powers are assiduously wielded by new apolitical creatures — 'the technocrats of repression'. Unfortunately, the repressive character of the West German state succeeds in winning approval from the masses, who, Enzensberger concedes, act rationally — if shortsightedly — in giving their support. Needless to say, Enzensberger is pessimistic about the Federal Republic: 'The political reality we are dealing with is a mess'. But is not liberal democracy by its nature a very messy arrangement? It is too easily forgotten in Germany that most Western democracies face problems of the same order, even though they may appear in different forms.

THE MECHANISMS OF CONSENSUS: A SYNTHETIC APPROACH

The performance of the Federal Republic must still be counted as remarkable, even if we allow for the case made by sceptics and critics, and that is true whether judging the republic comparatively or against previous German history. But we are always faced with the difficulty of explaining why parliamentary democracy enjoys such a smooth passage. In one sense, any 'secret', if there is one, must be rather open: it is to be found in the nature of the West German consensus, and it is seen in the absence of sharp political and social cleavages, in the successful management of potentially divisive conflicts, in the strength of political leadership, and in the successive votes of confidence accorded to the established parties.

Yet those indicators tell us little about how the political system operates and maintains a consensus. Whilst we can appreciate that there has been a fundamental change in political culture, that finding is an incomplete answer, since its present form is a result rather than a cause of development. Moreover, the cultural dimension requires an institutional connection, and yet, on the other hand, we do not receive much help from the catalogue of political institutions, for on the whole they are ones that are well represented in parliamentary institutions. It is true that some — such as the Bundesrat in directly representing the *Länder* governments — show interesting variations, but they can hardly bear a large weight of explanation.

It is even less likely that some kind of 'secret constitution' is operated behind the façade of the Basic Law. That would imply the knowing collusion of several elite formations, a political establishment that was able to dispose of the public agenda in private, a parallel to the theory of 'consociational democracy' that has been applied as an explanation of the stability of the smaller European democracies. Yet why, if the West German consensus is as strong as it appears, should resort be made to such a device? Indeed, there is a case for saying that government in the Federal Republic is palpably open, that there are no unified elites — in class, party, or educational terms — capable of keeping 'the system' intact by their own efforts, and that almost every political move is widely scrutinised and debated.

In that sense there are no mysteries to be explained. But following the spirit of Walter Bagehot's account of the real working of 'The English Constitution', we can examine the Federal Republic to see whether, there too, an 'efficient secret' operates. In Germany, an answer has to be sought in the areas of political culture and institutions as well as in the way the two interlock. The danger is that in the attempt to make the connections an analysis will tend towards embarking on a total appreciation of the Federal Republic, together with its history and even prehistory.

The 'synthetic' account presented here avoids that problem by concentrating on those aspects of consensus maintenance that appear to make a special contribution. They do span a large part of the political system, but their importance lies in the fact that they all display a certain ambivalence of function. These 'dualities' are significant in their own right, but — it is argued — their vital contribution as the 'mechanism' of consensus results from the mutually supportive fashion in which they work.

THE TWO FACES OF THE VOLKSPARTEI

It is natural to look first at the party system, since much of the success of post-war German democracy is ascribed to the role played by the CDU and the SPD, both in securing a mass support from the voters and in providing stable government. They are usually described as *Volksparteien*, with the CDU the first to become a party of general social integration. It succeeded in this through avoiding an oversharp ideological appeal, a strategy that the SPD was only able to follow at a distance, and it did so by underwriting the 'social market economy' in all important respects. By the end of the 1950s the party system had acquired its present and apparently fixed pattern.

The changes that occurred in Germany are usually read in the context of developments that were taking place elsewhere in Western Europe, and they follow general interpretations, especially those arguments advanced by Otto Kirchheimer to explain the 'transformation' of Western European party systems.[5] In Kirchheimer's view, a decrease in the extent of social polarisation implied a concomitant decrease in political polarisation. In an era of 'mass consumerism', the parties had to obey a new 'law of the political marketplace', and that law forced them to jettison any distinctive ideological position. In the effort to win over new, uncommitted voters, the parties also shed their important expressive function towards traditional supporters and members.

Kirchheimer's line of argument was influential, but — quite apart from the fact that many of the suggested developments have not materialised in practice for many countries[6] — there is a danger in accepting the 'transformation' thesis uncritically for Germany. That is especially so because Germany is one of the few countries that appear to fit Kirchheimer's prognosis in all major respects. In fact, what Kirchheimer presented was a 'soft' version of the *Volkspartei*, one that is characterised chiefly by its bland accommodative ability. There is, however, an alternative 'hard' type of *Volkspartei*, and arguably the parties in the Federal Republic provide the best examples.

One way of expressing the distinction between the two is to point to the differences in the *causes* of their rise in the first place, since their origins have nothing in common, even though their observable *effects* may be much the same. The causes of party change in Germany have to be related to the particularities of her history — the experience of the Weimar Republic and National Socialism, the impact of defeat in the Second World War, and its aftermath in the occupation and subsequent division of Germany — rather than being put down to general, wider changes in European society. The effects on Germany were profound, and together we can say that they led to an enforced 'modernisation' of her society. But it must also be evident that the political changes were substantially different from those brought about by a slower and more natural decrease in social polarisation.

Whilst the soft version of the *Volkspartei* points to the gradual decay of ideology, the hard one requires the active rejection of divisive ideologies by the parties. The soft, 'catch-all' type implies a pronounced centripetality in terms of party competition and in electoral response, but the German equivalent is more appropriately summed up by the term 'centrality', with the implication that the parties deliberately refrain from taking up strong ideological positions for fear of re-opening old wounds with all the consequences that might follow.[7] In the German context, one can see that the extremes of Right and Left — for very different reasons scarred in political memories — have been excised from the party system just as much as they have withered away electorally.

The concept of 'centrality' does not preclude the parties having a strong ideological base. On the contrary, the absence of distinctive ideologies in the hard *Volksparteien* only partly conceals the powerful ideological underpinning given to the political system as a whole. Any impression that the two pillars of the West German state, the CDU and the SPD, are merely supine vote-gatherers is far from the reality. Kaste and Raschke go so far as to describe the German *Volkspartei* as a '*Kampfbegriff*', introducing the idea of a 'combative ideology' that is surely incompatible with an exclusively 'soft' evaluation.[8] Nor can it be an accident that both the CDU and the SPD have continued the German tradition of being strong membership parties, a feature that is quite at odds with a supposed decline of party interest in maintaining an expressive function.

If there are, in fact, two faces to the German *Volkspartei*, what are the implications for the functioning of the political system? One consequence is immediately evident for the nature of the party system: the *Volkspartei* enjoys a double security against any erosion of its dominant position. Firstly, it gains through the centripetal effect, principally in its continuing ability to make a wide electoral appeal. Secondly, the force of centrality hinders any attempt to polarise the system on the part of an outflanking alternative beyond the wings of the major parties.

The iron grip exercised by the CDU and the SPD is almost without parallel in Western Europe, for in recent years many party systems have been under severe pressure. Perhaps the healthy survival of the FDP could be taken as evidence that other possibilities are feasible, but in reality it is the two-bloc alignment that is significant, and the Free Democrats may be secure only as long as they continue in federal alliance with the SPD. The failure (federally) of 'Greens' or others shows the position of the FDP as a small party to be exceptional; and the basic consensus at the electoral level, heavily reinforced by the nature of the parties, is quite compatible with large shifts in support from any one of the three parties to the others.

This fluidity has an important effect in keeping the parties in line with one another. Despite the considerable conflict over specific issues, often marked by vituperative political debate, neither major party can afford to persist for long or go very far in proposing radical change: compromises have to be sought and they are eventually found in a clearly delineated area.

INSTITUTIONAL AMBIVALENCE

It would be rather too facile to try to use the *Volkspartei* as an all-purpose key to the West German political system. Its general integrative capabilities are beyond dispute, but the parties also have to work within a complex institutional structure. Indeed, the parties may at times appear to occupy a subordinate role when all the ramifications of the other institutions are taken into account. That rendering can be appreciated by examining the constitutional order and the spirit motivating the Basic Law.

Of course, the constitution does show an unswerving commitment to the principle of parliamentary government and therefore to that of majority-party rule. A chancellor, after all, owes his position to direct election by the Bundestag and he has no option but to govern through a majority constellation. To that extent the Federal Republic is indistinguishable from other parliamentary democracies. But the Basic Law was also concerned with the wider question of how to anchor the doctrine of 'constitutionalism' in the new state. That endeavour was a reaction to the flaws of the Weimar Republic and to the excesses of National Socialism. In the late 1940s it was felt inadequate to rely on the balance of party competition alone to secure the foundations of the republic, and the emphasis on 'other means' showed a caution, a mistrust even, towards untrammelled popular democracy. It may be that the devices of constitutionalism — how to achieve 'limited' government as opposed to unqualified majoritarian rule — have taken on an anachronistic colouring in the contemporary world. Yet undoubtedly the Basic Law looks back to a golden age of 'checks and balances', but it does so without a marked reliance on a separation of powers.

Both the political process and the powers of central government are deeply affected by the conception guiding the Basic Law. The deliberate containment of the 'political arena' was realised through the wide power of judicial review given to the Federal Constitutional Court, but the Court could scarcely have proved so resilient if it were not for the presence of a powerful cultural support: the belief that there are certain objective criteria, expressed in the Basic Law, against which even the details of public policy have to be judged. This normative value together with the institutionalised *Rechtsstaat* puts the West German political system in a quite different position from other European democracies, for the constraints placed on governments are more than just awkward obstacles to be circumvented. The same can be said of the federal system, for even though the German tradition of federalism is generally thought to be 'weak' in the sense that the *Länder* exercise few original and independent powers, the federal government faces all kinds of restrictions on its ability to impose its own, unified policies. No one restriction is at all decisive, but there is a constant awareness that the authority of the federal government, and with it of the Bundestag, is circumscribed: the powers and interests of the *Länder* can never be brushed aside.

Now it can well be argued that this resurrected formula of 'checks and balances' amounts to a recipe for political *immobilisme*, an invitation to a squabbling inanition that could eventually lead to a real crisis of the state.

Yet precisely the opposite has happened. The rather old-fashioned constitutionalist view of the political system has been successfully reapplied in modern circumstances — ones that require the demands of a large number of well-organised and articulate interests to be satisfied. This ambivalence — on the one side the deliberate restriction and division of political authority, on the other a fashioning of a unified outcome to policy — belongs to any account of the consensus mechanism.

Rainer Lepsius has argued that a leading attribute of the Federal Republic lies in the peculiar fashion in which an 'institutional aggregation' of interests is achieved.[9] That is in contrast with the normal picture of an aggregation secured primarily through the efforts of the parties. One result of this partial displacement of function is seen by Lepsius in the significance of 'inter-institutional conflict' for the West German system. This effect can be seen most clearly in the operation of federalism. It arises because of the special 'administrative' emphasis in the German federal tradition: the federation possesses the bulk of legislative initiative whilst the *Länder* have the major administrative competence, a division that gives rise to a complex interpenetration of political and administrative authority — a *Politikverflechtung* — knitting the federal and *Länder* governing systems into a tight web of continuous bargaining, carried on by numerous political-administrative hierarchies, and operating within well-defined structures and rules.

The federal system provides a secure network within which group interests can be voiced and harmonised. Clearly, their ability to operate successfully at the national level is of cardinal importance, but the decentralised character of the state also requires organised interests to adapt to that structure. One result is that the leading interests are themselves based on a federal or confederal pattern. That arrangement allows them many points of access to policy-making, but it requires them also to accept a degree of public responsibility, and that emphasis reflects the German view which is somewhat removed from the unbridled competition of plural interests. It is an association rather than a collusion, however, and it accords with the idea of 'liberal corporatism' even though deviating from Lehmbruch's criteria.[19]

UNPOLITICAL POLITICS?

The third element of the consensus mechanism differs from the contributions of the *Volkspartei* and the formal institutions stemming from the Basic Law. This third duality can be expressed in the contradictory idea of an 'unpolitical politics'; it refers to a style of political behaviour that cuts across the institutions rather than appearing as a feature of any one part of the political system. However, the 'style' is also securely anchored in the structures, so that any impression of an imprecise — or conveniently vague — turn of phrase should not linger too long.

Kenneth Dyson has analysed the twin processes of 'politicisation' and 'depoliticisation' that have characterised the development of the Federal Republic, in his words, as a 'state democracy'.[11] In order to appreciate the force of his argument, it is important to consider these expressions in their German context, and in particular the tenacity with which the prevailing state tradition held out against the encroachment of 'society' on the 'state'. In a basic way, the state remained depoliticised, its ethos intact despite the German Revolution of 1918 and the Weimar Republic. In a sense it can be said that National Socialism succeeded where democratic efforts failed, but the totality of Nazi politicisation — the effective fusion of state and society — swung the balance so far the other way that it could just as well be said that Germany became totally depoliticised.

It is with the background of a 'battle for the state' that the developments in the post-war era can be viewed. In a way there was a fundamental democrat-isation of the state machinery, although it took the form of a *party* politicis-ation and led to a state bureaucracy — and more generally the public service — which fully accepted the dictates of party rule. Party politicisation of public office has been carried through in Germany as far as in any country in Western Europe. The implications are various, but in the train of argument presented here the important connection can be made between the role of the *Volkspartei* and the institutional structure of the state. Even though the concept of 'institutional aggregation' can be counted as valid, the fact that the self-same institutions are shot through with party influence puts a different gloss on interpretation. It is, in fact, the peculiar inter-twining of 'party' and 'institution' that modifies the influence of both.

Yet the extent of politicisation is met by an entirely contrary process of depoliticisation. Partly, it has to be conceded, this latter effect belongs to the German tradition of politics. It may be rooted in a political culture that tended to 'shun politics' and which showed itself in a reliance on proven expertise and a proclivity towards seeking an 'objectively-based' consensus. The belief that there are always 'objective constraints' (*Sachzwänge*) — what Mary Parker Follett would have called 'the law of the situation' — leads to a search for a consensual solution, and in this respect the over-worked sense of 'crisis' has a particular functional value in hastening a general search for a resolution. Possibly, there has also occurred a bureau-cratisation of politics — a price that was exacted in reverse for politicisation.

That view might be confirmed by examining the changing nature of the parties themselves: in shedding their partisan ideological positions, they came to accept the tenets of a broader state ideology, and in so doing became *Staatsparteien* as much as *Volksparteien*. This acceptance, especially when a party is committed to a governing role, entails the acquiescence towards an essentially managerial function, one that has little to distinguish it from the 'party-politicised' bureaucracy, and therefore allowing a major influence of the bureaucracy on the formation of policy.

At this point we can refer back to another source of depoliticisation, namely to the influence of constitutional norms on political behaviour. The 'deliberate containment of the political arena' set by the terms of the Basic Law, and referred to earlier, affects the parties in two related ways. One is provided by the actual power of constitutional jurisdiction given to the Federal Constitutional Court; there comes a point at which the political process gives way to a judicial one. The other follows from the fact that the parties — whether in government or opposition — face a common pressure in that they are at all times aware that the case they present will at least be partly judged on its compatibility with the dictates of the constitution; and the style of political discourse is coloured accordingly.

These two contrary indications — politicisation and depoliticisation — are not at odds with one another. At certain times and at different levels, one or the other may, of course, be predominant. But it is the total effect of their combination that is really significant. It means that the political arena is both widened *and* narrowed at the same time: on the one hand, political consider-ations extend much further than they did in the past or is the case in many other countries; on the other hand, the chances of securing a 'straight' political resolution of particular issues are diminished. The outcome might be expressed in terms of a 'diffusion' of political activity, and the contribu-tion towards the overall 'mechanism of consensus' will be apparent. It is principally shown in the need to fashion policies that require more than simple majoritarian support, but also in a government's reliance on bureaucratic and other expertise to fashion policy as well as to implement it. Finally, once policies have been adopted there is a strong pressure to maintain them, not only on the part of the government but also as an implied constraint on the opposition. In consequence, the political system is geared to making only gradual changes of course in any field of policy and putting stress on the virtue of continuity.

CONCLUSION

The three elements examined here produce a powerful drive towards consensus-seeking especially since they act in combination, but their strength is due in part to the fact that they have independent origins and expressions, so that a weakness at one point may be redressed at another. There is also an interdependence: thus without the presence of the *Volkspartei* it is doubtful whether the checks and balances of the consti-tutional structure would actually have acted in an integrative fashion. Furthermore, although party politicisation has given the Federal Republic an important basis of legitimacy, the consequences of that process could have been divisive if it had not been modified, even blunted, by the counter-vailing tendencies of depoliticisation, and a similar type of modification has been evident in the functioning of the institutional system. The strength of the synthesis has to be admitted; its hallmark is the value placed on securing wide agreement, and its style is best suited to the slow accretion of policies in well-defined directions that are generally understood. It amounts to a version of politics posited on consolidation rather than change. A successful leader appreciates how the elements of consensus are composed and the limits within which changes can be made.

All this is not to say that we should regard the political system as inflexible or unable to respond to challenges. What is required is that the need for change should be signalled well in advance, precisely reflected in the long-range forecasting of 'crisis', in order that various lines of solution may be thoroughly tested. This need is evident when one considers the slow-moving responses of the *Volkspartei*, a characteristic that is accentuated by the coalition-oriented nature of the party system. The inability of the parties to sustain a 'fruitful polarity' is taken further by the nature of the structures in which they operate, since they are suited to becoming strongholds of particular interests. Finally, the net effect of politicisation/depoliticisation is to bring about a harmony between the political and bureaucratic realms; it is not a dynamic relationship.

These reservations do not point to pressing and immediate problems. It is true that there is, in certain groups at least, a mood of disenchantment evident in the Federal Republic, a frustration felt with the system or more precisely focused on the parties, a *Parteienverdrossenheit*. But such resentments do not amount to a direct challenge, and many of the claims — say, for greater participation — can probably be met in good time. Even if the republic should experience a *sudden* reversal of fortune, the inherent resilience of the *Volkspartei* should not be underestimated, not least because of the ideological unity that the parties share. There is, however, the lurking suspicion that should the republic have to move to another stage beyond the present 'era of consolidation', then the mechanics of consensus would have to be basically refashioned. A new era could be ushered in by a changing and worsening economic climate, with political consequences following. The existing consensus was predicated first on economic recovery and then on continuing economic growth; it remains to be seen whether the consensus holds good in one direction only. But that query — and ones of a similar kind — may be just another way of re-introducing the baneful spirit of crisis, as opposed to its positive counterpart, and without as yet any firm indications or evidence.

It also takes us beyond our original brief and question. That concerned the nature of the consensus mechanism, and an answer might be that we should reverse Bagehot's phrasing and say that the German secrets are reasonably dignified and the façades quite efficient. A present-day formulation of the German Question is the dichotomy of 'problem or model',[12] but Western Germany is better seen neither as a special problem nor as a recommended example for others to follow.

NOTES

1. R. Dahrendorf, *Society and Democracy in Germany*, Weidenfeld and Nicholson, 1968, p. 14.
2. D. P. Conradt, 'Changing German Political Culture', in G. Almond and S. Verba (eds), *The Civic Culture Revisited*, Boston: Little, Brown, 1980, p. 265.
3. Representative of this kind of formulation is Joachim Hirsch, 'Developments in the Political System of West Germany since 1945', in R. Scase (ed.), *The State in Western Europe*, Croom Helm 1980. He regards the Federal Republic as an *'Ausnahmestaat'*, a 'State of Emergency', and frequently alludes to a supposed 'deterioration and exacerbation of living standards' in the Federal Republic.
4. H-M. Enzensberger, 'A Determined Effort to explain to a New York audience the Secrets of German Democracy', in *New Left Review*, No. 118, Nov./Dec. 1979.
5. O. Kirchheimer, 'The Transformation of Western European Party Systems', in J.

LaPalombara and M. Weiner (eds), *Political Parties and Political Development*, Princeton University Press, 1966.

6. In particular, there has been no general diminution of numbers of parties represented in West European party systems, a logical requirement of the 'catch-all' thesis. See, S. Wolinetz, 'The Transformation of Western European Party Systems Revisited', in *West European Politics*, Vol. 2 No. 1, Jan. 1979.

7. For a more detailed discussion of the idea of 'centrality', see G. Smith, *Democracy in Western Germany*, Heinemann, 1979, pp. 209-15.

8. H. Kaste and J. Raschke, 'Zur Politik der Volkspartei', in W-D. Narr (ed.), *Auf dem Weg zum Einparteienstaat*, Opladen: Piper, 1977, p. 26.

9. In a colloquium given at the Institut für Zeitgeschichte, Munich, in Nov. 1980 on the theme of 'Social Change in Britain, France and Germany since 1945'.

10. G. Lehmbruch, 'Liberal Corporatism and Party Government', in *Comparative Political Studies*, April, 1977. For a recent evaluation, see Ulrich von Allemann, 'Verbändestaat oder Staatsverbände: Die Bundesrepublik auf dem Weg vom Pluralismus zum neuen Korporatismus', *Die Zeit*, 19 Sept. 1980.

11. K.H.F. Dyson, 'The Ambiguous Politics of Western Germany: Politicisation in a "State" Society', *European Journal of Political Research*, Vol. 7 No. 4, Dec. 1979.

12. See, P.J. Katzenstein, 'West Germany in the 1980s: Problem or Model?', in *World Politics*, Vol. 22 No. 4, July 1980. (Review Article).